Governance Through Social Learning

THE CENTRE ON GOVERNANCE SERIES

Governance is about guiding: it is the process whereby an organization steers itself. Studying governance means probing the distribution of rights, obligations, and power that underpins organizations and social systems; understanding how they co-ordinate their parallel activities and maintain their coherence; exploring the sources of dysfunction and lacklustre performance; and suggesting ways to redesign organizations whose governance is in need of repair. Governance also has to do with the complex ways in which the private, public, and civic sectors co-ordinate their activities, with the manner in which citizens produce governance through their active participation in a democratic society, and with the instruments and processes required to ensure good and effective stewardship.

This series welcomes a range of contributions – from conceptual and theoretical reflections, ethnographic and case studies, and proceedings of conferences and symposia to works of a very practical nature – that deal with particular problems or nexus of issues on the governance front.

Director   Gilles Paquet

Editorial Committee   Caroline Andrew
                          Robert de Cotret
                          Daniel Lane
                          Donna Winslow

Centre on Governance http://www.governance.uottawa.ca

IN THE SAME SERIES

David McInnes, *Taking It to the Hill: The Complete Guide to Appearing before (and Surviving) Parliamentary Committees, 1999*

Governance Series

Gilles Paquet

Governance Through Social Learning

University of Ottawa Press

Canadian Cataloguing in Publication Data

Paquet, Gilles, 1936-
Governance Through Social Learning

(Governance)
Includes bibliographical references.
ISBN 0-7766-0488-0

1. Corporate governance—Social aspect.   2. Public administration—Social aspects.
3. Social learning.   I. Title.   II. Series: Governance (Ottawa, Ont.)

JF1351.P36   1999   658   C99-900359-3

JF
1351
P 343
1999

University of Ottawa Press gratefully acknowledges the support extended to its publishing programme by the Canada Council, the Department of Canadian Heritage, and the University of Ottawa.

UNIVERSITY OF OTTAWA
UNIVERSITÉ D'OTTAWA

Cover design : Robert Dolbec

Cover photograph: Used with permission of Canadian Information Processing Society
and Design 2000 Communications

ISBN 0-7766-0488-0
ISSN 1487-3052

© University of Ottawa Press, 1999
   542 King Edward, Ottawa (Ont.), Canada K1N 6N5
   press@uottawa.ca   http://www.uopress.uottawa.ca

Printed and bound in Canada

TABLE OF CONTENTS

Introduction – Governing, Governance, and Governability 1

Part I – A Framework

1. New Patterns of Governance 23
2. Tackling Wicked Problems 41

Part II – Social Learning in Action

A – International Perspectives

3. Elegant but Not Helpful to Navigation:
   Social Sciences Research and the Free Trade Debate 55
4. Science and Technology Policy Under Free Trade 79

B – National Perspectives

5. A Social Learning Framework for a Wicked Problem:
   The Case of Energy 93
6. The Environment–Energy Interface: Social Learning
   Versus the Invisible Foot 109

C – Social Perspectives

7. Multiculturalism as National Policy 127
8. Liberal Education as Synecdoche 137

D – Administrative Perspectives

9. How to Scheme Virtuously: The Role of Public Service
   Commissions in Meeting the Needs of Changing Societies 153
10. Granting Councils in Search of Excellence:
    Dynamic Conservatism Versus Social Learning 169

Part III – New Directions

11. The Strategic State 183
12. Betting on Moral Contracts 205
13. Distributed Governance and Transversal Leadership 217

Conclusion – The Burden of Office, Ethics,
and Connoisseurship 233

References 247

INTRODUCTION

GOVERNING, GOVERNANCE, AND GOVERNABILITY*

> Je ne crois pas aux choses
> mais aux relations entre les choses.
>
> – *Georges Braque*

Over the past 10 years, I have worked on the problems raised by the governing, the governance, and the governability of complex organizations and socio-economic-political systems. This terrain has been explored by many researchers. Indeed, over the last 10 years, these themes have become the centre of important debates on every continent (Kumon 1992; Kooiman 1993; Castells 1996). However, governance studies are still in their infancy. Although many interesting approaches and perspectives have been proposed, there is still no consensus on the best way to handle these issues, nor is there agreement on a lexicon or vocabulary for formulating these questions.

This compendium of papers is a progress report on work that strives to generate new responses to these problems. These studies are unified by the choice of a particular strategy for dealing with governance problems. It is not intended to be *le dernier mot* on these matters, but only a *premier effort* to clarify the issues, using a method that has proved useful — the social learning approach.

CHANCE EVENTS AND INSTITUTIONAL SUPPORT

The research program on which this volume is based originated in 1988–89 during a sabbatical leave from the University of Ottawa, but the original plans evolved as a consequence of many chance events and help from friends and colleagues at certain junctures.

The first chance event was an invitation from Rod Dobell, president of the Institute for Research on Public Policy, to spend my sabbatical at the Institute.

---

* This chapter contains excerpts from "States, Communities and Markets: The Distributed Governance Scenario." In Courchene, T.J. (editor), *The Evolving Nation-state in a Global Information Era: Policy Challenges*. Kingston: John Deutsch Institute for the Study of Economic Policy, 1997, pp. 25–46.

At the time, the Institute was very much a forum interested in exploratory thinking. My work there was entirely curiosity-oriented, but I had an opportunity to discuss the results of my first analyses with Peter Dobell, Rod Dobell, Jeffrey Holmes, Steven Rosell, and Walter Stewart. Each of these colleagues forced different perspectives on these issues of governance on me, and they all had an impact on the reflections that stemmed from my sojourn at the Institute.

The second chance event was David Zussman's invitation to present a paper on these issues at the Aylmer Conference of the Liberal Party of Canada in November 1991. This was an opportunity for a synthesis of work that, at that point, remained somewhat scattered and issue-oriented. Preparing a synthetic piece on the Strategic State was an occasion to refine my approach considerably and to sketch, however roughly, a research program that is still unfolding. A fragment of this paper was published in the proceedings of the conference early in 1992; a three-part document covering the same terrain much more thoroughly was published in *Ciencia Ergo Sum* (Paquet 1996a, 1997a,b). The latter version is included in this volume (Chapter 11).

A third determining event was an invitation to become a senior research fellow at the Canadian Centre for Management Development (CCMD) in 1992. This opportunity, offered by Ralph Heintzman, who was then vice-principal (research) at CCMD, together with my extensive involvement with the teaching faculty at the Centre, at the request of Lise Pigeon, provided an extraordinarily rich cauldron in which these ideas could be stirred, debated, and further distilled. From 1993 on, various working papers were used in the classroom at the Centre; in them, the ideas were tested and polished through discussion with hundreds of senior executives in the federal public service. A number of papers emerged from this extremely rich experience at CCMD; a few have been collected here.

The final important event was the creation of PRIME (Program of Research in International Management and Economy), which John de la Mothe and I pressed into existence in 1993 with the support of Dean Jean-Louis Malouin. This organized research unit brought together a number of colleagues (Robert de Cotret, Georges Hénault, Luc Juillet, David Large, Paul Laurent, Morris Miller, Christian Navarre, Jeffrey Roy, Robert Shepherd, Chris Wilson, and others) and a number of associates from the private, public, and civic sectors. The PRIME group has produced a stream of papers and books, in which we have all become more and more concerned with problems of governance.

The success of the PRIME experience — both in terms of the interest it generated in the community and the financial support it elicited from the Social Sciences and Humanities Research Council, Industry Canada, Statistics Canada, etc. — prepared the way for our 1997 petition to the University of Ottawa for the creation of the Centre on Governance. The Centre is an umbrella organization for a variety of programs of research and organized research units with an interest in governance issues. The support of Vice-Rectors Howard Alper and Gilles Patry and of Deans Caroline Andrew (Social Sciences) and Jean-Louis Malouin (Administration) was most important in efforts to create the Centre and to assure sustained funding for its development phase.

The purpose of the Centre is not only a certain *mise en visibilité* of the research personnel of the University of Ottawa and their partners, affiliates, and associates, but also, more importantly, the development of a particular *manière de voir* — an approach to governance issues that holds the promise of revealing important dimensions hitherto not accorded the attention they deserve, of leading to explorations of novel sorts of governance, and of providing opportunities to develop clinical interventions to ensure greater effectiveness for a number of organizations and sociotechnical systems.

UNE MANIÈRE DE VOIR

Since the early 1970s, it has been my view that the overly simplistic and mechanistic ways of examining the problems of coordination and governance in modern socioeconomies are grossly inadequate (Paquet 1971). The triumphant belief — still in good currency in the 1960s — that the simple modeling of rational economic actors (with their target-and-instruments-type policymaking) could cure all ills had been all but discredited by the 1970s. But this view is still living on, even though the intervening years have revealed that most coordination and governance problems are "wicked" — the goals are ill-defined and uncertain and the means–ends relationships unstable and unreliable. It has become clear that neither the market mechanism nor rational policymakers (neither presumed perfect competition nor presumed perfect computation) can ensure that the socioeconomic system will be governed perfectly. An alternative way of looking at the coordination problem was needed.

A major alternative to the mechanistic models of the 1960s and 70s was the systems approach, which emphasized the dynamics of interaction and interrelationships among actors. General systems theory, in particular, proposed a holistic way of thinking. Ludwig von Bertalanffy, a former faculty member at the University of Ottawa, was a most important voice preaching the systems approach gospel against the mechanistic stimulus–response view of the world that was in vogue. But his perspective was not taken very seriously. Indeed, many opinion molders regarded it as suspect because of its link to discredited theories of vitalism, which held that organisms and organizations were directed from within by a soul-like force (von Bertalanffy 1968; Davidson 1983).

Yet, von Bertalanffy's perspective was never vitalistic. It focused on organizations as open systems and on a reality best represented as a many-layered architecture of organizational entities. It searched for laws (progressive integration, differentiation, mechanization, centralization, etc.) that might apply to every layer of the system, from cell to biosphere. But this gambit was perhaps too ambitious, for, in the 1960s and 70s, the systems approach seems to have lacked sufficient heuristic power to shake off the seduction of the language of management science.

The management science approach to governing presumed that public, private, and civic organizations were strongly directed by leaders who had a good understanding of their environment, of the future trends in the environment if nothing were done to modify it, of the inexorable rules of the game they had to put up with, and of the goals pursued by their own organization. Those were the days when the social sciences were still Newtonian and pretended to explore a world of deterministic, well-behaved mechanical processes where causality was simple because the whole was the sum of the parts. The coordination–governance challenge was relatively simple: building on the well-defined goals of the organization, it was to design the control mechanisms likely to get the organization where its leaders wanted it to be.

Many issues were clearly amenable to this approach, and many still are. But as the pace of change accelerated and the issues grew more complex, private, public, and civic organizations were confronted more and more with "wicked problems" (Rittel and Webber 1973). In dealing with such problems, inquiry can only mean "thinking and acting that originates in and aims at resolving a situation of uncertainty, doubt and puzzlement" (Schon 1995: 82). This calls for a new way of thinking about governance. At best, one can hope for pattern causality: the gradual construction of a "causal" story on the basis of background knowledge of the system that is often tacit, and "working back," as plumbers do when tracing a leak to its source. In this quantum world, there is no objective reality, the uncertainty principle looms large, events are at best probable, and the whole is a network of synergies and interactions that is quite different from the sum of the parts (Becker 1991).

Three important forces have played a central role in generating this quantum world: the rise of the international, flexible production system, the accelerating pace of technological change, and the new global financial structure. As a result of these, governments and state authorities have lost much of their dominion over national economies and societies, and there has been a decline in state legitimacy (Morales 1994; Strange 1996).

This erosion of the power and legitimacy of the state has had two important impacts: first it shifted attention to the nonstate authority, to the other loci or sources of power; and, second, it brought nonpurposive action and unintended consequences to the centre of the stage (Galston 1998). A number of important studies have explored these different sites of power and tracked down the ways in which much of the state authority has become diffused to nonstate agents in economy, polity, and society (Horsman and Marshall 1994; Held 1995; Strange 1996). This phenomenon has given rise to a new distributed and not entirely purposeful governance shared among the different stakeholders as the new emerging social technology.

The Boulding Triangle

Even in the old world of governance, the boundaries between the economic, political, and civic spheres were never well-defined either conceptually or statistically; they did not correspond to a rigid frontier, but rather to a wavering and evolving fracture zone between subsets of organizations and institutions integrated by various mechanisms. This has become even more true in the new world of governance.

Economists have explored this terrain for quite some time. François Perroux (1960) and Kenneth Boulding (1970) proposed a simple conceptual map. Both identified three generic ensembles of organizations dominated more or less by a different mechanism of integration: *quid pro quo exchange* (market economy), *coercion* (polity), and *gift, solidarity, or reciprocity* (community and society). These mechanisms had been explored by Karl Polanyi (1957) as dominant features of the concrete socioeconomies of the past. Perroux and Boulding fleshed out the idea and applied it to the modern context.

In this approach (Figure 1), the organizational terrain is roughly divided into three domains where the rules or mechanisms of coordination are based on different principles: the economic/market domain (B) where the forces of supply and demand and price mechanisms are the norm; the state domain (C) where the rules are based on coercion and redistribution; and civil society (A) where cooperation, reciprocity, and solidarity are the integrating principles. This corresponds roughly to the partitioning of human organizations into economy, polity, and society (Wolfe 1989).

A careful survey of many advanced sociopolitical economies reveals that society, economy, and polity each occupy approximately one-third of the terrain and that the central point is a rough approximation of the centre of gravity of the organizational triangle. This does not correspond to the

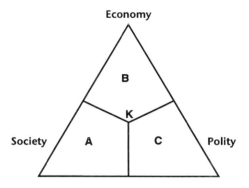

**Figure 1. A modified version of Boulding's triangle,
mapping the organizational terrain based
on three mechanisms of integration.**

statistical portrait emerging from official agencies, mainly because zone-A activities are grossly underreported; activities in the home, within not-for-profit associations, and in general beyond the market and the state are poorly recorded and remain largely underground (Paquet 1989a).

These three sectors have not always had equal valence and need not have similar weight. A century ago in Canada, the state portion was quite limited and the scene was dominated by the other two sets of organizations. From the late 19th century to the 1970s, government grew in importance to the point where probably half of *measured* activities fell into the general ambit of state and state-related activities. The boundaries have been displaced accordingly over time. More recently, a vigorous counter-movement of privatization and deregulation has caused a reduction in the state sector and a reverse shift of the boundaries (Chapter 11).

In parallel with these swings, there has been a tendency for the new socioeconomy to trigger the development of an ever-larger number of *mixed* institutions, blending the different mechanisms to some extent (market-based public regulation, public–private–social partnering, etc.) to provide the necessary signposts and orientation maps in a new confused world. In the recent past, this has translated into a much denser filling in of the Boulding triangle. Mixed institutions have been designed that are capable of providing the basis for cooperation, harmonization, concertation, and even co-decision-making involving agents or organizations from the three sectors (Leroy 1990; Burelle 1995; Laurent and Paquet 1998).

Heterarchy and Co-evolution

A modification of the governance process necessitates some rearrangement of the role of each sector and, therefore, entails a shift of the boundaries between A, B, and C. Any such shift corresponds to a new division of labour among the three sectors, but there is not necessarily a hierarchy among those sectors.

Indeed, the great weakness of most analyses of the scope of government has been that they ascribe to the state either a dependent and somewhat secondary role vis-à-vis the market or a domineering role vis-à-vis economy and society. In the first case, the state is required to attend to matters only when neither the market nor civil society is able to take care of it; in the second case, the state is imposing hegemonic constraints on the other sectors. Both these positions are misleading ideologic stands. In reality, the relationships among sectors are *heterarchical*: it is a world without a pecking order. Heterarchy introduces "*strange loops*" of authority "under conditions of time and place" very much like the "game of paper, rock, and scissors where paper covers rock, rock crushes scissors, and scissors cut paper" (Ogilvy 1986–87). *Any sector may at times have dominion over the others; indeed, the three sectors co-evolve.*

The ecological concept of *co-evolution* is an apt way to synthesize the links among these three universes. Co-evolution in biology refers to an evolutionary process based on reciprocal responses of closely interacting species. Reference has been made to the co-evolution of the beaks of hummingbirds and the shape of the flowers they feed from. The concept can be generalized to encompass feedback processes among interacting systems (social, economic, political) going through a reciprocal process of change. The process of co-evolution becomes a form of *organizational learning*, that is, of joint learning and interadjustment of economy, society, and state (Norgaard 1984).

The central characteristics of this jointly evolving process are *resilience* (the capacity for the economy–polity–society nexus to spring back undamaged from pressure or shock through some minor rearrangements that do not modify the nature of the overall system) and *learning* (the capacity to improve present performance as a result of experience through a redefinition of the organization's objectives and a modification of behaviour and structures as a result of new circumstances). These *governing relations* are in creative tension (resilience calls for preservation, while learning means change) and must be balanced. This does not call for a rigid division of labour among the spheres, but rather, for a capacity to switch to a greater or lesser dependence on one family of integrative mechanisms or another as circumstances change.

One may identify a variety of mixes of political, social, and economic mechanisms (and different modes of interaction among government, business, and society) in different parts of the world. The Anglo-American system (Canada, United States, United Kingdom, Australia, New Zealand, and South Africa) is prone to ascribing a dominant valence to the market mechanism, to the point of belittling the scope of state and civil society. Other parts of the world (Western Europe, Asia, etc.) have chosen to assign a much greater role to the state, but also to community, culture, citizenship, and social cohesion (Dahrendorf 1995).

In this process of co-evolution, adjustments are not the result of the workings of some invisible hand. The state has an important role in maintaining healthy communication in the forum and workable competition in the market. It also has an important intelligence function if it is to act as catalyst in an innovative learning process (Wilensky 1967; Lundvall 1992).

"Glocalization" and Dispersion of Power

To cope with a turbulent environment, organizations must use the environment strategically, in much the same way a surfer uses a wave: to learn faster, to adapt more quickly. This calls for *noncentralization*, for an expropriation of the power to steer held by the top managers in an organization. This is very different from a unilateral decentralization that can be rescinded. There must be constant negotiation and bargaining with partners. Managers must exploit all favourable environmental circumstances and the full complement of imagination and resourcefulness in the heart and mind of each team player; they must become team leaders in task-force-type projects, quasi-entrepreneurs capable of cautious suboptimizing in the face of a turbulent environment (Leblond and Paquet 1988).

This sort of strategy calls for lighter, more horizontal and modular structures, for the creation of networks and informal clan-like rapports (Bressand et al. 1989). This is the case not only in the public sector; in the private sector, the "virtual corporation" and the "modular corporation" are now the new models of governance (Business Week 1993; Tully 1993).

These new modularized private, public, and civic organizations cannot impose their views on their clients or citizens. The firm, very much like the state or civic organizations, must consult. Deliberation and negotiation are everywhere, moving away from goals and controls and deeply into intelligence and innovation. A society based on participation, negotiation, and bargaining has more and more replaced one based on universal rights. The strategic organization has to become a broker, a negotiator, an animateur; and, in this network, a consultative and participative mode obtains among the socioeconomy, the firm, the state, and communities (Paquet 1992a, 1994a; Cassells 1996).

All this triggers a paradoxical outcome that has been analyzed by Naisbitt (1994) and christened *"glocalization"* by Courchene (1995). As globalization proceeds, economic integration increases, and the component parts of the system become more numerous. The central question is how to organize for faster learning. And it would appear, according to Naisbitt, that the game of learning is going to generate more innovation if those components confronted with different local realities are empowered to make decisions on the spot. Thus, globalization has led to localization of decision-making, to empowerment, to the dispersion of power, and to a more distributed governance process.

DISTRIBUTED GOVERNANCE

In times of change, organizations can only govern themselves by becoming capable of learning both what their goals are and the means to reach them *as they proceed*. This is done by tapping the knowledge and information that active citizens possess and getting them to invent ways out of the predicaments they are in.

This leads to a more distributed governance that deprives the leader of his or her monopoly on directing the organization. For the organization to learn quickly, everyone must take part in the *conversation* and contribute each bit of knowledge and wisdom that he or she has that has a bearing on the issue (Paquet 1992a; Webber 1993; Piore 1995).

Distributed governance does not mean only a process of dispersion of power toward localized decision-making within each sector. It also entails a dispersion of power over a wide variety of actors and groups within the Boulding triangle, because of the fact that the best learning experience in a context of rapid change can be brought about through decentralized and flexible teams woven by moral contracts and reciprocal obligations negotiated in the context of evolving partnerships (Nohria and Eccles 1992; de la Mothe and Paquet 1994).

A Triangle-wide Governance System

Distributed governance is embedded in a set of organizations and institutions built on market forces, the state, and civil society. But it is most importantly nested in transverse links relating these three families of institutions and organizations and allowing them to be integrated into a sort of neural net.

These transversal links neither echo the traditional, functional top-down organization nor the matrix form of organizations, where vertical–functional and horizontal–process rapports are supposedly keeping one another in check. Rather, in a transversal world, processes are dominant, and the reaction to external challenges is for the different stakeholders to coalesce laterally to create informal links and multifunctional teams capable of promoting faster and more effective learning (Tarondeau and Wright 1995).

Under ideal circumstances, this multifunctional *esprit de corps* provides a most fertile ground for social learning. It is based on the existence of a social capital of trust, reasonableness, and mutual understanding that facilitates the debates and generates a sort of basic pragmatic ethic likely to promote interaction and synergies among the many potential partners in each of the three families of organizations. But this entails mobilization of all participants through a wide array of coordination maps and institutions all over the Boulding triangle, and this may prove much more difficult to realize than is usually presumed. Indeed, not all social learning is feed-forward in nature, and, consequently, the neural net arrangements may encompass only a portion of the Boulding space, may link the various components only loosely, and may also generate "low" learning.

In these forums that cut across bureaucratic hierarchies and vertical lines of power, fraught with overlapping memberships, personal ties, temporary coalitions, and special-task organizations, "the organizational structure of the future is already being created by the most as well as the least powerful" within the new paradigm (Hine 1977). Indeed, to the extent that middle-range regional and transnational networks are cutting across the usual structures, the interactions distill, in an evolutionary way, an always imperfectly bounded network (Strange 1996).

Transversal Governance and Meso-innovation Systems

Our exploration of the evolution of the governance process suggests that this new pattern tends to evolve in two directions: its centre of gravity shifts downward toward the subnational level with a pattern of power distributed more broadly along the supra- to infra-nation-state axis; and its area spans a broader terrain involving a larger number of institutions and coordinating maps from the economic, political, and civic sectors.

The addition of a major component of *associative governance* to the more traditional state and market governance mechanisms triggers a major qualitative change. It introduces the network paradigm within the governance process (Cooke and Morgan 1993; Castells 1996, 1997), and this paradigm not only dominates the transactions of the social sector, but also permeates the operations of both the state and market sectors (Amin and Thrift 1995). For the network is not, as is usually assumed, a mixed form of organization existing halfway along a continuum ranging from market to hierarchy. Rather, it is a generic name for a third type of arrangement, built on very different integrating mechanisms: networks are consensus or inducement-oriented organizations and institutions (Kumon 1992; Acs et al. 1996).

Networks have two sets of characteristics: those derived from their dominant logic (consensus and inducement-oriented systems) and those derived from their structure. The consensus dominant logic does not abolish power, but means that power is distributed. A central and critical feature of networks is the emphasis on voluntary adherence to norms. Although this voluntary adherence does not necessarily appear to generate constraints, per se, on the size of the organization, it is not always easy for a set of shared values to spread over massive disjointed transnational communities: free riding, high transaction costs, problems of accountability, etc., impose extra work. So the imperatives of leanness, agility, and flexibility have led many important multinationals to choose *neither* to manage their affairs as a global production engine *nor* as a fully decentralized system, but as a multitude of quasi-independent units working in a loose confederated structure (O'Toole and Bennis 1992; Handy 1992).

The structural characteristics of the network nicely complement the collaborative and adaptive network intelligence (Kelly 1994: 189). The network externalities and spillovers are not spreading in a frictionless world; they cast much more of a local shadow than is usually presumed: "Space becomes ever more variegated, heterogeneous and finely textured in part because the processes of spatial reorganization... have the power to exploit relatively minute spatial differences to good effect" (Harvey 1988). So a network does not extend boundlessly; instead, it tends to crystallize around a unifying purpose, mobilizing independent members through voluntary links, around multiple leaders in overlapping and superimposed webs of solidarity. This underscores the importance of "regional business cultures" and the relative importance of networks of small and medium-sized enterprises as a source of new ideas (Putnam 1993; Lipnack and Stamps 1994).

Reciprocity, based on voluntary adherence, generates lower costs of cooperation and, therefore, stimulates networking as social capital accumulates with trust. Not only do the networks generate social capital and wealth, they are also closely associated with a greater degree of progressivity in the economy, that is, with a higher degree of innovativeness and capacity to transform because networks cross boundaries. Indeed, boundary-crossing networks are likely to ignite considerable innovativeness because they provide an opportunity for reframing. In the face of placeless power in a globalized economy,

seemingly powerless places, with their own communication code on a historically specific territory, are fitful terrains for local collaborative innovation
networks (Acs et al. 1996).

Renaissance-style Interdependency

In the transition period from the current nation-state-dominated era to the
newly emerging era of distributed governance and transversal coordination,
there will be a tendency for much devolution and decentralization of decision-
making, i.e., for the meso-level units in polity, society, and economy to become
prominent and for the rules of the game of the emergent order to be couched
in informal terms. Moreover, the emergent properties of the new order (be it
a public philosophy of subsidiarity or another set of workable guiding principles) are likely to remain relatively unpredictable (Ziman 1991; Norgaard
1994; Paquet 1993a, 1995).

This multilayered structure is something very like a neural net of the kind
found in a living brain: a layered system of many signal-processing units
interacting in parallel within and between layers. This sort of system can learn
(i.e., transform) in reaction to external stimuli and develop a capacity for
pattern recognition and for adaptation through experience. Indeed, the
resiliency of the neural net (in the brain or in an organization) is due to the
redundancy of connections that allows the information flow to circumvent any
hole or lesion.

The new form of transversal coordination now in the making may not
suffer as much as some fear from the loss of central control and the weakening
of the national state imperium. A different sort of imperium, adapted to the
age of networking, is emerging — reminiscent of the Roman empire under
Hadrian, where the institutional order was a loose web of agreements made
to ensure compatibility among open networks (Guéhenno 1993).

ADDITIONS TO THE LEXICON

To analyze this drift in the governance process, it is important to develop a
lexicon capable of differentiating the various aspects of the transformation.
Borrowing to a large extent from systems analysis, we must first distinguish
between, on the one hand, the organization as an open system and, on the
other, its environment and recognize that there is continuing interaction
between them.

The environment of the organization may be characterized in broad terms
by its texture. And the texture of the environment has an impact on the system
itself. Depending on whether the environment is placid, randomized, clus-
tered, disturbed reactive, or frankly turbulent, organizations will have to vary
and transform themselves in different ways to cope effectively with these
challenges (Emery and Trist 1965). The texture of the environment has become
much more complex, diverse, and dynamic over the last while, and it has

changed much more rapidly than it used to. Problems are more often than not the result of a confluence of different factors, knowledge is dispersed over many actors, and there is much uncertainty and dissent about the nature of the objectives pursued. This has created new pressures on the organization as an open system.

The governing activities of any single actor have become rather ineffective. Purposeful action by stakeholders is likely to encounter resistance from highly organized groups in these complex, dynamic, and diverse environments. Unintended consequences, external economies and diseconomies, and feedback of all sorts are likely to ensure that the intended outcomes will not be achieved. The interaction and composition effects, the coordination and "collibration" (co-equilibration) efforts, and the important degree of integration, differentiation, and hierarchization that are likely to materialize, are bound to generate a pattern of governance that may have little to do with the original plans.

Indeed, the pattern of governance is likely to *emerge* rather than being crafted.

> Governing and governance are subjected to a permanent process of mutual interaction. Actors who govern, or try to govern, also influence the governance structure.... Some (more powerful) actors have the possibility to rewrite some "rules of the game" but no one has complete control. There is always some intended and unintended change, which creates maneuvering space for actors willing to change the existing pattern. [Kooiman 1993: 258–259]

We are entering an era where the governance process is a game without a master. This raises the question of whether such systems are governable. Governability is a measure of the organization's capability to govern itself within the context of broader systems of which it is part, and the environment within which it is nested. Governability makes no sense in a static context; it corresponds to the organization's capacity to transform, its capacity to modify its structure, its process, and even its substantive guidance mechanism and orientation. To ensure governability, some balance must be maintained between *autonomy* and *responsibility*. Moreover, there must be some match between the *needs* and *potentialities* of the required organizational resources for the governability dynamics to be viable. Finally, governability requires substantial equilibration between *effectiveness* and *legitimacy* (Kooiman 1993: 259–260).

Governing, governance, and governability are obviously in continuous interaction: the gaps between governing needs and capabilities are likely to modify governing behaviour and transform the governance pattern. This is likely to trigger the emergence of a fitful degree of centralization, differentiation, and self-governance; to give rise to a variety of partnerships and joint ventures to respond to the challenges posed by knowledge dispersion, motivation, and implementation problems; and to correct some of the important side-effects of the existing governance structure.

The emerging institutional order may not correspond to one ensuring optimal governability, for it is not determined on the sole basis of efficiency; the most important dimensions are legitimacy, fairness, ethics, learning, etc.

The overall objective is to maintain enough coherence over time to maintain the organization as a bundle of coordination mechanisms, but not so much that it would prevent the organization from developing new instruments, new perspectives, and new purposes (Laurent and Paquet 1998).

This subtle search for the right degree of coherence calls for a new *political* language to replace the traditional *engineering* language in the world of governance. The dynamic new realities of alliances, power, influences, and constituencies have replaced the old static realities of property, structure, planning, and control. In a world where the new assets are intangibles and mainly in the control of stakeholders, the challenge of governability is the challenge of transforming mercenaries, owing loyalty only to themselves, into members of a community interested in and capable of allegiance and reciprocal commitment (Handy 1998).

This calls for significant modification in the form of our organizations. First, it confirms the need for modular and federal structures better able to mobilize loyalty. Second, it requires that trust be nurtured, as it must be in the bloodstream of the organization for it to be effective even though it is only loosely structured.

This does not eliminate the responsibility of the state for "the infrastructure of life" (Handy 1998: 223) in the new governance. Without it, governability is in doubt. This new strategic role of the state is bound to be more modest than it has been in the last 50 years, but it is a most fundamental role in providing help to ensure that appropriate organizations can evolve, that citizens connect themselves better with the market, and that civic engagement and entrepreneurship are rekindled through permissive and supportive framework interventions (Handy 1998; Paquet 1999).

SOCIAL LEARNING

In the dynamic, innovative, and cooperative environment of the learning economy, the capacity to learn increasingly determines the relative position of individuals, firms, and national systems. New modes of production of knowledge and new modes of collegiality, alliances, and sharing of knowledge have evolved (Gibbons et al. 1994; Lundvall and Johnson 1994).

The learning economy is the source of wealth creation and is rooted in a social or collective mobilization of knowledge: learning is harnessing the collective intelligence of the team as a source of continuous improvement (Florida and Kenney 1993). This, in turn, commands a degree of cooperation to take advantage of positive externalities, economies of scale and scope, and strong cumulative experience–learning processes (Jacquemin 1995). But this process does not necessarily work perfectly.

Although much know-what and know-why has been ever more effectively codified and can be produced and distributed as a quasi-commodity, know-how and know-who have remained tacitly and socially embedded (Foray and Lundvall 1996). Consequently, the production and distribution of these latter forms of knowledge have been more problematic; they depend a great deal on social cohesion and trust, on much trespassing and cross-fertilization among disciplines and on the development of networks capable of serving as two-way communication links between tacit and codified, private and shared knowledge, between passive efficiency-achieving learning and creative–destructive Schumpeterian learning (Boisot 1995). There are ample possibilities for coordination failures that can slow down the process of learning (de la Mothe and Paquet 1997).

Interaction and Conventions

Interaction is necessary to generate effective learning. It focuses on the desirable form of imperfect competition or mixes of competition and cooperation characterized by product-based learning. Learning entails "the mutually consistent interpretation of information that is not fully codified, and hence not fully capable of being transmitted, understood, and utilized independently of the actual agents who are developing and using it" (Storper 1996: 259). It is of central importance because of the fact that knowledge is dispersed and exists in a form that is not fully codified. This calls for conventions or relational transactions to define mutually coherent expectations and common guideposts. These conventions differ from sector to sector: they provide the requisite coherence for a common context of interpretation and, for some, "cognitive routinization of relations between firms, their environments, and employees" (Storper 1996: 259).

Such coherence results in nimbleness in the network economy. Yet, a good learning network must not be too coherent: the nodes should not be too similar nor the ties too strong or too routinized. This is the sense in which one may speak of "the strength of weak ties" (Granovetter 1973); a certain degree of heterogeneity and, therefore, social distance, might foster greater potential for innovation because the different parties bring a more complementary body of knowledge to the "conversation." More fruitful synergies ensue.

Ideal-types of Transaction Structures

To analyze the different types of transaction structures, Max Boisot (1995) has suggested a three-dimensional space — information space — which identifies an organizational system in terms of the degree of *abstraction*, *codification*, and *diffusion* of the flow of information within it (Figure 2). This three-dimensional space defines three continua: a vertical axis indicating increasing codification of the information (i.e., the more its form is clarified, stylized, and simplified); an eastward-pointing axis along which information is more widely diffused and shared; and a westward-pointing axis measuring increasing abstraction of the information (i.e., the more general the categories in use) (Boisot 1995).

To illustrate the use of the information space, Boisot has identified several transaction structures corresponding to different loci. First, he identifies as "fiefdoms" the type of organization where information is very concrete and is

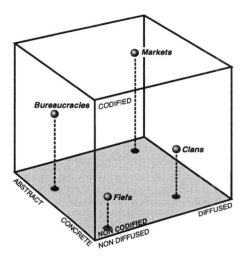

Figure 2. The three dimensions of the flow of information
in organizations. Source: Boisot (1995).

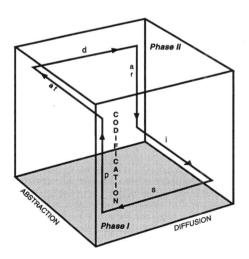

Figure 3. The social learning cycle. Source: Boisot (1995).
Note: Phases I and II are each made up of three steps: s, scanning the environment; p, stylizing the problem; at, abstraction; d, diffusion; ar, absorption; and i,
impact.

neither much codified or widely diffused because of the fact that the core transactions are based on the savoir-faire and personal authority of the leader. Second, he characterizes the world of bureaucracy: information is more abstract (monthly reports, etc.) and codified in precise rules, but available only on a need-to-know basis within the organization and, therefore, not shared much. Third, is the market organization, where price information is very abstract, highly codified, and widely diffused. Finally, Boisot labels as "clans" some organizations based on shared values and personal contacts: in the clan, information is concrete, noncodified, and widely diffused.

In each of these subspaces, governing and governance connote rather different realities. In fiefdoms and bureaucracies, governing is based on top-down command and governance is rather hierarchical; in markets and clans, governing is much more a lateral endeavour, and the pattern of governance much more horizontal and transversal.

The Learning Cycle and Learning Blockages

Within the cube, Boisot has attempted to stylize the operations of the social learning cycle to capture the different phases of the processes of production and diffusion of information in organizational learning. This cycle is presented in two phases with three steps in each phase (Figure 3): phase I emphasizes the cognitive dimensions of the cycle, phase II the diffusion of the new information.

Learning begins in phase I with some scanning of the environment and of the concrete information that is widely known and diffused (s) so as to detect anomalies and paradoxes. In step 2, one is led to stylize the problem (p) posed by the anomalies and paradoxes in a language of problem solution. The third step purports to generalize the solution of the specific issue to a broader family of problems through a process of abstraction (at).

In phase II, the new knowledge is diffused (d) to a larger community of people or groups. Step 5 is a process of absorption (ar) of the new knowledge by the population and its assimilation so that it becomes part of the tacit stock of knowledge. In step 6, the new knowledge is not only absorbed but has an impact (i) on the practices and artefacts of the group or community.

Boisot also notes the possibility of blockages at each step in the learning cycle. For example, in phase I, cognitive dissonance in s may prevent the anomalies from being noted, epistemic inhibitions of all sorts in p may stop the process of translation into a language of problem solution, blockages preventing the generalization of the new knowledge because of the problem definition being encapsulated within the *hic et nunc* (at) may keep the new knowledge from acquiring the most effective degree of generality. In phase II, the new knowledge may not be diffused appropriately because of property rights (d), certain values, or very strong dynamic conservatism which may generate a refusal to listen by those most likely to profit from the new knowledge (ar) or because of difficulties in finding ways to incorporate it (i).

It is important to note that the social learning cycle does not pertain only to the search of new means to reach well-defined ends. It is double-looped in the sense that as the learning proceeds, anomalies and paradoxes are generating the redefinition not only of the means but also of the ends (Argyris and Schon 1978).

Interactivity

Social learning is organization-based and interactive. It stems from creative interactivity. Interactivity is a form of dialectical relations among agents and their evolution through time. It connotes the process through which four aspects of organizations become harmonized: the various capabilities or competences (technical, organizational, strategic, learning) of organizations; the particular capacities of the different organizations (to solve problems, to absorb knowledge, to innovate and experiment, and to incorporate new knowledge in its functions); the interactions with the environment and with other organizations; and the degree of dynamic increasing returns for organizations in learning by learning.

Interactivity brings some sort of cumulative process of learning built on externalities of all sorts, with great potential for irreversibility and inflexibilities of all sorts (Le Bas 1993: 13). But it mostly provokes the genesis of institutions: a set of guideposts, the locus for the memorization and transmission of routines and tacit knowledge through conventions, contracts, and contraptions that form a cognitive framework that guides the learning process and constrains the nature of the exploration and exploitation of new knowledge: they orient the directions of learning (March 1991; Llerena 1997).

The nature of the ethos and of the culture can have an important impact on the shape of the learning cycle. One might find the learning cycle jammed in a narrow band close to the abstraction–codification plane on the left when learning is restricted only to a very limited community, or the learning cycle may rotate almost exclusively within the bureaucratic world or the market world, or it may be disjointed into several separate or quasi-separate loops within the Boisot cube.

New types of relationships have developed in this new context: new open self-elective communities transcending borders and generating new bonds of a nonnational sort have emerged. But there has also been much *stunting* of the existing pluralistic relationships: the rise of reactive exclusionist "identity groups" defined by a total allegiance to a single club — be it tribe, race, gender, ethnicity — that can only lead to the politics of divisiveness and the prevention of the sort of ongoing conversation that leads to social learning (Piore 1995).

Design Rationality

In this new fluid setting where precarious new associative relationships develop, not only is the *citizen* somewhat uprooted, but the whole *process* through which the sociopolitical system learns and gets transformed becomes ill-defined as it is pulled at the same time toward the supranational and the subnational levels, and coordination tends to become much more complex as it becomes based less on hierarchies and more on associative networks of cooperation (Paquet 1997c,d).

These looser forms of coordination may rise organically, but not necessarily. It is not always easy for a set of shared values to spread over massive communities. There are organizational diseconomies of scale. This is why networks do not extend boundlessly, and why their development often depends on shocks (the moral equivalent of a war or the sociological equivalent of a defeat that sometimes provides the requisite *esprit de corps*) or on crises revealing a lack of trust, a lack of the requisite amount of social capital, and the erosion of communities.

These looser forms of coordination build much on tacit knowledge, and tacit knowledge and incomplete knowledge create difficulties and bottlenecks. But it can be argued that excessive codification may well also be a source of inertia and deceleration in the process of learning and change (Foray and Lundvall 1997). Mode 2 production of knowledge is the world of "delta knowledge," i.e., of practical transdisciplinary knowledge as a result of reflection-in-action (Gilles and Paquet 1991). This sort of knowledge is not new, but it has become immensely more important in the recent past, as the intensity and complexity of interactions between actors in organizations has increased.

The pressure to organize, learn, and innovate has generated the emergence of value-creating partner systems in which core competencies are often embodied in forms of knowledge that are idiosyncratically synergetic, i.e., in some form of connoisseurship or practical wisdom, or savoir-faire, that remains largely tacit but is fundamental nonetheless. This form of knowledge has been so neglected and the more traditional form of technical and codified knowledge has been so celebrated that very little has been done to uncover the ways in which delta knowledge is produced and diffused. Even if the capabilities on which this sort of connoisseurship is built are highly regarded, they are often considered as inimitable and noncontestable, so little is known about ways to augment them.

The accumulation of reservoirs of tacit knowledge emerges from *a conversation with the situation* and from a process of exploration and learning driven by *design rationality* (Schon and Rein 1994). Such a process embraces error as the only way to learn, as the way to fuel creative deliberations. This process of learning through a conversation with the situation and as a result of errors (the difference between what is expected and what happens) is at the core of the learning organization, but it is also a quagmire that few have explored seriously. Consequently, we often count on the forces of instrumental rationality and logical processes only because of the fact that these are regarded as the only source of valuable knowledge. Only when the full array of different types of knowledge becomes legitimate and when we have probed the way in which nonlogical processes can be fully tapped can we hope to make the greatest and best use of mode 2 knowledge production.

PROPOS D'ÉTAPE

The essays in this volume were written over some 10 years, and they do not form a systematic study of governance, as they lack the sustained argument of a monograph. However, the whole is more than the sum of the parts. Together, they convey an understanding that separately would be missing. This is the rationale behind my decision to publish them in this form.

Part I contains two chapters that act in lieu of a fully developed conceptual framework. Chapter 1 develops more fully the argument presented in this introduction. Chapter 2 presents, in a succinct way, the social learning approach I have elected to use as our compass and makes passing references to a number of papers presented in part II as an illustration of the heuristic power of this approach.

Part II is a collection of papers in which the social learning approach is used as the analytical framework that is most likely to serve as a set of useful organizing ideas.

- At the international level, this approach covers a vast terrain: a deconstruction of the free trade debate, and an outline of what a science and technology policy might be under free trade.

- At the national level, the social learning approach is used to study the aborted process from which an energy policy might have emerged, and the treacherous problems raised by the environment–energy interface.

- At the social level, the social learning approach is used to examine two thorny policy areas: multiculturalism and liberal education. These areas are ill-structured and poorly understood; my hope was, at best, to provide a provisional lay of the land.

- At the administrative level, I have examined two areas — public service commissions and granting councils — where extraordinary opportunities have been missed as a result of a systematic underestimation of the power of administrative mechanisms as a basis for reform.

Part III attempts to draw some conclusions from these preliminary studies. It sketches the contours of the emerging strategic state, explains the importance of moral contracts in the new governance, and explores the way in which distributed governance and transversal leadership may materialize.

The conclusion raises the question of the burden of office of citizens and officials alike in the new governance, examines the central issues of accountability and ethics at the core of social learning, and identifies the sort of connoisseurship necessary to survive in this world of 360-degree accountability.

Finally, I would like to thank Vicki Bennett, Sandra Garland, and Marie Saumure for their help in getting this manuscript through the production process.

Part I

A Framework

CHAPTER 1

NEW PATTERNS OF GOVERNANCE*

> C'est pas toujours le capitaine
> qui voit premier venir le vent.
>
> – *Gilles Vigneault*

The globalization of production, the dematerialization of economic activity, and a wave of democratization, together with sweeping demographic changes and much social upheaval have generated growing complexity, turbulence, and interdependence in the world's socioeconomic environment. This has led to a loss of the stable state. The foci and substance of the governance process have been modified dramatically (Schon 1971).

Yet, despite these major developments, some features of the governance system have endured. The nation-state is 200 years old, and it would appear to be in very good health. The purposes for which it was invented (to organize and use social violence, to express a sense of political and social identity, to write and then execute the rules by which a society chooses to govern itself, to organize economic life) are still paramount in the consciousness and high among the values and beliefs of citizens (Economist 1990). Indeed, one might even speak of a convulsive in-gathering of nations these days: nation-states are becoming more and more centres of identification and adherence. Therefore, the problem of governance by nation-states continues to be of central concern.

In Canada, the problem of governance is posed with particular acuity. In a survey published in *The Economist*, John Grimond (1991) suggests that Canada is "the first post-modern nation-state, with a weak centre acting as a kind of holding company." Therefore, hierarchical and centralized control is no longer workable, and there is a real danger of anarchy and chaos if the forces of entropy were to make the nation-state rudderless. What then is the pattern of governance in such a context? In what direction is it drifting?

Governance is about guiding. It is "the process whereby an organization or society steers itself" (Rosell 1992: 21). This process is complex and changing,

* This chapter is a revised version of a paper presented at the Canadian Centre for Management Development's (CCMD) annual university seminar in Touraine (Quebec) on 18 February 1993. This work has benefited from discussions with the participants at CCMD's Advanced Management Course in 1991–92, participants at the seminar, suggestions from Ralph Heintzman, and conversations with Lise Pigeon.

but it hinges on the dynamics of communication and control. Consequently, in a globalized, democratic, and knowledge-based society, the pattern of governance is different from what it was in a closed, authoritarian, and natural-resource-based society: the nation-state may have endured but the governance process and the precise way in which the state plays its role in it have evolved and will continue to evolve.

Because a number of important changes in the sociopolitical environment and in the guiding values are already detectable, some have argued that the contours of the governance system in advanced socioeconomies in the 21st century — in the private, public, and civic sectors — may be surmised in a general way, that already a new set of rules is in the process of crystallizing: complexity is the new reality and perplexity the new frame of mind.

A CONCEPTUAL FRAMEWORK

Those attempting to read the auspices or search for directions are confronted with competing paradigms. A paradigm is a "cluster of fundamental principles guiding the perception and organization of data... a widely shared system of assumptions and beliefs operating at a basic, almost unconscious level of experience" (Ogilvy 1986–87). The most popular categorization of paradigms pertaining to the governance of the nation-state suggests three scenarios: the dominant *hierarchical* paradigm, the also popular *minimal government* paradigm, and the emerging *heterarchical* paradigm of decentralized planning (scissors cut paper/paper wraps stone/stone breaks scissors) (Ogilvy 1986–87).

This categorization, though suggestive, provides neither a sufficiently detailed description of the terrain nor a sufficiently rich heuristic. The difficulty with these simple paradigms is that they quickly run into paradoxes and dilemmas as soon as one uses them. Such anomalies or insoluble puzzles are signs that the paradigm is unable to explain what is happening. A paradigm shift or a reframing is then probable. But shifting back and forth from one of these paradigms to another is a game that has not proved very fruitful.

To produce a diagnosis and to be able to design new systems of governance in the post-modern state requires a guiding analytical framework. In the language of Harvey Leibenstein (1976), an analytical framework is "a set of relationships that do not lead to specific conclusions about the world of events (but constitute) ... the mold out of which the specific theories are made." A conceptual framework is much more in the nature of an approach, of a preliminary way to organize objects of the inquiry. Such a framework is not easy to construct, for it must build on a synthesis of work done in isolation in the fields of industrial organization, strategic management, the contractual theories of organization, etc. (Charreaux et al. 1987; Alt and Shepsle 1990; Milgrom and Roberts 1992). Each group celebrates its own interpretation of reality with little or no reference to the work done by the other groups.

Our approach may not offer the ideal synthesis but it allows for a degree of syncretism and might prove to be a powerful heuristic.

Information and Organization

A wide array of models and theories provide guidance for discussion of governance and organizations. Oliver Williamson (1975, 1985), who has done some of the most interesting work in this area, uses a framework emphasizing the cost of transacting. Other groups single out property rights as a guidepost. Others suggest that one can dissolve the organization into a web of explicit or implicit contracts, and still others postulate that the organization emerges from complex dynamic and somewhat implicit interdependencies. Whatever the model, a basic feature remains constant: organizations may be regarded as a way of structuring and sharing information. In that sense, one may x-ray organizations via their informational dimensions without any a priori commitment to any of the causal explanations in good currency (Ouchi 1980; Boisot 1987; Stinchcombe 1990).

One of the simplest presentations of this approach is the synthesis of Max Boisot (1987) (developed from the work of William Ouchi and others) in which he suggests that organizations might be mapped in a two-dimensional *culture space* which defines the extent that information is codified and diffused: the farther from the origin on the vertical axis, the more codified is the information (i.e., the less ambiguous, the less fuzzy, the more stylized the code, the more structured the information), and the farther from the origin on the horizontal axis, the more readily diffused is the information (i.e., the more widely the information is shared). Boisot partitions that *culture space* into four subspaces (Figure 4) in which is a reduced form of Figure 2.

This partitioning carves out different families of organizational arrangements where

• transactions are based on personal knowledge and authority imposing a sort of *dominion* in a *fiefdom* where information is not very codified or diffused (lower left quadrant);

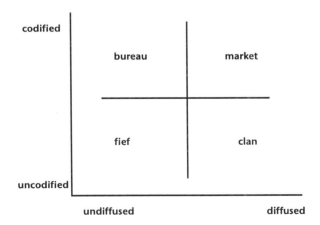

Figure 4. Organizations in a two-dimensional culture space.
Source: Boisot (1987).

- transactions are based on well-codified, proprietary knowledge not generally available outside the organization and hierarchically coordinated transactions in *bureaucracies* (upper left quadrant);
- transactions are based on impersonal information and knowledge very neatly codified in the form of price signals and widely diffused in *market-type organizations* (upper right quadrant); and
- transactions based on shared values, personal contacts, and implicitly-conducted negotiations among peers in *clans* (lower right quadrant).

Evolution of Governance

Boisot (1987) uses this simple tool to sketch the evolution of the firm: from the fiefdom of the small family firm dominated by its authoritarian owner, to the more bureaucratic forms of management in large firms; from bureaucracies to the multidivisional or holding-company administrative forms that have emerged, introducing some form of market coordination as the centre acts as a sort of capital allocation mechanism among units dominated by bottom-line considerations; and from these quasi-market organizations to the loosely coupled organisms regarded by Peter Drucker (1988) as the "coming new organization."

This template may be used to explore a number of hypotheses about the dynamics of information and organization. For instance, one may use it to stylize the diverse corporate culture of the various departments within a firm: the research and development department might be organized as a fiefdom, the production department as a bureaucracy, the sales department as a market, and the board as a clan. One may also use this approach to examine certain hypotheses about the structuring of organizations, for instance, the hypothesis put forward by Arthur Stinchcombe (1990: 6) that "the structure of organizations [is] determined by their growth toward sources of news, news about the uncertainties that most affect their outcomes"; one may gauge whether the crystallization of an organization's form can be ascribed to this major force. Such a template also helps us make sense of the new organizational forms that have been much celebrated in the recent past (many forms of highly decentralized and less formal networks) which would be located roughly in the right-hand quadrants (Leblond and Paquet 1988; Davidow and Malone 1992; Peters 1992).

One might even conjecture, on the basis of ethnographic evidence, that, both in the private and the public sectors, there has been a systematic drift away from bureaucracy toward forms of organizations that are based on more diffused information, because they are more effective in getting the news. This *dispersive revolution* in private, public, and civic organizations has often been celebrated as forms of "privatization" and "deregulation." What has not been heralded is the fact that this quasi-disintegration of bureaucracies has been paralleled by a quasi-reintegration using very different instruments: moral contracts and other clan-type ligatures (Badot and Paquet 1991; de la Mothe and Paquet 1994).

In a nutshell, our hypothesis is that the governance system of the different sectors is in the process of moving to an organizational form characterized by a less-codified information structure and more diffuse information sharing, i.e., toward the lower right quadrant in Boisot's model.

CRITIQUE OF THE STANDARD PARADIGMS OF GOVERNANCE

Even though fiefdoms have not disappeared entirely, bureaucracies and market-type organizations are the standard forms in the public and private sectors. Indeed, at times, much of the current debate on governance appears to revolve around the different ways in which private and public bureaucracies might be freed from their arteriosclerosis through some marketization: closer links with the customers, more competition, total quality imperatives, etc.

These debates have revealed that the simple introduction of market incentives and competition will not suffice to meet the challenges at hand. Market-type mechanisms have been shown to be relatively inefficient compared with negotiated arrangements, and competition much less effective than presumed in both the public and private sectors (Cova and Cova 1991). So the traditional bureaucratic governance system is under siege, and nothing less than a radical departure from the hierarchical model (more or less enriched by market paraphernalia) seems to be called for.

External Pressures

External pressures on domestic firms and governments have originated first and foremost from one major nexus of interconnected forces: the emergence of a knowledge-based and technologically sophisticated global economic order. Innovation has become the determining source of economic advantage; the globalization process has introduced a fair degree of fuzziness in the very notions of "domestic firm" and "national economy" (Paquet 1990a). Both these forces have triggered a new strategy of coordination and control and a metamorphosis of the rules of the game.

On the one hand, heightened competition and the search for competitive advantage generated by the process of international integration have demanded maximum mobility, fluidity, and flexibility in the process of continuous adaptation by both government and business. On the other hand, the centrality of knowledge and information has set in place a new logic: new types of technological ensembles built on "untraded interdependencies" or synergies among sectors, technologies, and firms have constrained the possibilities of recombination, generated the need for new compacts, and created focusing devices and guideposts that have greatly influenced firms and governments.

Accelerated change has forced them to become multiterritorial, to cope with fierce time-competition, and to experiment with networking and strategic alliances not only with clients, suppliers, venture capitalists, or research laboratories, but also even with governments. In this process, centralized insensitive Taylorian structures are a strategic handicap: such structures do not learn fast nor grow toward the source of news. This was IBM's fate: "It grew complacent and failed to innovate" (Stewart 1993).

The emerging transnational–technological context has imposed new strategically crucial tasks on national governments while considerably limiting the scope of independent policies that national governments can pursue (at least without major social costs). The complexity of the issues facing governments generates more and more "wicked problems" in policy formation: unclear and uncertain objectives, given the general turbulence and interdependence, and a great uncertainty and instability in the means–end relationships at least with reference to standard policy tools. In the face of "wicked problems," simple rules are no longer available; governments must learn as much about their goals as about the means likely to help them achieve them (Rittel and Webber 1973).

In this context, governance has ceased to be a matter of defining organizational targets and designing simple control mechanisms to ensure their attainment. When the ground is in motion, governments and firms have to rely much more on intelligence and innovation, to develop smarter ways and strategic alliances, and to promote innovation.

Simply injecting competition into the governance system is not enough. More competition has brought *some* benefits (Barzelay 1992), but the intricacies of the "virtual corporation" and "virtual government" (i.e., the new types of sophisticated networks coming together quickly to exploit fast-changing opportunities) require a high degree of cooperation and trust, and the market mechanism by itself does not nurture sufficient cooperation.

As a result, there has been a shift from a narrow celebration of competition (as a government-free environment), to concerns for competitiveness (which encompasses the broader sociopolitical context of cooperation), to insistence on development power, as it has become amply clear that many features of the competitive advantage of firms and nations flow from active private and public entrepreneurship, from government policies, and from new forms of partnerships between governments and firms (Dahmén 1988; D'Cruz and Rugman 1992).

Internal Constraints

At a time when governance systems are strained by external pressures, a family of sociodemographic and ideological–legal pressures has emerged from within nation-states, considerably weakening their power bases. New demands by citizens and clients whose expectations know no bounds have revealed both the extraordinary weaknesses in the bureaucratic paradigm's ability to cope with these heightened demands and the serious difficulties raised by the loss of legitimacy of that state and the rigidities introduced by charters of rights and misdirected accountability (Marquand 1988).

In Canada, these questions have been and are important. Seven million Canadians were born between 1950 and 1966. This "baby boom" is the most important social phenomenon of our time, and the "boomers" have changed the face of the nation. A "new kind of people" has been produced: more sharply differentiated, more demanding, more alienated, more balkanized, and with a greater capacity for violence (Kettle 1980). In the last 20 years, the sharp increase in immigration has brought "new faces in the crowd" and a much more polyethnic and multicultural country. The nature of the demands on government and business has become more variegated and has contributed to some attenuation of the solidarities and of the consensus on which the old governance system had come to depend (Hardin 1974).

Ideologies can energize and motivate, but they can also paralyze the nation-state. On the one hand, we witness heightened expectations on the part of the citizens and less willingness to accept centrally controlled organizations using Taylorian methods to extract their contribution as suppliers. This has created a growing tension as the requirement to provide a larger quantity and a higher quality of service has come more and more sharply into conflict with less malleability of the workforce. The failure to live up to expectations has raised important questions about the efficacy and even the legitimacy of the state.

On the other hand, the post-modern ideology has challenged the legitimacy of existing institutions and organizations. Indeed, post-modernism questions all the major interpretative schemes: it raises questions about the destructive effects of the rationalization of society under the influence of the managerial state and of bureaucracies in general; it also generates the emergence of new guiding values and social movements (women, ecologists, transculturalism, etc.) that offer alternative interpretations of society. Everything becomes contestable and unanimity disappears. As a result, the modern state has imploded: contested and balkanized, it has lost its guiding legitimacy.

Moreover, social relations have grown tense and the degree of litigiousness has increased, as we observe a shift in power from the legislative and executive branches of government to the judiciary and as precise methods focused on rules enforcement and centralization are less and less effective. Even when market-related arrangements (such as user fees or merit rating) have been added to the panoply of instruments used by bureaucracies, the fundamental intent to control and enforce responsibility is ever present. Governance has, therefore, become more and more unwieldy, and bureaucratic organizations (even when they have been gingered by market-driven contraptions) are increasingly unable to cope effectively with the tasks at hand without going beyond authority, rules, procedures, and administrative systems.

Anomalies and Paradoxes

The real test of modern organizations is their capacity to meet the new challenges from without and the new constraints from within, i.e., their capacity to read and understand the environment and to respond swiftly and creatively to the challenges of the new context. The old hierarchical, centrally controlled organizations are inefficient at that sort of adaptation for, as was noted in connection with IBM's difficulties in the recent past, they "suppress innovation, crush aspirations and retard productivity" (Mills 1993).

The large hierarchical private and public organizations suffer from a form of arteriosclerosis that prevents them from taking steps to resolve their problems. Indeed, the way out of the present predicament calls for paradoxical and seemingly contradictory strategies for which such organizations are rather ill-equipped: organizing/focusing on one hand and disorganizing/de-integrating on the other, to be both smaller (as firms break up) and bigger (as their networks grow), to have more autonomy and power but to form more partnerships (Peters 1992).

Successful organizations are those that find ways to accommodate and resolve these contradictory needs — promoting competitive pressure and network cooperation at the same time. These countervailing pressures raise the question of the source of the requisite amount of trust, unrequited transfers, and the like that are necessary for such islands of cooperation to be built in a sea of competition.

Such anomalies and paradoxes call for a reframing of the very way in which we think about public and private organizations. The new forms of organization require more than mere tampering with structures; they cannot simply be quasi-disintegrated and quasi-reintegrated in a more modular or decentralized form according to the old rules of social architecture and using the old materials. The very notion of effective governance has to be rebuilt on an entirely new set of principles and values. It is not simply a weighted average of markets and hierarchies. The degree of turbulence and the speed of change is such that innovation, motivation, and speed of response are the new norms. Moreover, coordination cannot be accomplished successfully through the simple magic of stylized signal prices or the utterance of commands. It must be effected through the development of shared values and shared understanding. This is the only way to achieve the right balance between delegation and control. This calls for new styles of organization and new managerial competencies (Morgan 1988).

A new evolutionary model of organization is needed: one providing an approach to coordination through voluntary adherence to uncodified norms, which can best serve as guideposts because of their informal nature, and of the "jurisprudence" allowing them to evolve as circumstances dictate and new contexts command.

THE ORGANIZATION AS CLAN

The road to a pattern of governance that is less heavy-handed and more flexible, less directive and more participative, more diffuse and less technocratic may appear at best somewhat utopian and at worst a hybrid form of organization that might unleash the most ungodly exclusive coalitions. These objections have been voiced in a very articulate way, yet neither is warranted. Clan-type networks exist in the private, public, and civic sectors, which should be enough to rid us of the label of impractical idealist. Moreover, successful clan-type networks are open, inclusive, pluralist, and coherent, which should dispel the fear that clans must degenerate into conspiracies (Hine 1977; O'Toole and Bennis 1992).

This *new evolutionary model of organization* — under a number of labels — has "emerged" in the private and public sectors, but also within a wide range of social "movements" as the most effective governance system. Anthropologist Virginia Hine (1977) has used the clumsy phrase "segmented polycephalous network" (SPN) and emphasized the central role of the "ideological bond" or "the power of a unifying idea" as adding the sort of glue necessary to make the organization live and prosper. To underline this key dimension, Hine has labeled the new form of organization SP(I)N where I stands for ideology.

The organization chart of an SP(I)N/clan would look like "a badly knotted fishnet with a multitude of nodes and cells of varying sizes, each linked to all the others directly or indirectly." Examples might be the Audubon Society, the Sierra Club, ABB (Asea Brown and Boveri), or the Confederaziun Helvetica (Hine 1977; O'Toole and Bennis 1992).

A central and critical feature of the notion of clan is the emphasis on *voluntary* adherence to norms. Although this voluntary adherence does not necessarily generate constraints on the size of the organization (as some of the examples mentioned above indicate), it is not always easy for a set of shared values to spread over massive disjointed transnational communities: high transaction costs, problems of accountability, etc., impose extra work. So the benefits in terms of leanness, agility, flexibility are such that many important multinationals have chosen *not* to manage their affairs as a global production engine, but as a multitude of smaller quasi-independent units coordinated by a loose federal structure, because of the organizational diseconomies of scale in building a clan (O'Toole and Bennis 1992; Handy 1992).

This nonhierarchical constellation of units is glued together by a common vision, a covenant that binds the allegiance of the units to the basic purpose. The clan (1) is working on a project that has a hologram function (i.e., each part contains a perception of the whole project and of its place in it) and (2) is capable of learning through dialogue, networking, feedback, and self-organization (Sérieyx 1993).

The same generic language can be used to analyze the new process of governance of the state and the new form of corporate governance: in each case, the form/design and the content/strategy of the organization is dramatically modified as it acquires clan status. Indeed, this new organization form is characterized by a different anatomy and physiology, and a different form of organizational glue, leadership, and ethics.

Anatomy

The new form of organization, in the private, public, and civic sectors, is a result of contradictory forces: the word *federal* is often used to characterize the ongoing tensions between big and small, global and local, noncentralized and coordinated, pluralist and coherent, etc. It is also modest, suppletive, and fundamentally designed according to the subsidiarity principle (Handy 1992; Millon-Delsol 1992).

The word "subsidium" means "reserve army": this is the source of help when needed. The subsidiarity-based organization is designed to help those in need. It does not derive its authority from basic or primary rights of individual citizens or clients, but from an assessment of their incapacity (if left to themselves) to contribute effectively to the common good and of the consequent need to help the citizens or clients through the intervention of the level of "authority" that is closest to the citizen or client — family, locality, region, etc. — a responsibility being delegated upward only when it is impossible to do the work at a lower level (Millon-Delsol 1992).

The notion of subsidiarity (and its insistence on needs) raises questions about the ideology of egalitarianism that underpins the concept of universal and generalized programs without any attention paid to the capacity of individuals to deal with the underlying problem. With reference to the private sector, it raises parallel questions about the wisdom of mass production in the face of personalized demands. Conversely, subsidiarity would appear to legitimize a sort of *"devoir d'ingérence"* that is both precise and limited, but might appear to violate the independence and autonomy of citizens. In this reframed version of the organization, a number of basic features stand out (Paquet 1993b).

Scheming virtuously: The need to cope with a turbulent environment forces the organization to adopt a design that enables it to use the pulsations of the environment the way the surfer uses the wave: organizations must use the environment strategically to develop more actively plausible scenarios, to learn faster, to adapt more quickly. This calls for *noncentralization*, for expropriation of the steering power from the top leaders of the organization. We are very far from unilateral decentralization that can be rescinded. There must be constant negotiation and bargaining with nature and partners. Managers must exploit all favourable environmental circumstances and the full complement of imagination and resourcefulness in the heart and mind of each team player. They must become team leaders in taskforce-type projects, quasi-entrepreneurs capable of cautious suboptimizing in the face of a turbulent environment (Emery and Trist 1965; Leblond and Paquet 1988).

Modular structures: This sort of strategy calls for lighter, more horizontal and modular structures, networks and informal clan-like rapports (Bressand et al. 1989) in units freer from procedural morass, empowered to define its mission and its clienteles more precisely, and to invent different performance indicators. This is not only the case in the public sector: in the private sector, the "virtual corporation" and the "modular corporation" are now the new models (Business Week 1993; Tully 1993).

"Modular" should not convey a sense that the organization chart is a linear set of blocks. This new organization is patterned after neural networks incorporated into flexible and evolutionary structures of relations and *filières*. These structures are in a process of continuous self-reorganization. This is happening in government with the proliferation of executive agencies, commissions of inquiry, i.e., all sorts of "temporary networks" getting together to solve urgent issues, very much as it is going on in the private sector to exploit fast-changing opportunities.

Interactive meso-forums: Modularized private and public organizations cannot impose their views on clients or citizens in a Taylorian way. The firm, much like the state, must consult. Deliberation and negotiation are everywhere: away from goals and controls and deep into intelligence and innovation. A society based on participation, negotiation, and bargaining is replacing one based on universal rights. The strategic organization has to become a broker, a negotiator, an animateur; in this network socioeconomy, the firm and the state are always in a consultative and participative mode (Navarre 1986; Paquet 1992a; see also Chapter 11).

In these forums that cut across bureaucratic hierarchies and vertical lines of power and are fraught with overlapping memberships, personal ties, temporary coalitions, special-task organizations, "the organizational structure of the future is already being created by the most as well as the least powerful" within the new paradigm (Hine 1977). Indeed, to the extent that middle-range regional and transnational networks and forums are cutting across the usual structures, the interactions distill in an evolutionary way the always imperfectly bounded network.

Partnerships and moral contracts: The networks are consolidated by partnerships and moral contracts that must be based on a few basic, shared assumptions. Rigid rules are not useful, as the environment is evolving rapidly and new directions are always in the process of being crafted and recrafted. Protocols cannot be stylized, routined, or written down. In such a multinodal neural network, the density of interchange is maximized, redundancy of connections is the rule, and communication is protocol-free. This is the way the brain resolves problems and also the way clan-type networks operate.

Physiology

At the core of the physiology of the clan-type organization is a process of social learning. The efficacy, resilience, and usefulness of the new organizational pattern stem from its capacity to learn. Organizational learning occurs when

> Members of the organization act as learning agents for the organization, responding to changes in the internal and external environments of the organization by detecting and correcting errors in organizational theory-in-use, and embedding the result of their inquiry in private images and shared maps of the organization. [Argyris and Schon 1978]

Organizational learning occurs through flexible networks held together by moral contracts based on reciprocal negotiated obligations. Nothing is black or white: all is grey. The moral contracts contribute to the solution of the potential prisoner's dilemma that might plague clan-type networks by defining, often tacitly, the corridor or boundaries within which one must stay to honour the agreed-on expectations (Paquet 1991–92a).

There are many definitions of the learning organization (Friedmann and Abonyi 1976; Senge 1990), none of which covers the whole range of learning mechanisms and activities. One can describe organizational learning very simplistically:

- the process of acquisition of new information is enhanced by the promotion of experimentation, the use of planned, temporary systems-like taskforces;

- the process of retention and use of the new information is improved by teamwork, mutual respect, good communication, and sharing of experiences; and

- the capacity for continued learning and self-renewal of the organization is ensured through mechanisms to evaluate experiences and orderly discarding of dysfunctional ways.

The process of *organizational learning* itself is acquiring particular characteristics in the face of complexity. The environment is turbulent, the ground is in motion, uncertainty is omnipresent, and the policy/strategy problems are ill-structured and/or wicked. Three main principles appear to drive the learning process under these circumstances (Morin 1990):

- The *dialogic principle* posits the coexistence of contradictory logics at the very core of the problem definition. Social learning in the clan occurs through the maintenance of complementary/antagonistic forces. This is the only way to tackle a world marred by paradoxes, anomalies, and contradictions: for example, the tension between organizing and focusing, disorganizing and deintegrating, accountability and teamwork, autonomy and partnership, smaller and larger that confront all organizations at present (Peters 1992). Maintaining these contradictions is inherent to the "federal principle" and it is seen as crucial to the functioning of organizations like ABB (divided into some 1200 companies with an average of 200 employees and subdivided into some 4500 profit centres with an average of 50 employees, but with only 100 professionals at the Zurich headquarters). To its CEO, Percy Barnevik, "ABB is an organization with three internal contradictions. We want to be global and local, big and small, radically decentralized with centralized reporting and control" (O'Toole and Bennis 1992).

- The *organizational feedback principle* establishes that the clan produces not only output, but also itself. On a given day, the members of clans are different from what they were the day before: they have sharpened their roles, the technology has drifted ever so slightly, the self-image or theory of the organization has improved or deteriorated, and in the process the functioning and governance system has evolved. The clan is a self-organizing form in which simultaneously the clan shapes its members and the members shape the clan.

- The *hologram principle* echoes the neural nature of the network: the quasi-totality of the information contained in the whole clan may be accessed through any member of the clan. It is a way to transcend the dichotomy between fixation on the whole or on the parts. In the brain, learning gets incorporated into neural nets, and even if a portion of the brain is destroyed the information can be retrieved. In the same manner, social learning proceeds in a two-way process of enrichment of the whole by the parts and vice-versa (Morgan 1986).

These three principles are interactive: they represent a way to approach complexity that challenges the Manichean casts of mind that suggest that only one logic must underpin an organizational form, that organizations are programmed by a "syndrome" that is not evolving but self-reinforcing, and that the duality between whole and parts must be resolved instead of being self-reinforcing.

The Ideological Glue

One fundamental dimension of the clan-type network is the syndrome of images/theory/values that gives it unity, stability, and dynamism. This bond is defined in a variety of ways but is always presented as a central glue — a common appreciative system, a shared vision, or a common set of values.

Jane Jacobs (1992) reminds us that "syndrome" comes from the Greek, meaning "things that run together." She boldly proposes that different ethical or theoretical glues bind together different types of organizations and divide them under two general headings: the guardian moral syndrome underpinning the hierarchical system, and the commercial moral syndrome underpinning market-type organizations.

Jacobs sketches the main features of these two syndromes. The guardian syndrome shuns trading, exerts prowess, adheres to tradition, hierarchy, discipline, ostentation, largesse, honour, fortitude, and deception. The commercial syndrome shuns force, celebrates voluntary agreements, adheres to collaboration, competition, industriousness, thriftiness, and dissent. Jacobs then declares, on the basis of a rather unpersuasive argument based largely on anecdotes, that any attempt to mix the two syndromes can only lead to "monstrous hybrids." Indeed, much of her book is a relentless declaration that when one syndrome encroaches on the other, "crazy things happen." In principle, Jacobs is willing to entertain the possibility that syndrome-friendly inventions and adaptations of one syndrome in the direction of the other are possible and that flexibility on this front may produce good results, but her main thrust is a forceful assertion that these two "systems of survival" do not lend themselves to much beneficial mixing.

Jacobs' Manichean approach is wrong-headed. It is built on much misunderstanding of the paradoxical realities of modern society. Monstrous hybrids are often the result of a hypocritical mask or rhetoric borrowed from one syndrome being slapped on a reality that is clearly defined by the other (Sérieyx 1993: 274). Contrary to Jacobs, our argument is that symbiosis between syndromes can occur and does occur *without* corruption. This is not only possible, it is mandatory and essential in the modern context. Indeed, such mixing constitutes the major challenge for the implantation of the new pattern of governance.

A clan requires a system of survival that combines the two appreciative systems underpinning hierarchy and market. Only such a combination can elicit a mixed system that has the capacity to overcome the hegemony of vertical linkages (imposed by hierarchical arrangements) and of horizontal linkages (embedded in market mechanisms) to promote the dominion of *transversal* linkages weaving together the network-type clan.

This new "mixed" syndrome (calling, for instance, for the capacity to play the market game when it is called for while recognizing the necessity of playing the guardian game in the face of crises) corresponds to the imperatives of the new reality. In a complex world, one cannot rely on simple radar, based on permanent rules. The key decisions have to be taken in full cognizance of changing and turbulent circumstances. Indeed, one needs not only to elicit transparent ways to mix these syndromes or to establish mechanisms through which one can switch at the right time between syndromes, but to develop the capacity for the mixed syndrome to evolve as circumstances change.

Already, some work on animal collectivities and on sophisticated social organizations has revealed that one may identify communities where the dual syndrome is in place and performs most effectively; although swift and radical guardian-type interventions are made during a crisis to secure the collective survival, the commercial syndrome takes over as soon as the crisis dissolves. Indeed, Japan is referred to as having found a particularly effective and idiosyncratic way to solve this very problem with great success (Vertinsky 1987). But this may not be sufficient. Nothing less than a syncretic meta-syndrome or a meta-set of rules is necessary.

The reason for this is rather simple. If one is interested in change or in changing rules, one must be in a position to discuss the rules about changing rules. In a legal framework, laws, rules, and regulations are established. The rules about defining rules are defined in the constitution — the constitution being a meta-rule. If one wishes to change the constitution (i.e., the rules about changing rules), one must shift the debate to a higher plane: the rules about changing rules about changing rules. In many countries, this requires a referendum. In the case at hand, what is needed to arbitrate and finalize the appropriate mix of syndromes and/or the switching mechanism between syndromes are some basic values that might act as meta-rules (Orgogozo and Sérieyx 1989).

What might serve as meta-rules appears to be rooted in an emerging ideology of participation. Until now, liberal democracies have emphasized rights and negative freedom (i.e., protection against interference with individual choices). This has led to an expropriation of the central ruling work of the citizens. Participation emphasizes positive freedom (i.e., the person being able to do this or be that and the duty to help others in that respect). In a rights society, the dignity of the individual comes from the fact that he has rights; in a participation society, freedom and efficacy come from the fact that the individual has a recognized voice. This participatory model obviously presupposes a "strong sense of community" (Taylor 1985). "The segmented organizational pattern that emerges involves individual participation in more than one segment. Participants... interact with several different nodes in the network" (Hine 1977).

This ideology of participation will bolster the clan as a pattern of governance and help spread it like wildfire. It is still *en émergence*, but it is in the making. It is embodied in an evolving pragmatic ethic that establishes a corridor within which the language of rights, individualism, and markets prevail, map the area beyond the corridor where the language of good would supersede it, and work out a language of problem solution for border issues: a pragmatic compromise of communicative procedures (commercial syndrome) *and* communitarian substance (guardian syndrome) that binds the multitude of participants in the sociocultural system in a sort of transversal neural network (Paquet 1991-92b).

THE NEW COMPETENCE

The new pattern of governance demands that managers have competencies quite different from those required in the past, and this has an important impact on the mix of education, training, and personal development likely to enable leaders and managers to be ready for the future. Because the new organization has to become a learning organization, the new "federal" leader or manager cannot ordain or command any longer: he or she must consult, negotiate, act as coach, animateur, designer, advocate, etc.

Families of New Competencies

The competencies that are going to be essential in this new world have not been fully documented yet, and there would be much disagreement in any discussion about what should be on any priority list. But one can draw up a provisional list from the work of Donald Michael (1980, 1988a,b) and Gareth Morgan (1988). The new competencies appear to fall into four general groups: contextual competencies; interpersonal and enactment skills; creating an effective corporate climate; and systems values.

Contextual competencies: This group consists of a number of important competencies and tools that are unlikely to be developed in management programs: acknowledging uncertainty, recognizing the full implications of the fact that there is no reliable theory of social change, the capacity to entertain two logics at the same time, embracing error, building bridges and strengthening links, reframing problems to explore new solutions, and the capacity to prospect the regulation though values and norms.

Interpersonal and enactment skills: This group contains the whole range of communication skills and tools that are going to be required in a variety of contexts: consultation, negotiation, deliberations, conflict resolution, facilitation, action as a broker, a preceptor, an educator, an animateur. There is also the capacity to adopt new roles and attitudes.

Creating an effective corporate climate: In this group, one might retain the central importance of facilitating a shift toward perceiving the organization as a learning system; this requires a capacity to enable and truly empower individuals and a culture of productivity, responsiveness, creativity, and learning.

Systems values: This group focuses on the new ethic driven by the new reality of interconnectedness and interdependence: "our values still emphasize rights and autonomy while the actual circumstances of life make imperative the acceptance of obligations and interdependence" (Michael 1988a). This ethic is one that forces a redefinition of leadership: away from leaders as generals to leaders as leaders of leaders — those removing obstacles that prevent followers from making creative and effective decisions themselves (O'Toole and Bennis 1992).

Experiential and Action Learning

These new competencies cannot be acquired solely through a bookish mode of instruction or solely through action. One is not simply attempting to develop a broader knowledge base, or a few particular skills (although much of that is also happening) but to promote personal development. Indeed, as David Kolb (1984) would put it, in a true sense, learning is "the process whereby development occurs." This relatively novel way of looking at learning denies the cleavage between learning and personal development, between learning and experience. It calls for ways to effect this learning by going through all of the steps of the "wheel of learning": questioning, theory, action/experience and reflection (Handy 1990).

The current debates on management education have revealed its extraordinary weaknesses (Fry and Pasmore 1983; Porter and McKibbin 1988; Paquet 1992a). It has become clear that the educational establishment tends to break down experience or action into bits and pieces and write off too quickly the knowledge that can only result from one's own experience. As a result, it has failed to provide the sort of learning that is required. The need to change the paradigm has been captured by the new emphasis on *leadership*, a word that may fail to connote something very precise, and indeed has a protean quality, but captures very well what Vickers and others have been grasping for since the postwar period.

In leadership, what is at stake is "the ability to stay the course while rocking the boat, to enhance organizational readiness and competitiveness in an unpredictable environment" (Vicere 1992). This ability cannot be imparted effectively except through experiential and action learning. This form of intelligence — *mètis* as the Greeks called this complex but coherent set of mental attitudes and intellectual behaviour that combines "*le flair, la sagacité, la prévision, la souplesse d'esprit, la feinte, la débrouillardise, l'attention vigilante, le sens des opportunités*" and is applied to "*des réalités fugaces, mouvantes, déconcertantes, ambiguës, qui ne se prêtent ni à la mesure précise, ni au calcul exact, ni au raisonnement rigoureux*" (Détienne and Vernant 1974) — cannot be imparted in any other way.

The links between *leadership* and *mètis* and the intricate links between these concepts and the concept of *phronesis* ("*union entre un jugement sain et l'acte qui est l'expression correcte de ce jugement*") is a terrain that Aristotle explored in some details. Contrary to Plato who condemned this sort of intelligence *tâtonnante*, Aristotle celebrated it as the result of a dialogue with the situation that transforms, with experience, into *incorporated prudence and vigilance* (Paquet 1992b).

One can design programs likely to improve those needed competencies, and much experience has been gained in the design of such programs by the executive leadership team at CCMD. Such a program is profoundly inspired by the experiential learning theory of development that builds on the four learning modes:

> Affective complexity in concrete experience results in higher-order sentiments, perceptual complexity in reflective observation results in higher-order observations, symbolic complexity in abstract conceptualization results in higher-order concepts, and behavioral complexity in active experimentation results in higher-order actions. [Kolb 1984]

But this amounts to "reinventing education" (Handy 1990), to put in place an educational organization providing services, as tailor-made and individualized as possible (to the extent of designing individual contracts for each learner), but also emphasizing the development of the many types of "intelligences" (not only the analytical skills measured by IQ tests) and the need to build much more explicitly on the possibility of educational credits being granted for all sorts of experiences that are now neglected or ignored when formally appraising the status of learners (Handy 1990; Authier and Lévy 1992).

CONCLUSION

Over the last decade, new patterns of governance have evolved in the public and private sectors to meet the challenges posed by this new complex, turbulent, and interdependent world. Side by side with the dominant bureaucracies and market-type organizations, clan-type networks have evolved. They have proved rather flexible and effective. Fluid alliances have woven "virtual" organizations and temporary networks in both sectors that are in a process of continuous self-reorganization and self-reconfiguration.

We have identified some of the anatomical and physiological features of this new type of organization, and probed into the nature of the *mixed* ideological bond or glue necessary to provide this new organization form with unity, stability, and dynamism. Moreover, because such organizations require new sorts of competencies in their executives, we have looked at the new ways in which such competencies might have to be acquired.

Geoffrey Vickers (1965) anticipated much of this new state of affairs in his classic book on the art of judgment. He showed how much depends on mental skills, institutional processes, a capacity for reflection-in-action, and dynamic interaction with context — all elements that can be constructed. So the new patterns of governance may not be all that new. Indeed, it may be that we are in the process of rediscovering a new form of intercreation and leadership within organizations that have been allowed to disappear because of our excessive confidence in the efficiency of markets and hierarchies.

In a discussion of the particular qualities of Gildardo Magana (who took over the Mexican Revolution after the assassination of Zapata), John Womack (1969) echoes the workings of a good forum and the aptitudes and qualities of an official carrying the burden of office well, i.e., having become himself the locus of effective argumentation:

> What he had learned was to mediate: not to compromise, to surrender principle and to trade concessions, but to detect reason in all claims in conflict, to recognize the particular legitimacy of each, to sense where the grounds of concord were, and to bring contestants into harmony there. Instinctively, he thrived on arguments, which he entered not to win but to conciliate.

This may well correspond to the model of the new leader in a system of governance resembling evolving neural networks.

CHAPTER 2

TACKLING WICKED PROBLEMS*

> The expert as expert... cannot by
> his nature learn anything new, because
> then he wouldn't be an expert.
>
> – *Donald N. McCloskey*

There have been many important changes in the socioeconomics of advanced nations over the last decades and they have had a significant impact on the role of the state and on the nature of the policy process.

First, the globalization of production has generated new worldwide networks and greatly increased global competition. Few national economies have escaped some fracturing as a result of these external pressures, as their exposed and sheltered sectors have crafted quite different strategies and followed disparate paths. Such modifications in the fabric of the socioeconomy have added to the menu of problems that governments must address both domestically (coordination, redistribution, etc.) and transnationally through concerted action at the global level (environmental issues, urbanization processes, technological change) (OECD 1979).

Second, the dematerialization of economic activity, i.e., the shift from goods-oriented production to the dominance of services, information, and knowledge, has also relaxed some of the geotechnical constraints. Because information and knowledge are not handled well as simple commodities, the need for nonmarket and state coordination grew considerably with the development of the information economy (Paquet 1987a).

Finally, a wave of democratization has forced all organizations to become more sensitive to a number of sociocultural dimensions — gender, employee rights, race, etc. The workplace has been transformed; we are no longer living in a Taylorian world. This has also led to a growing involvement of states and governments in matters of culture and values, as new rights and sensitivities and varied forms of affirmative action have emerged: administration has become more and more philosophy-in-action (Hodgkinson 1983).

* Material in this chapter is based on "Policy as Process: Tackling Wicked Problems." In Courchene, T.J., Stewart, A.E. (editors). *Essays on Canadian Public Policy*. Kingston: Queen's University School of Policy Studies, 1991, pp. 171–186.

These three nexuses of forces — among others — have generated growing complexity, turbulence, and interdependence in the global socioeconomic environment and led to loss of the stable state. In such a *turbulent* environment, it is no longer possible to regard the state as a simple policeman enforcing certain rules, acting as protector and provider, as was the case when the environment was *placid*. Such functions persist but governments have had to develop additional capacities to act as animators, facilitators, and negotiators. With accelerating change and related uncertainty, circumstances have evolved in such a way that no simple rule will do: judgment is called for (Emery and Trist 1965; Vickers 1965).

One of the important consequences of this *remue-ménage* has been that the state has had to confront more ill-structured problems, and as a result, the foci and substance of public policy as process have been modified dramatically. In place of the old state, content with housekeeping and offset functions, a *strategic state* (Navarre 1986) has invaded new realms, pursued new polymorphous and often ill-defined goals, targeted new objectives, and evolved in new ways. Yet, the prevailing model of policy analysis does not appear to have been adjusted accordingly. Policy research has remained trapped in the models that evolved in the decades following the Second World War.

The main message of this paper is that policy research must be taken in for repairs. In the following sections, some of the inadequacies of the standard models are outlined and an alternative approach is suggested.

POLICY AS PROCESS

First, a few definitions are called for. Policy connotes a course of action, a pattern of actions. As such, it is different from individual decisions or actions performed by some official. Policy agenda refers to a set of topics or issues that receive policymakers' attention. Policymaking consists in maintaining or modifying the actual course of affairs in line with certain norms or governing relations. By policy process, I mean the procedures through which problem identification leads to a place on the policy agenda, and then to the formulation of proposed courses of action to deal with the problem, but also the manner in which such courses of action are legitimized or authorized, then implemented in an interactive way by the administrative "machinery"(Buchholz 1985).

Policymaking is a rather complex, messy, and poorly understood process that evolves through time as participants, perspectives, situations, and base values change. It is embodied in institutions and organizations that influence our processes of recognizing and classifying situations and issues, and constitutes an ongoing way to regulate the social system, i.e., to set and reset norms and standards in line with the underlying appreciative system and in response to changing circumstances (Vickers 1965; Lasswell 1971).

The Standard Models of Policymaking

Whether it has been presented as the outcome of "elitist planning" or "pluralist exchange," the best known stylizations of public policymaking are very close to the technocratic model propounded most eloquently by economists and based fundamentally on a notion of instrumental rationality (Stokey and Zeckhauser 1978; Manzer 1984). They are *outcome-oriented* and rooted in an explicit statement of a preference function (either derived from the priorities of the elite or of the citizenry), in a careful exposition of the constraints limiting the realm of possibilities and of the alternative actions open to the policymaker. By relating these constraints and actions to the preferences, an efficient choice among the alternatives ensues. This is a characterization that is very close to what Graham Allison (1971) has called the rational actor model.

The notion of policymaking underpinning this stylization is rooted in the presumption of a guiding macro-rationale and of a set of priorities (objectives and actions) developed from it. A policy or a plan is stylized as the outcome of a well-behaved process defined by five sets of statements summarizing (1) the state of nature, (2) the future state of nature in the absence of any action, (3) the rules of the game, (4) the goals pursued, and (5) the actions called for to attain (4), given (1), (2), and (3). Policy research in this context is designed as a process of clarification of each of these components.

This stylization has been widely criticized: the state of nature may never be fully describable; the future state of nature is at best guessed at; the rules of the game are many-layered and evolving; the goals are unknown, ambiguous, or in conflict; and the means–ends relationships are highly uncertain and unreliable, so no unambiguous set of actions can be chosen. Moreover, as it is impossible to determine a priori the appropriate ends of public policymaking, one cannot avoid facing the problems of the legitimacy of policies for the community and of the extent to which these policies satisfy or fail to satisfy basic needs (Manzer 1984).

As a result of criticism of the rational actor model, a loosely defined incrementalist countermodel has evolved under diverse names. These alternative formulations have in common an effort to relax some or many of the strictures inherent to the technocratic model and to place at centre stage a set of procedures likely to approximate more aptly the *process* of policymaking observed in real socioeconomies.

Whether the emphasis is on organizational process (focusing entirely on bureaucratic procedures), governmental politics à la Allison (1971), muddling through à la Lindblom (1959) (focusing on an essentially incremental — leaderless, remedial, fragmented — process in which all the stakeholders mutually adjust), emergent strategies à la Mintzberg (1985), or the more extreme case of the "garbage can model" (Cohen et al. 1972) in which everything floats randomly, all these alternative models add much messiness, but not necessarily much enlightenment for they are all trying to escape from the limitations of the rational actor model without proposing explicit and programmatic alternatives.

The contrast between the instrumental rationality of the econocrats — those *"terribles simplificateurs"* — and the administrative rationality of the situationologists — with decision-making occurring almost by a process of fermentation — has been such that, despite the hopes expressed by practitioners, no satisfactory synthesis has yet been produced. To prepare the ground for such a synthesis, the very different rationalities underpinning these broad families of models must be examined more closely. Although I use the labels econocrats and situationologists, Hartle I and Hartle II might also do if a classification with a Canadian twist is required, for Douglas Hartle (1978) has probably best described the conversion from econocrat to situationologist on the Canadian federal public policy scene.

Econocrats Versus Situationologists

Econocrats: This is what Torgerson (1986) calls the first face of policy analysis: an echo effect in this field of the positivist craze. It represents a tradition that reached its peak in the 1960s in Canada (French 1980). It is the world of *Zweckrationalitat*, i.e., of instrumental rationality (Weber, in Ramos 1981). In this world, knowledge is supposed to replace politics.

Econocrats are blinded to political reality, to values, to the intricate process of legitimation and implementation. They attempt to extend the naive model of rational choice developed at the psychological level to situations where it would appear to focus "on the wrong unit of analysis" or to deal with "an inaccurate characterization of the preferences involved" (March 1978). This extension of calculating rationality has failed to provide public administration with anything more than a solution to trivial problems — not unimportant but trivial — like routing interlibrary loans or locating facilities for meals on wheels.

Such a Hobbesian notion of rationality (Ramos 1981) presumes that public policy is connected consciously and meaningfully to knowledge about goals and future outcomes and it completely ignores both the extraordinary complexity of the interrelated games (electorate, politicians, bureaucrats, special interest groups, media) that generates public policy and the dynamics of unintended consequences that often takes over (Trebilcock et al. 1982). Moreover, it endows public policy decisions with "a certain deliberate quality, a relative permanence... an objective character which decisions do not possess" (Majone 1980).

Situationologists: Situationologists give priority to politics over knowledge and offer a broad array of alternatives, all more or less based on some "systemic rationality." James March (1978) has formulated the problem aptly:

> Suppose we imagine that knowledge, in the form of precepts of behavior, evolves over time within a system and accumulates across time, people, and organizations without complete current consciousness of its history. Then

sensible action is taken by actors without comprehension of its full justification.

March shows that "there is intelligence in the suspension of calculation" and searches for the location of these "precepts of behavior."

One possible location is in the sociocultural underground of the "collective game" — "where interdependence is strong, the group is more efficient as a decision-making body than individuals acting in isolation" (Hirsch 1976). The sociocultural underground might best be described in the language of Geoffrey Vickers (1965) as "an appreciative system" — "a set of readinesses to distinguish certain aspects of the situation rather than others and to classify and value these in this way rather than that."

The notion of systemic rationality resembles what Max Weber calls *Wertrationalitat* — substantive rationality determined "independently of its prospect of success" (Ramos 1981). But the recognition that there is such a thing as a basic systemic rationality and that *governing relations* may guide the process cannot suffice; one requires a clear statement of where they are located and how they operate. Allison's (1971) models II and III or even the emergent policy à la Mintzberg (1985) do not provide much of a framework for developing a policy analysis. At best, they provide ways to describe ex post facto how a policy process has unfolded.

The Search for a Third Way

In this search for a third way, a guiding light has been policy problems as they are, i.e., as *practical problems* calling for a mix of formalization, judgment, and craft for their resolution and most certainly calling on both prudential and moral reasoning (Manzer 1984). However, one feature of the new problems facing public policymakers has been of paramount importance in the design of that third way: a recent recognition of the extent to which important policy issues pose ill-structured problems — wicked problems to policy analysts and policymakers. Once this central issue has become clear, a reframing of the challenge facing policy analysts is in order. For policy problems are seen as having two major characteristics most of the time: (1) the goals are not known or are very ambiguous and (2) the means–ends relationships are highly uncertain and poorly understood (Rittel and Webber 1973).

To deal with ill-structured problems, policy analysts must learn on the job about both the configuration of facts and the configuration of values. They must also manage to learn from the stakeholders at the core of the policy game and from the many groups at the periphery who are in possession of important *local knowledge*: without their participation, no policy can be implemented. A third way must then synthesize, reconcile, and transcend the ways of the econocrat and of the situationologist by setting the issues within a dialogue of the policymaker with the situation and with the clients.

A number of new trails have been opened up in this general field and most of them deserve some attention. Only a few papers are referred to explicitly to illustrate the directions being taken. Three approaches have the merit of being somewhat complementary and may well add up, as a whole, to a promising alternative. What they have in common is that they are somewhat *constructivist*, i.e., they suggest that we are unavoidably bringing about what appears to be happening, that we are not only observers but also participants. Moreover, they suggest to different degrees that policymaking is both a matter of craft and a matter of transforming communications and perceptions.

A clinical approach: Archibald (1970) has suggested a fruitful avenue inspired somewhat by the work of the Palo Alto School, especially Erving Goffman (1969). For her, policy analysis focuses on organizational, i.e., informational, problems, and policymakers approach the issue very much like an agent of change facing a client system. This clinical approach borrows from the work of psychotherapists and their patients and builds on participatory decision-making, on the acceptability of the decision within the organization, and on the realization of some sort of "social rationality." In all this, the policymaker is a proactive agent of change at the level of perceptions and communication to resolve conflicts.

Because of the importance this approach places on implementation and acceptability of policies by clients, it is likely to initiate much organizational change that was not planned, as the situation is reframed. It is also likely to make extensive use of values, creativity, and innovation in the dialogue between expert and clients. However, the approach — at least the version suggested by Archibald (1970) — remains somewhat vague and most certainly not programmatic.

A social learning approach: Friedmann and Abonyi (1976) proceed one step further. They suggest that social experimentation, practice, and learning are the principal methods for public intervention. For them, social learning can only occur in the context of social practice, and they suggest a process — an open-ended exploration as a way to recast the problem and the image of reality into a more desirable form.

Very much like Archibald, Friedmann and Abonyi insist that policymaking must include interaction with the clients and focus on perceptions, "images" à la Boulding. For them, social practice is an experiment in which core images of reality are substantially reorganized through experiential learning. They are daring and precise in their recommendations: they propose nothing less than an epistemology of practice to replace the standard epistemology in academic work and a precise and detailed strategy to initiate the process of social learning likely to generate the "new reality."

A radical practice approach: More recently, in papers developed independently from earlier work and based on entirely different perspectives, Manzer (1984) and Torgerson (1986) among others have revived the central idea of policymaking as "practical reasoning." Manzer has suggested ways to rebalance prudential and moral considerations in policymaking by reshaping institutions; Torgerson has illustrated the necessity of dialogue between experts and citizens in the realization of the practical task of policymaking using the Berger inquiry as a model. In both cases, if in a somewhat subdued manner, social learning becomes not only a way to create a new reality or to suggest a reframing of reality, but a mode of emancipation, a way to recover the political community and civil society and to effect a contextual reorientation.

This work illustrates the broad drift that has occurred in the perception of policymaking over the last decades. John Friedmann (1987) has reviewed this evolution in a recent book. Although we have not attempted to synthesize these new currents into a final integrated version of what policy might be in this ideal third way, in the next section we suggest nothing more than a gambit that builds on the work of Friedmann and Abonyi. Its programmatic content has been developed relatively more fully than has been the case for the other versions available, and it has proved more powerful heuristically and more capable of accommodating other components in a provisional synthesis.

The Paradigm of Social Practice

Friedmann and Abonyi (1976) have stylized a social learning model of policy research to deal with wicked problems. It combines a detailed analysis of four subprocesses: (1) the construction of appropriate theories of reality, (2) the formation of social values, (3) the gaming that leads to the design of political strategies, and (4) collective action. These four interconnected subprocesses are components of a social learning process: any change in one affects the others (Fig. 5).

Block B is the locus of dominant values that provide normative guidance either in the transformation of reality or in the selection of strategies for action. Theory of reality (block A) refers to a symbolic representation and explanation of the environment. Political strategy (block C) connotes the political game that generates the course of action chosen. Social action (block D) deals with

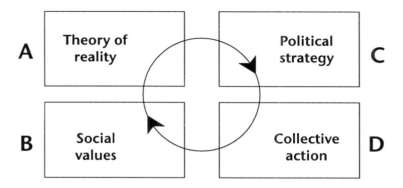

Figure 5. A paradigm of social practice in policy research.
Source: Friedmann and Abonyi (1976: 88).

implementation and the interaction with the peripheral groups. Together these four subprocesses come to life in concrete situations.

Traditional approaches to policy research focus on attempts to falsify hypotheses about some objective reality according to the canons of scientific experimentation. This is too narrow a focus when the ground is in motion. For the *social practitioner*, what is central is an effort "to create a wholly new, unprecedented situation that, in its possibility for generating new knowledge, goes substantially beyond the initial hypothesis" (Friedmann and Abonyi 1976: 938). The social learning paradigm is built on reflection-in-action, dialogue, mutual learning by experts and clients, i.e., on an *interactive or transactive style of planning* (Schon 1983):

> The paradigm makes the important epistemological assumption that *action hypotheses* are verified as "correct" knowledge only in the course of a social practice that includes the four components of theory (of reality), values, strategy and action. A further epistemological commitment is to the *creation of a new reality*, and hence to a new knowledge, rather than in establishing the truth-value of propositions in abstraction from the social context to which they are applied. [Friedmann and Abonyi 1976: 938]

When dealing with broad policy issues like multiculturalism, one must be aware of the limits of existing tools: one cannot hope to produce anything more than incomplete answers. In the words of Alvin Weinberg (1972), in policy research we need a "trans-science": we are confronted with trans-scientific questions that cannot be answered by science, that transcend science. Engineering (physical and social) and many of the policy sciences are plagued with such questions: answers may be impractically expensive, the subject matter too variable for scientific canons to apply, moral and esthetic judgment may be involved, etc. What is required is a new understanding built on "usable ignorance," for "by being aware of our ignorance, we do not encounter disastrous pitfalls in our supposedly secure knowledge or supposedly effective technique... institutions should be designed with the ignorance factor in mind, so that they can respond and adapt in good time" (Collingridge 1982; Ravetz 1986).

Coping with ignorance requires *a more transactive and transparent policy process*, a deliberate dialogue designed to tap local knowledge and, therefore, a change in the way in which policy research is carried out. It has been argued that the transaction costs of running such a system are higher, but the outcome is more than proportionately improved.

SOCIAL LEARNING AS A TOOL

The tradition of social learning has deep roots in the works of John Dewey and, as a result, shares a number of shortcomings with them: a certain rationalistic bias and the presumption that there is a high degree of communicative competence guiding the process of social learning toward a consensual state. This is probably somewhat utopian. In fact, there is a need to add some dimensions to social learning: an explicit macrosocial theory to underpin its action, a recognition that people and groups have differential access to social power and that social communication may be distorted, and a realization that social learning is a highly normative field (Friedmann 1987). Many of the adjuncts to the basic Friedmann and Abonyi approach suggested by Palo Alto inspired clinical work or by attempts to institutionalize or serialize social learning have been designed to enrich the basic approach and to make it more effective.

The case for the paradigm of social learning might have been developed in a variety of ways. We have attempted to illustrate how it can help answer four basic questions: (1) how social learning can effectively mix prudential and moral reasoning, (2) how it can show the limits and perversions of the policy process, (3) how it can serve as a diagnostic tool and help trigger Pygmalion effects, and (4) how it can serve as a guide in the process of social architecture.

Practical Reasoning

David Gauthier's (1963) analysis of practical reasoning and its use in analyzing public policymaking (Manzer 1984) provide the lead here. These works help us to understand the full extent to which the econocrats put exclusive emphasis on prudential reasoning and the situationologists on moral reasoning, while a good picture of public policymaking as practical judgment involves both considerations. The paradigm of social practice recognizes that social learning need not result in integrative action that would give all components the same weight. At times, what is feasible (A) will dominate, at others what is morally acceptable (B), what is politically generated stability (C), or what is collectively implementable (D). Policymaking as a learning process allows for conflicts and strains between these components.

Table 1: Characterization of public policy institutions.

Predominant approach to problem-solving	Predominant approach to practical reasoning	
	Moral	Prudential
Incremental–reactive	Judicial policymaking	Budget policymaking
Comprehensive–anticipatory	Commission policymaking	Ministry policymaking

Source: Manzer (1984: 589).

In that sense, social learning gives appropriate consideration to both moral and prudential reasoning. It can most certainly serialize the use of each set of norms as policymaking represents, of necessity, a diachronic or developmental activity involving many kinds of decisions (Manzer 1984). Moreover, it allows also — as suggested by Manzer — the crystallization of subinstitutions predominantly dominated by one or the other component of practical reasoning given the nexus of constraints that are operating.

Manzer has identified a few public policy institutions characterized predominantly by moral or prudential reasoning and by incremental-reactive or comprehensive-anticipatory problem-solving (Table 1). This configuration of institutions was arrived at as a result of a process of historical social learning and indicates the extent to which social practice may underpin a variety of organizational forms.

Critical interpretation

If social learning serves extremely well in the rational reconstruction of the strategies of different policy organizations, it also enables one to appraise critically the process through which the policy was researched, crafted, and elaborated, and it may serve to show where and when it went afoul. In that context, the Friedmann and Abonyi model is essentially a checklist, an organizing principle to ensure that all aspects are appropriately dealt with.

A fair example of this use of the framework is provided in the analysis of the energy options inquiry carried out in Canada in the late 1980s (see Chapter 5). It is possible to synthesize the strategies of the different stakeholders and to identify why they have been led to adopt partial and limiting approaches to the energy problem. The energy options inquiry was originally designed as an effective social learning process, but it is fairly easy, using the social learning framework, to show how the process was derailed. In the Friedmann-Abonyi language, Block A issues came to dominate the scene completely and poor coverage of blocks B, C, and D led to a virtual suppression of these dimensions in the final report.

In the same manner, it has been possible to analyze a complex policy field like multiculturalism using the Friedmann and Abonyi scheme to unveil the extent to which it had evolved perversely as a result of a dominance of block C issues to the point where block A, B, and D issues were systematically downplayed and the dynamics of intercultural relations very poorly understood and managed (Laurent and Paquet 1991; Paquet, this volume, Chapter 7).

Diagnostic Approach

The Friedmann-Abonyi scheme not only allows one to effect the appropriate mix of prudential and moral reasoning or provide a checklist for a critical analysis of imperfect policies, it can also guide the analyst toward a diagnosis within the clinical relationship between experts and clients and suggest directions for reframing the situation. This aspect is much emphasized by Archibald (1970) and is central in the socio-intervention that is meant to create a new reality.

The scheme has proved useful in designing a new national policy on entrepreneurship in Canada. It has suggested ways to transform perceptions of people and groups and, through such a change, get them to become more entrepreneurial. Interventions of this sort have also worked well at the community level: perceptions have been reframed in much the same manner as Palo Alto psychotherapists reframe the perceptions of their clients. Nothing less than a Pygmalion effect at the community level has often ensued (Watzlawick 1978; Paquet 1989b; Errens and Paquet 1990).

The idea that the Friedmann-Abonyi approach might act as a mobilization device represents a way to overcome the limitations of the social learning approach as perceived by Friedmann (1987) in his *auto-critique*. Clinical interpretation of the social learning framework by revealing a capacity to reframe deliberately the sociocultural context opens the door to effecting the sort of catharsis likely to generate a new sort of behaviour or a new form of policy context.

Design Capability

The Friedmann-Abonyi scheme is also a useful guide in social architecture; it is likely to guide the sort of dialogue necessary for a useful exercise of building public institutions with the requisite variety and qualities (Perlmutter 1965) and to serve as a radar in an inquiring system trying to design them.

The process through which the new institutions are going to be crafted may benefit much from the guidance of such a scheme (Paquet 1989c, 1990b). It might improve practical reasoning to such an extent that a more appropriate social architecture might ensue. Indeed, the usefulness of the scheme as a guide in the design of improved institutions for the year 2000 has been demonstrated (see Chapters 9 and 10).

CONCLUSION

The poor state of policymaking cannot be entirely ascribed to the poor state of policy analysis or to the slowness of governments, bureaucrats, and citizens in recognizing that policymaking is a form of social learning. But a good portion of the problem may indeed be a result of these factors. This calls for a new competence and for a reframing of policy analysis: the organization of public policymaking has to become a learning organization (Michaels 1980).

For this reframing to occur, a revolution is required in the mind of policy analysts. The few illustrations mentioned above were only meant to whet the appetite of interested parties. If the argument appears to be persuasive and there is a wish to transform policymaking in this way, the first stage in the acquisition of the new competence has been completed. At the individual level, this is equivalent to the decision to visit a psychotherapist. The next phase calls for much experimentation with the social learning scheme, in the context of ongoing public policy debates, to develop some sort of *connoisseurship* — a sort of expert knowledge in the precise experience of specific contexts. Some of the exercises mentioned above, and others developed more fully in Part II of this book, may be useful in this apprenticeship for it is impossible to impart connoisseurship without reflection in action. It is only later that one can hope to produce a blueprint for a procedure likely to guide the policymaker's steps in the design of a meaningful social learning exercise in the context of social practice. Such a procedure would not provide a mechanical contraption applicable to all cases, but simply a guide in the practical use of such tools as search conferences and other instruments of this type (Williams 1979).

But fundamentally, reflection in action requires first and foremost a willingness to act. In the words of Heinz von Foerster (1988: 69), *"si tu veux voir, apprends à agir."*

Part II

Social Learning in Action:

A – International Perspectives

CHAPTER 3

ELEGANT BUT NOT HELPFUL TO NAVIGATION: SOCIAL SCIENCES RESEARCH AND THE FREE TRADE DEBATE*

> "Beware of the man who works hard to learn something, learns it, and finds himself no wiser than before," Bokonon tells us. He is full of murderous resentment of people who are ignorant without having come by their ignorance the hard way.
>
> – *Kurt Vonnegut*

From time to time, major issues of public interest provide an opportunity for social scientists to unpack their gear and show what new insights their *"outillage mental"* can generate and what new solutions their analyses suggest for tackling urgent and complex social issues. Such moments are always greeted with enthusiasm by practising social scientists as an occasion to prove their social usefulness; however, it is fair to say that most of those challenges have turned out to be somewhat catastrophic for the reputation of the social sciences when such "insights" and "solutions" have been assessed with a bit of hindsight.

Such failures are not so much ascribable to the incompetence of the practitioners as to the fact that social sciences in Canada and elsewhere have promised more than they could possibly deliver: they have been living beyond their means. Nowhere is this more evident than when social scientists leave their ivory tower to go to the forum.

In this chapter, it is suggested that one of the major sources of this failure of the social sciences may be traced back to the positivist revolution that led social scientists to ape the postures of their colleagues in the physical sciences in the hope of achieving respectability by following the recipes physical scientists were using. The social sciences input into the free trade debate is critically reviewed, and its limited usefulness is revealed. We speculate on the

* This chapter also appeared in Maslove, A.M., Winer, S.W. (editors). *Knocking at the Back Door: The Political Economy of Canada–U.S. Free Trade*. Montreal: Institute for Research on Public Policy, 1987, pp. 165–198. I am grateful to Allan Maslove and Stan Winer for offering me an opportunity to explore the implications of this work in the context of the free trade debate. The assistance of A. Burgess, G. Kippin, and H. Nicoll is gratefully acknowledged.

likely contours of refurbished social sciences and on what such an *"outillage mental"* might be able to contribute to the free trade debate. In conclusion, some hopes for refurbished social sciences are shown to be less unrealistic than might first appear.

SOCIAL SCIENCES RESEARCH: A GENERAL DIAGNOSIS[1]

Although there has been much dissatisfaction with the drift of the social sciences into positivism, there has also been considerable praise for this development. Consequently, the social science community has been split into two factions: one group betting on the form of *explanation* propounded by positivism, the other defending *a mix of explanation and understanding* as the only warranted strategy for a sound social scientist (von Wright 1971). Most practitioners have chosen positivism; a minority is on the other side.

Syntax Versus Semantics

Much of the success of positivism in the social sciences is ascribable to the success of the physical sciences in explaining much of what is observed in nature through mechanical cause–effect connections. The machine model of reality worked well in the physical sciences and, since the 19th century, has slowly come to be regarded as more or less the only acceptable model in the social sciences as well.

But to explain a phenomenon, in the physical sciences sense, one must presume it has coherent identity and is repeated (Latouche 1984). But social phenomena are rarely, if ever, truly recurring or identical. Consequently, social phenomena must be reified, i.e., be given definite content and form, for explanations to take hold.

As a consequence of this process of reification (perpetrated on social phenomena to make them amenable to explanation), the social sciences have drifted further and further from the original questions that led to inquiry into social phenomena (Monnerot 1946; Schrag 1980). They have come to focus more exclusively on method and methodological procedures instead of on content and meaning. The social world has been reduced to a set of *facts* and knowledge made exclusively synonymous with the output of certain methodologic procedures. Epistemology has been reduced to simple methodology and methodology itself to certain procedures that were successful in the physical sciences (Habermas 1971; Paquet 1988a). A hypertrophy of syntax in the social sciences has ensued, much to the detriment of semantics. The social sphere has been reified, physicalism and analytical methods have become hegemonic, a polytechnician attitude prevails, and unrealistic ambitions have flourished within the social sciences community (von Hayek 1952[2]).

Parsimony, Normalization, Regulation

The drift toward positivism has permeated social sciences over the last 40 years. Originally, positivism had been only one of many research strategies or approaches, but it has slowly become a set of norms imposed on the practice of social science and then the basis for a control apparatus to ensure the hegemony of those norms. There has been a *progressive sociologization* of positivism. Positivism is a parsimonious way to look at social reality. It constructs a collapsed, flattened, and shriveled version of the social world, a reduction to a single order, a single true version of the world — an order that positivism is supposedly best equipped to investigate (Hirschman 1985).

This parsimonious attitude would have been of little consequence, were it not that the social sciences of the 19th century had the tendency to respond to accusations of practical irrelevance or theoretical failures in a bizarre way. They were not so much led to take a less parsimonious view of reality, but rather to neutralize such criticisms by efforts to normalize and regulate the practice of the social sciences. This is the purpose behind the production of *rules of method* codifying *the only way* to acquire meaningful knowledge.

But every time a *rule* defining a norm — what is normal and what is not in the practice of any activity — is made, there must be reference to a regulatory power with the capacity to separate the normal from the abnormal. There is a need for a regulator. The dynamic of construction of regulatory instruments has been spelled out succinctly by Katouzian (1980: 119–122). He ascribes the emergence of the rigid paradigms in good currency in the practice of the social sciences to the growth of professionalism: the growth of a population of full-time mental workers operating in discipline-bound fields. There, narrow disciplinarian leaders rule through their control not only of the instruments of publication and dissemination of ideas but also of the mechanisms of research funding. In such a world, being normal translates into a higher probability of being hired and promoted, i.e., into a probability of survival in academe.

This enforced balkanization of the social sciences into fragmented disciplines has had important consequences for their usefulness. There has been a tendency toward a high degree of hyper-specialization, toward the concentration of the effort of full-time mental workers on the solution of real or imaginary problems defined by the leadership of the disciplinary professions, and toward a proliferation of publications for the sake of publications, i.e., much printed material with comparatively little addition to knowledge (Beam 1983; Paquet 1978a, 1985a).

In practice, this perversion has resulted in the social sciences' developing a predilection for small questions, an unmistakable theoretical twist, and a tendency to follow "in the footsteps of Monsieur Pangloss and Dr Bowdler" (Andreski 1974; Gordon 1970, 1975). The smoke screen of jargon has grown exponentially, and analytical/tautological developments have mushroomed to the point where Nobel laureate Wassily Leontief has gone on record as deploring the drift away from relevance and meaningfulness of much of the work in current journals in economics. The methods used to maintain intellectual discipline in the most important departments of economics, says Leontief (1982), "occasionally remind one of those employed by the marines to maintain discipline on Parris Island."

The Need for Interpretation

These trends in the current practice of the social sciences are well known even though they are not always appropriately acknowledged. Some continue to argue that positivism is the only way to make the social sciences truly scientific; however, a view that is becoming more widely held is that only through a more judicious mix of interpretation and explanation can we hope to extract the social sciences from their present crisis of confidence.

Daniel Bell (1984) has argued that a "turn to interpretation, in the broadest cultural sense, signifies the turn of the social sciences — or of those practitioners of this art — from the models of the natural sciences and their modes of inquiry, to the humanities."

Interpretation is an ancient method of inquiry. It was the traditional method in vogue among scholars until the physical sciences developed and imposed their model on the production of knowledge in all areas. What makes *interpretation* a necessary ingredient in the social sciences has to do with the nature of the human sciences. The difference between mechanical or animal societies and human societies mainly rests with the fact that human action is based on plans, i.e., on mental constructs elaborated before the action is effectively carried out. It is not really possible to reduce all human activities to such plans (which are often not carried through) or to the perception or significance such plans might have for the main actors, but it is not possible either to exorcize those dimensions from any meaningful effort to understand such actions.

This qualitative difference between the human sciences and the physical sciences commands a different methodological strategy. It focuses mainly on institutions as instruments of coordination of activities for human agents, as rules of the game, as social armistices likely to reveal the meaning of such actions.

Institutions are the fabric of World 3 in Karl Popper's (1972) parlance: a sort of efficient reconciliation of the pressures emanating both from World 1 (the world of material realities) and from World 2 (the world of plans, values and *"faits de conscience"*) (Lachmann 1971; Shapiro and Sico 1984). World 3 is a complex "text" that the human sciences must interpret in order to understand it. This sort of interpretation would not be unlike a close interpretation of a collective agreement to reveal the texture of conflicts that it has refereed.

THE FREE TRADE DEBATE

The free trade debate between Canada and the United States is a multilogue among various groups on both sides of the border about the number of impediments to trade between the two countries that should be tolerated. As such, it should be analyzed like a multifaceted conversation. The instruments used for such analysis must obviously draw on the body of theories and techniques in vogue in the study of rhetoric. For what is involved in this debate are attempts to persuade and, in assessing those attempts, rhetorical norms are in order. Indeed, much of science is rhetoric: "What distinguishes good from bad in learned discourse... is not the adoption of a particular methodology, but the earnest and intelligent attempt to contribute to a conversation" (McCloskey 1985: 27).

In such a context, the central question has to do with the standards of persuasiveness: whether the conversation about free trade is working well, whether the arguments put forward are persuasive. Our general point will be that the conversation about free trade is *not* working well, and that social scientists as persuaders have failed miserably in that debate.

Anatomy of the Free Trade Debate

One of the basic difficulties that might explain the poor performance of social scientists as persuaders in this debate may have to do with the confusion among three interrelated questions, all subsumed generally under the same rubric: *free trade as an idea*, *free trade as a bout of negotiations*, and *free trade as construction of a new socioeconomic space*. These are quite different issues, although obviously interconnected, but they have been debated interchangeably without taking care to specify which issue was addressed.

Free trade as an idea does not refer to the design of a free trade arrangement. It pertains to the inception of the idea of a free trade arrangement as a source of opportunities for business. As such, it is a potent economic force, even though it may never be realized. New opportunities are entertained and the prospective and plausible futures are significantly altered by the sociopsychological setting created by the beginning of a "conversation" about free trade.[3]

Because one might speculate on many different ways in which this idea might be implemented, everything is plausible, for the idea of free trade embodies what Leland Jenks (1944) would call "the dream of developing communities, regions, the continent." Corresponding to any number of different social partitionings of the community, one may identify clusters of groups grappling with the idea, speculating on whether the costs and benefits are of comparable magnitude or not for them. This is the paradise of *simulators*, i.e., those who have a simulacrum of the socioeconomy on which they are willing to play, for a fee, any imaginative scenario one might fantasize or build on this free trade idea. The simulacrum may be a simple supply-and-demand scheme, an "issue-machine," or an elaborate econometric caricature of the socioeconomy, but the process is largely of the same nature: a mechanical analogue of the socioeconomy is used to forecast growth in various allocations and distributional impacts.[4]

Whether these simulations are anchored in a "realistic" model is not the issue. As any mechanical analogue is a reification of the socioeconomy — even if behavioural reactions and policy triggers are built in — such a construct is unlikely to generate very persuasive results. Indeed, the wide variability of "results" developed through those simulations has provided their consumers with very little in the form of robust persuasion. The main reason is that too much of the reality of the socioeconomy as instituted process is expurgated from even the most sophisticated simulations. An additional reason is that any built-in forecast of the reactions of different groups to changes in the rules of the game in matters such as our trade relations with the United States is unlikely to be gauged reasonably well by a simple rule. Consequently, most of the results generated by such exercises are not very robust when they are not simply tautological.

One cannot expect much better results from social science analyses of the *free trade debate as a bout of negotiations*. Modeling such an interactive process is so difficult that most analysts have been satisfied with simple general descriptions. To perform a meaningful simulation of a game of negotiations, much is required: (1) an explicit set of actors together with their domains of possible actions, (2) a clear specification of mutual interdependencies, and (3) a correct gauging of the extent of consciousness of each group of actors and (4) of the degree to which any group is aware that all groups are aware of each other's perceptions and of their interdependencies.

Leif Johansen (1979) asserts that standard social sciences do not admit of most of those points: in general, analyses considerably emasculate (2) and (3), do not deal with (1) very well and fail altogether to take (4) into account. There have been some efforts to develop *the game paradigm*, but the results to date are not very promising when one is confronted with complex non-zero-sum games with more than a few actors. The great merit of that paradigm has been to throw some light on the essential *social* character of the social sciences and on some of the requirements that status imposes on the practice of social sciences (Coddington 1968; Cross 1969; Shubik 1982; Schellenberg and Druckman 1986).

The contribution of the social sciences *to the process of bargaining* in the free trade debate has been rather limited. Although a certain amount of intelligence is necessary in such a process, the Macdonald Commission (1985) report noted that there is a significant gap in the expertise of Canadian academics about the structure of the American political system and its behaviour. Therefore, whatever contribution might have been legitimately expected from the social sciences in ascertaining what our trade partners are all about has not been provided. Although this is partly ascribable to a lack of expert personnel, it is not entirely clear that their contribution (if it had materialized) would have been that significant, largely because of the limits of their tools.[5]

As for *free trade as construction of a new socioeconomic space*, the process is so full of unforeseen and unintended consequences that social scientists have a rather limited ability to grasp its full scope. Attempts to gauge such broad transformations in the social architecture of socioeconomies have been attempted through the use of *counterfactuals*, i.e., alternative versions of the world to ascertain the net effect of a particular transformation or feature. Counterfactuals have to be reasonably precise to be of use. A common weakness of most general equilibrium analyses of counterfactuals is that they leave so much unspecified that nothing categorical can be stated with certainty from comparisons between the "world as it is" and the counterfactual version of it.

A good example, again taken from economic history, is the comparison made by Robert Fogel (1964) between a world with and without railroads in the United States. One is hardly persuaded by simple quantifications of the "social savings" generated by railroads, when they are based on a naive comparison of the costs of transportation by rail with the costs of transporting the same goods to the same places using the pre-existing mode of transportation. The assumption is that the same goods will be transported to the same places before and after the introduction of railroads. But if anything is clear, it is that railroads have triggered a complete transformation of the matrix of transported goods (Fogel 1964, 1979). Therefore, the comparison is really meaningless and the notion of social saving thus defined somewhat spurious. The same general weakness plagues all attempts by social scientists to gauge the effects of the long-run adjustment to a "reality of free trade."

A sweeping transformation of the tariff arrangements between two countries is likely to promote efficiency, but this is not certain. It may also promote economic growth through the expansion of trade, but it is not certain exactly how the benefits emanating from such a transformation will be shared by the different segments of the new socioeconomic space. Depending on the assumptions one makes about reactions, adjustments, etc. one may obtain dramatically different although not necessarily inconsistent results. Moreover, many have expressed doubts about the wisdom of this policy initiative as a mechanism to solve Canada's economic problems: tariffs are not the issue any more,

> The real issue is non-tariff barriers, such as regional tax incentives, government procurement policies, the treatment of foreign-owned firms, and the setting of currency exchange rates. These are the tools used in advanced industrial countries to pursue industrial strategies.... These tools are central to the economic power of the modern state, the key to sovereignty in the late twentieth century, just as tariffs were in the nineteenth. [Laxer 1986: 11][6]

Because social sciences can throw no uncontroversial light on the impact of the "idea" of enhanced trade arrangements between Canada and the United States, nor on the best way to bargain for it, nor on the efficiency, economic growth, and wealth redistribution the new socioeconomic space is likely to trigger, nor even on the wisdom of such a policy initiative, it is hardly surprising that rhetoric has played such an important role in this debate. What has been accomplished in terms of public awareness and in terms of persuasion is not so much a result of arguments soundly based on thoroughly persuasive social sciences research as rhetorical devices. Rhetoric may be inescapable, but even the conversation about free trade might be conducted more persuasively with the use of an enriched *"outillage mental."*

Some Paradoxes

Three paradoxes illustrate the degree to which social science research is bogged down in terms of illuminating the current debate.

Second-best results: One of the depressing results of economic analysis of the post Second World War period has been the development of second-best theorems in economics. This disquieting feature of general equilibrium analysis may be summarized as follows: there are many conditions to ensure welfare maximization in an economy; if for any reason, *one* of the conditions is unobtainable, it may be necessary to depart from *other* welfare-maximizing conditions. Because of the fact that perfect competition rarely exists (governments intervene via all sorts of taxes and subsidies, external economies and diseconomies exist in production and consumption, etc.), it cannot be assumed that all marginal social costs and benefits are equal in every segment of the economy. Because this means that some welfare-maximizing conditions are not met at some point in the economy, it becomes impossible to know with certainty whether a policy designed to remove a restriction to free trade (supposedly to bring the socioeconomy closer to the point of maximum welfare for all) will leave members of the community economically better off.[7]

This shattering result has not received the broad diffusion it required. Second-best is still regarded as an advanced subject and is not discussed in most intermediate textbooks. Yet, one may infer from it that there are very few a priori propositions that economists may offer to policymakers. Obviously, the more we know about the *facts* of the economy, the more we are in a position to compute *ad hoc* second-best optima. However, as the number of violations of efficiency conditions increases and as the complexities of interdependency grow, computing such second-best solutions is both difficult and, of necessity, based on disputable assumptions.

In the great debate that surrounded the decision by Britain to join the European Economic Community, economists were very divided, and even free trade defenders like Harry Johnson (1971) campaigned against Britain joining the EEC on the ground that "the obvious economic benefits to Britain of joining are negligible and the obvious economic costs are large" (Hutchison 1977: 181). Other economists took a quite different stand, and their view prevailed; however, the force of their argument was much more rhetorical than substantive. The same conundrum faces experts when asked whether Canada should enter into a free trade agreement with the United States.

The broad consequence of this predicament is that there is no agreement among economists a priori about the desirability of free trade even as an idea.

When confronted with facts that can be read in a variety of different ways, one is faced with very different viewpoints. The full extent of the confusion can best be summarized by saying that it no longer appears inconsistent for an economist to say that even if economic integration is likely to generate more efficiency and growth, it cannot be presumed that economic disintegration is likely to generate inefficiency and slower growth.[8]

The framing of decisions: A second major paradox has emerged from the experimental work of Tversky and Kahneman (1981): if one modifies the framework of presentation within which a decision is made, one may dramatically transform the nature of the decision. For instance, their studies have shown that medical personnel may be led to choose diametrically opposed strategies for treatment if the "objective" information is cast in terms of probability of death instead of probability of survival.

This work raises fundamental questions about the predictability of decisions by groups and, therefore, about the reliability of simulacra, as it would appear that "objective" conditions are *not* the determining factor in decision-making. This increases even more the importance of the rhetorical elements in debates such as the one about free trade. For the activities of the "*définisseurs de situation*" will trigger continuous "reframing" of the decision context, and consequently a modification of the decisions. In the case of complex issues, it is futile to model decisions and strategies anchored in "objective" conditions. This casts a shadow on much work based on rational man and his predictable behaviour.

In the free trade debate, much is based on presumptions and assumptions, and the complexity of the choices proposed are of such a magnitude that the framing dimensions are even more determining than they might be in laboratory circumstances. Consequently, there is little hope of developing an objective database on which to construct a sound simulation of decisions to be expected from different groups. Not only are the knowledge and database that are necessary for good social science work nonexistent, but also, even if they could be established, nothing would lead us to believe that the objective facts would have a determining impact on real decisions. In this world, interventions by opinion molders using the instruments of rhetoric have more chance of being determinant than the so-called basic facts of the case.

Balkanization and multistability: The efficiency, growth, redistribution effects of a freer trade arrangement are unclear, but the relative weights of these performance indicators in a dynamic socioeconomy existing through extremely rapid change and transformation are not clear either. Departure from the world of perfect competition does not only deprive economists of simple rules for policy advice, it also imposes a different set of weights on those different performance dimensions. In a world of perfect competition, it is argued that "there is an optimal amount of instability and inequity; this is the one that makes the human economy as efficient as possible in the broadest sense."[9]

This may be questionable even in a world of perfect competition, but it is clearly neither warranted nor reasonable in a world that departs from the competitive ideal. In such a context, the whole notion of performance indicators has to be "reframed," and the problem must be addressed by a decision to "select *a set of targets or objectives for the economy* and then analyze the performance of particular sectors of the economy in terms of whether or not this performance aids or impedes the achievement of these overall goals" (Herendeen 1975: 230). *De facto*, the pursuit of equity and stability (or of growth/employment objectives, the construction of a particular socioeconomic structure, or the achievement of some cultural goals) overrides the concern for efficiency (Paquet 1978b: 46).

This shift in emphasis in evaluating performance has not always been given sufficient recognition in the practice of social scientists, despite important work recasting the image of the economic system as a non-zero-sum game in which the parts devise rival strategies taking into account conjectures about what other parts might do and the interactions between strategies. Such work has shown our capitalistic socioeconomies to be dynamically inefficient and, therefore, call for the use of other performance indicators (Lancaster 1973).[10]

What makes this shift to other gauges of performance fundamentally important in the free trade debate is the fact that as soon as efficiency considerations cease to be dominant, there is little or no agreement on alternative gauges. Moreover, optimizing in other directions seems condemned to violate blatantly the efficiency norms. For instance, a fragmented, fractured economic system may be shown to be *multistable*, i.e., to have a relatively greater ability to adapt than a fully integrated one. Through the fragmentation of an economic system into "sub-systems subject to slightly different rules and interacting incompletely or only through the mediation of specific channels," one can ensure that an adjustment in some key or essential variables is "delegated, so to speak, to a partial system enabling the overall process to adjust to important shocks in the environment in a manner which would have been either impossible or very time-consuming had the overall process been forced to adjust *in toto*" (Paquet 1977, 1978b: 52).[11]

This might lead one to argue that although an expanded zone of freer trade might generate efficiency benefits, it might also reduce the capacity to transform of a socioeconomic system. It is possible to argue along the same lines on the basis of some fundamental social objective like the *primacy of culture* or the *preservation of sovereignty*: this leads to a situation in which no technical advice based on simple efficiency norms can ever be persuasive, for the ground has been shifted to moral choices and one cannot replace a fundamentally *moral* basis for decision with a *technical* argument.[12]

It is far from evident, therefore, that social science research can produce unambiguous answers to the questions of the day. The combination of second-best and framing-of-decisions constraints, together with the possibility that static and dynamic contexts or narrow and broader contexts might call for different policy initiatives, have led social scientists to make many statements in general (and, therefore, on the basis of the most extremely reductive assumptions) but to contribute little except some interesting rhetoric — nothing that might be regarded as providing solutions to the practical problems facing the community.

Anamorphosis of the Free Trade Debate

Over the last 2 years, an extensive literature has been triggered by the free trade debate in Canada. I do not wish to review that literature; I have only sampled it to identify some of the major strands of argument, to illustrate the interesting rhetorical ploys used, and to show the general unpersuasiveness of the social science contributions to that debate. Because the free trade issue has a dominant economic flavour, the place of economists in this anamorphosis may be larger than life. I have also tried to gauge what filtered down to people from the social sciences community through the press.[13]

Because I claim that rhetoric has played a dominant role in the free trade debate, an anamorphosis through the prism of the four tropes that have so generously spiced the economic discourse in the past has appeared useful.[14] Those figures of speech (metaphor, metonymy, synecdoche, and irony) have played a crucial role in the free trade debate. The pro-free-trade participants have tried to persuade by making use of them. Their opponents, in turn, have often used figures of speech in lieu of proofs. The rationale for such posturing is simple: neither side is really able to prove much.

Trade as synecdoche: A socioeconomy as an instituted process cannot be reduced to the process of trade: this is a synecdoche, i.e., taking a part for the whole. The manner in which the economic process gets instituted at different places and times invests that process with unity and stability and defines the nature of specific human economies (Polanyi 1968). A socioeconomy is fundamentally an organizational–institutional reality, of which trade is only a portion.

Any analysis of an economy partitions it into subprocesses. This reveals the extent to which trade is only a small part of the picture. One such partitioning that has proved particularly useful in analyzing the Canadian socioeconomy is based on six subprocesses — demographic, financial, production and exchange, distribution, and the state subprocesses, and the ecology of groups and their motives) (Paquet 1980).

By making trade relations *the fabric* of the economy, some social scientists have reduced the complex process of private, social, and public production, consumption, cooperation, and exchange to simple trading relations. This is a bold synecdoche.[15] In fact, one is led to postulate a frictionless world in which monads trade relentlessly in all dimensions and where any trade impediment generates waste in preventing the realization of best solutions in all dimensions.

This elevation of trade relations to absolute eminence has meant that all other dimensions have been either occluded (except for their trade-related traits) or at least emasculated to a great extent. For instance, the whole production process and its technological dimensions are naively simplified to a problem of scale economies.[16]

The mythical 100-million-consumer market: The trade bias leads naturally to an interesting metonymy — a procedure through which a thing associated with the matter under discussion becomes a symbol for it. The whole productive dimension of national economies has simply been subsumed under the rubric of *scale*. All the complexities of modern economies are reduced to one feature: the size of the market. Consequently, all problems of productivity and competitiveness are ascribed to lack of opportunity to gain access to a market of 100 million.

This is the foundation on which the Macdonald Commission builds its argument in favour of freer trade: without such a market, it is presumed that a socioeconomy cannot really achieve efficiency and, therefore, competitiveness. Yet there is more to the making of our daily bread (as McCloskey would say) than scale economies, and there is plenty of evidence that small open economies have succeeded in doing extremely well even without full access to a market of 100 million.[17]

This reduction of the whole productive side of the human economy to economies of scale and, therefore, the size of the market, has been challenged by most opponents to free trade as bogus. They argue that there is plenty of evidence that viable economies based on small domestic markets, but skilled productive capacity and good marketing strategies, have established a strong international presence in the world economy (de Wilde 1985; Drummond 1986). But the figure of speech has a great resiliency and it has had an extraordinary impact on the citizenry, as can be seen in the popular and financial presses, which have reproduced this argument hundreds of times. This is so despite the fact that the same financial press (Business Week 1984) has also shown unambiguously that economies of scale alone will no longer guarantee an advantage in manufacturing. Shorter product cycles and reliance on computer design and manufacturing have "made it economical to turn out products in small customized batches."

The metaphorical flavour of the basic argument: By focusing exclusively on trade and the extent of the market, pro-free-trade participants infer that from competition in a large market flows efficiency, and from efficiency flows welfare. This pivotal reliance on efficiency enables the pro-free-trade argument to stand; however potent the forces of competition may be, they cannot by themselves eliminate "natural protection" bestowed by transportation costs or "unnatural protection" bestowed by collusion, cartels, price manipulation, and other such techniques. Moreover, the surge of employment and per capita income purported to ensue from free trade (on the grounds that efficiency is the key to prosperity) depends on a large number of factors about which we know little. What about investment? What about the independence of Canadian policymaking? What about the differential institutions that characterize

Canada in comparison to the USA? On those matters, we can speculate, but we know little.

The trick of the free-trade promoters has been to force the argument on the grounds of competitiveness and efficiency and to presume that employment, growth, and welfare are *necessary* consequences flowing from efficiency. In fact, efficiency *may* promote growth, but it is hardly sufficient to ensure growth. Indeed, "inefficiencies" like tariffs appear to have been associated historically with periods of rapid growth in Canada (Drummond 1986).[18] The basic argument linking large markets-competitiveness-efficiency-growth to employment and welfare may hold as *a perfectly competitive world metaphor* but it does not capture the essence of real socioeconomies.

The thrust behind the basic argument is that the optimal amount of protection is zero. The counter-argument is that it is not so, that there is a "scientific tariff" (Johnson 1960) that may well be significant if one is intent on achieving certain social objectives like economic growth, the creation of jobs, or the pursuit of certain objectives of political sovereignty or cultural development. The counter-argument adds that there is an "imperialism of free trade" as present today as it was in the middle of the 19th century. Free trade as panacea or free trade as economic and cultural genocide are rhetorical stands that one cannot buttress with persuasive arguments.[19]

The use of irony in the free trade debate: Irony is the most sophisticated of the rhetorical techniques. It uses humorous or slightly sarcastic expressions in which the intended meaning is the direct opposite of their usual sense. The trade literature in Canada has always had a strong ironic strand: some may remember the famous Bladen Plan, a proposal to reduce tariffs on the import of auto parts but retain them on whole cars, which, even though designed to increase protection for local assembly plants, was billed as a step toward free trade.[20]

For instance, to defend his belief in a more aggressive and forceful effort toward a complete liberalization of trade, Ron Shearer (1986) characterizes the more careful suggestion of the Macdonald Commission to liberalize trade in industrial products only as "a new face of Canadian mercantilism."

In the face of attacks on the free trade initiative as a threat to Canadian independence, Simon Reisman (1985) refers to studies that supposedly show that "there is not much to worry about on the independence issue in a free trade context that we don't already worry about." This is an argument that Anthony Westell (1984: 22) also uses, although Westell reserves his most biting words for those "romantics" who keep referring to the "national character" and the "national identity." There is also something suave about the U.S.–Israel free trade agreement being proposed as a model for Canada. Or about the suggestion by the prime minister (in his television address of June 1986) that the growing protectionism in the United States (*Fortress U.S.A.*) is putting our markets in peril and the only way out is to negotiate a trade deal. The rest of the year showed how little the ongoing negotiations would affect the dynamic of countervails and how vulnerable Canadian sovereignty over its own policy instruments turned out to be!

The other side has shown itself capable of irony as well. James Laxer (1986) handled this trope exceedingly well, when he accused "economists of harbouring dark feelings about Canada" and he understood "that Canada is the scene of heinous outrages against economic theory." Mel Hurtig (1985) is also a master of irony in his many speeches and articles in which he uses variations on the theme of the famous blind leap of faith through the window of opportunity into the cold shower of international competition, ending up on a cement floor.

The final irony about the free trade debate is that the very notion of free trade connotes and has been made to connote explicitly in the mind of the public some sort of reduction of the importance of the state in trading relations. We are told that free trade, deregulation, and privatization constitute a trinity of policies designed to reduce the role of government in the socioeconomy. In fact, as Bruce Doern (1986) has shown, free trade is bound to mean expanded activities by the state (Baldwin 1986). In this context, it is enlightening to read the briefing document outlining the communications strategy of the Canadian government to sell free trade to the Canadian public. It shows clearly that the intent was not so much to educate the general public as to bamboozle the citizenry by emphasizing the *free* in free trade.[21]

It is hardly surprising that the free trade debate has generated more heat than light. Throughout, the notion of free trade has maintained a certain strategic vagueness nurtured carefully by all participants in the debate. Attempts to promote other versions of the notion (freer trade, enhanced trade) have been perceived as decoys for the real thing and never did take hold. This strategic vagueness compounded by a certain tactical imprecision regarding the coverage of any possible free trade arrangement (industrial production à la Macdonald or a wider coverage including services, agriculture, culture, etc.) and the shifts among free trade as an idea, as a game of negotiations, and as a redesigning of the socioeconomic space of North America have kept the debate out of reach of most Canadians.

The lack of focus of the conversation about free trade is obviously partly strategic, but it is also largely ascribable to the lack of rigour of the language of problem–solution provided by the social sciences. Otherwise, much of this mumbling would have been exposed forcefully much earlier. But as very little of substance can be generated from general social-scientific rules, debaters have been forced to construct ad hoc policy recommendations derived from analyses of second-best or third-best possibilities. The framing of decisions has become such a key variable that the same "objective" information is now seen as capable of triggering quite diverse reactions depending on the way it is presented: rhetoric is queen. This is nowhere more transparent than in the communications strategy document revealed on 20 September 1985. Government would appear intent on shaping the framework for decisions rather than attempting to deal with so-called "objective" dimensions of the issue.

The multilogue is fundamentally flawed: on a bold *synecdoche* of a socio-economy fully defined by trading relations, academics and bureaucrats have attached the *metonymy* that the only operative force in the productive process is economies of scale. This has served as a foundation for a metaphorical chain rooted in the extent of the market and leading to an efficiency-seeking policy recommendation that had to be free trade; an occlusion of key substantive features of the socioeconomy as instituted process ensued. Appropriately spiced with irony, all this could be tonic, but not enlightening.

WHAT REFURBISHED SOCIAL SCIENCES MIGHT CONTRIBUTE

An alternative practice of the social sciences might be able to go further and deeper in making sense of the free trade debate. In this section, a general sketch of what refurbished social sciences might look like is presented, together with the sort of new model for policy research that should ensue. This might carry the debate on free trade into more promising directions.

This is quite a voyage, deep into *terra incognita*. It cannot be certain, therefore, that we can deliver as much as we would like to promise. The intent at least should be clear: we wish to map out this new terrain in a preliminary way.

The Nature of the Repairs[22]

Refurbished human sciences must take a turn toward interpretation, and the fundamental *sociality* of the social sciences must become the central dimension of interest. To explore sociality, a new methodological strategy focused on institutions is necessary. This strategy calls for a reconstruction of the institutional schemata (as social armistices and parameters of possible actions) and for a recreation of their genesis; the central concern is not to explicate the reified social context from *without*, but to try to understand from *within* the unity, complementarities, consistency, permanence, and development of the institutional texture of World 3 (Bourdieu 1972; OECD 1979; Thompson 1981: 173).

But this cannot be done without some effort to go beneath the historical traditions to the real forces determining their shape. This is where hermeneutics comes in. It considers human social life as text-analogue calling for interpretation in the same manner as old incomplete and fragmented texts from past ages used to be interpreted. The contexted traditions are almost of necessity interpreted overtly by different actors or groups of actors in a biased, ideological way. This is why *depth interpretation* is in order.[23]

What is called for is not unlike a Freudian-type interpretation looking for unsuspected patterns of distorted communication, beneath the observed speech pattern of ordinary life, resulting from the repression of needs and wants. What appear to be forms of neurotic symptoms in the individual may transpire as forms of "false consciousness" and ideology in societies. Habermas (1971) suggests that in the same way Freud penetrated beneath the surface to underlying forces by methodical interpretation of dreams, behaviour, speech, etc., one can interpret societies' pathologies and unearth what might account for the false consciousness of groups in society.[24] Bringing out the latent repressed significance of the patient's life history leads the patient to place new significance on those repressed areas; Habermas hopes to apply the same therapy in social life. By revealing the preconditions of power and domination that gave rise to distorted communication, one might improve the degree of communicative competence within a socioeconomy and come closer to realizing a less imperfect community.

To do so, one needs a better decoder than the language of problem solution — the language of progress. This *language of progress is based on freedom as an absolute* and on a blind faith in continuing progress through the use of instrumental reason and technology. This has been the decoder used to analyze our societies. The language of progress is not capable of throwing any light on the essential *sociality* of human communities, on their intersubjective fabric or on the various ways in which communication can be and is systematically distorted within human communities (Ramos 1981). It decomposes the institutional fabric of our societies into reified rights and, thereby, dissolves it into a contractual texture that gives no voice or reality to those who have no contracting power: marginals, nonconformists, the unborn, etc. It cannot take into account fundamental categories like goodness or justice.

What is required is *a language rooted in what makes us human rather than in what makes us free*. Michael Ignatieff (1985) has proposed one such language — a language of the good, a language of needs — more capable of appreciating fully our essential sociality and consequently also the relevant deformations of the social space, i.e., deviations vis-à-vis situations promoting the good and the just (Schick 1984). Such a language rooted in civil society recognizes the centrality of good society, good polity, good economy, and strives to eliminate impediments standing in the way of their realization, i.e., a socioeconomy that meets not only efficiency standards, but also standards of reciprocity and stability.[25]

Toward a New Model of Policy Research

In most policy research on big questions, goals are ambiguous or in conflict *and* means–ends relationships are highly uncertain. It is hardly surprising that policy research should be of little use. Researchers have a great latitude to specify unreasonably narrow or naive goals or to presume some deterministic link between means and ends when there is at best a remotely possible one. However cleverly one may wish to package the results of such policy research, it is bound to be irrelevant.

This often leads to deception, but most of the time it results in some conniving between the producer of the metaphorical research and the policy-maker who has paid for it. The rationale for this connivance comes from the fact that such policy research is of no consequence: it leaves the policymaker entirely free to follow the strategy that proves electorally expedient. David Slater (1950) was not challenged when he wrote that little in the successes or failures of economic policy in the post-war period in Canada could be ascribed to economic research.[26]

The only way to generate policy research of import is to renounce scientism and develop policy research in the full context of social practice. This in turn calls for a simultaneous taking into account of four interactive subprocesses: "the formulation of a theory of reality, the articulation of relevant social values, the selection of an appropriate political strategy, and the implementation of practical measures or social action" (Friedmann and Abonyi 1976).[27] John Friedmann (1978: 86) has proposed one such model in which

> Cognition is linked to the world of events via social action (SA) and the results of that action. The adequacy of the theory of reality (TR) and/or the political strategy (PS) is, therefore, dependent on the results of action (SA) and the extent to which these results satisfy the given social values (SV). Such knowledge is useful in solving social problems, but it is not formally cumulative knowledge. Indeed much of the knowledge obtained may leave no visible traces of itself; it is experiential or tacit knowledge.[28]

Such a policy research model incorporates normative assertions explicitly instead of "smuggling" them in; it is based on a transactive style of planning that boldly accepts the underlying conflictive process implied in the political system. It is also based firmly on the belief that *social learning* must be promoted at all possible locations within a social system and that social experimentation should be promoted wherever possible. Indeed, it would appear to lead exactly to the converse of the current manipulative strategies hinted at in footnote 21. In a world freed from the totalitarianism of the knowledgeable elite, there is a "commitment on the part of the policy-maker to the idea of social experimentation, practice, and learning as the principal methods for public intervention" (Friedmann and Abonyi 1976: 939; on how one might implement such transactive planning, see Friedmann 1973).

Dimensions of Interdependence

The remaining question is whether refurbished social sciences might throw some new light on the free trade debate. I think it would. An attempt to examine the Canadian socioeconomy as a text-analogue and to *socioanalyze* it to unearth the foundations of the various ideological discourses we hear might indeed reveal a large amount of false consciousness in the Canadian political economy. Moreover, a model of policy research taking explicitly into account the sociocultural and the sociopolitical dimensions of the free trade arrangement might significantly redirect the thrust of the debate.

Many "deformations of the social space" might serve as *révélateurs*: Canada is a small, open, dependent, and balkanized socioeconomy living in the shadow of the United States but intent on preserving a separate and different cultural identity and social fabric. Whatever the rectitude of this view, the coherence and permanence of the existing Canadian social order is perceived as jeopardized by an economic *rapprochement* with the United States. Richard Lipsey (1986: 235) has labeled this sort of opposition to free trade "visceral rather than intellectual."

There are widespread concerns about free trade because it would seemingly lead irreversibly to a complete submission of the operations of the Canadian socioeconomy to the imperatives of the market. The strictly commercial dimension of the arrangement has already become hegemonic in all discussions. Culture, which for Canadians used to mean a profoundly different "program" in the sense that computer scientists use the word, i.e., a different way of life, a significantly different way to tackle issues and solve problems, is in the process of becoming synonymous with cultural industries. Social programs, that used to connote the style of society Canadians had chosen, are now referred to as forms of export subsidies.

If the *free* in free trade has been used to market the idea that Canadians could have their cake and eat it too, for other Canadians, the abandonment of their life-styles to the whims of the *free* market makes no sense. In many ancient societies, the market mechanism was used for the allocation of widgets, but banned in relation to food and essential goods, because it was believed that the free market might not allocate such essential commodities ideally (i.e., fairly and appropriately). The same might be said about such important intangibles as culture and social mores. Free trade has, therefore, been a major source of fear.

The only way to incorporate fully the social and cultural dimensions (but also the regional, distributional, technological, financial, human, political, and demographic objectives) into the discussion about trade is to recast the debate in terms of *fair trade* (Mégrelis 1980). This would ensure that, in the process of bargaining over trading arrangements, the collective goals that Canadians have chosen would be kept in perspective and explicitly brought forward in an attempt to negotiate a fair deal with the United States.

Fair trade is an expression which is likely to generate negative reactions from those who feel that *fairness* is not a sound enough basis to serve as a benchmark. Yet for years, courts have refereed cases on the basis of such criteria without too much difficulty. This is most certainly better than the "leap of faith" that might simply end up in a process of "Ukrainization" of Canada (Varzeliotis 1985: preface).

The fair trade scenario poses many important challenges to Canada. Such negotiations would have to be developed on the basis of the *Charter of the Economic Rights and Duties of Nations* approved by the General Assembly of the United Nations in 1974. The 34 articles of this charter (including the right to control foreign investment, the right to share in the advantages that result from technological and scientific innovations, the duty to cooperate to ensure fair terms of trade, etc.) were approved by a majority of 120 votes to 6, but the United States voted against the charter. Consequently, it is not certain that efforts to negotiate a fair commercial, technological, financial, and social deal with the United States would either be welcome or feasible. But is anything less than such an arrangement simply another form of "imperialism of free trade"? And if so, do Canadians really want it?

A social science research program intent on examining the new trading relations with the United States within the context of a model of social learning might reveal that, as it has been mentioned by some observers, free trade as an idea is not such a good one, that Canada may have been imprudent in jumping into such negotiations without the necessary preparatory work at the provincial and grassroots levels, and that the economic benefits from such a new trading space are doubtful (while triggering irreversible social, cultural, and political consequences). It might also dispel those fears and help prepare the documentation necessary for the negotiation of a fair deal.

Such a research program does not exist. Many intelligent appraisals of the situation have been put forward, but they are mostly speculations and opinions couched in different figures of speech. Little has been done to analyze the "deformations" of our social space, to dispel the high degree of false conscious-ness that inhabits the debate, or to hasten social learning about the price Canadians might be willing to pay to maintain "their good society." And when such analyses have been put forward, they have been ignored or disparaged as "nationalist" or "socialist." This has not helped the conversation about what a fair deal with the United States might be. Canadians have been bombarded with messages from many Cassandras and many Candides, or they have been simply dis-informed. What they need is an orderly framework for their thought. Only a refurbished social sciences can help in this construction.

CONCLUSION

It may be unduly optimistic to believe that, after a century of positivistic indoctrination, one might feel that a turn to interpretation is likely to bring a breath of some fresh air into the social sciences. Yet there are many signs that we are entering a crucial transition period. The disciplinary guilds have been led to excesses in their regulation and there has been "a crisis of abstraction" in the 1970s. As a result, it can be argued that the social sciences have become more disconnected from the original questions that led to their creation than ever in the past.

According to Katouzian (1980), no amount of moral suasion or sporadic dissent and no sermons will provoke the needed change, "only a combination of public consciousness and the growing proximity of the abyss" will do the job. Those two forces may be at work. A crisis of confidence has developed over the last 15 years within the social science community. It has been echoed within the broader social context as practical irrelevance and theoretical failures showed up more and more frequently. Consequently governments and patrons have become less willing to fund the activities of the social scientists. The matching grants policy of the Mulroney government should bring that crisis to a head.[29]

While not determinant in this process, the free trade debate may have exposed social scientists more than they would have liked. There seems to be a convergence of developments (both in current philosophical thinking and in the demands by society) that would appear to promote the development of "an epistemology of practice which places technical problem solving within a broader context of reflective inquiry, shows how reflection-in-action may be rigorous in its own right, and links the art of practice in uncertainty and uniqueness to the scientist's art of research" (Schon 1983: 69). An alternative to positivism now exists and there is a demand for it.

At a time when those who gave us positivism — the physicists — apply terms like *colour* and *charm* to the quark — this elusive and invisible ultimate element — it may be time for social scientists to recognize at last that they should cease to be slaves to some defunct physicist (Jones 1983).

NOTES

1. The diagnosis put forward in this section has been developed more fully in Paquet (1987b).

2. This is probably the most vehement denunciation of this perversion of the social sciences. Von Hayek (1952) shows how, from Francis Bacon to Auguste Comte, there have been efforts to reduce the human sciences to the status of natural sciences of man. Although there is much merit in this approach in many subareas of the study of man, it is unacceptable, says Hayek, to reduce all of social sciences to this subsegment.

3. In economic history, it is often argued that tariffs are not unlike "negative railroads," as the impediments to trade that they generate are the exact obverse of the facilitation of trade generated by the introduction of railroad transportation. L.H. Jenks (1944) has analyzed the impact of railroads on American development under three rubrics: railroad as an idea, railroad as a construction enterprise, railroad as a producer of transportation services. We have adopted a somewhat similar approach.

4. These mechanical analogs might be almost entirely unspecified (Culbertson 1986), although one may easily gather from the analysis what sort of model Dr Culbertson carries in the back of his head; or it might be a very elaborate econometric construct as in the case of the work of R.G. Harris and D. Cox (1985) or in the many simulations performed by management consultants like Informetrica for a variety of clients. Such elaborate constructs need not be economic in nature (Braybrooke 1974).

5. It is interesting to note that in many instances the "social scientists" who have been making the most interesting contributions to this debate have been those least constrained by the trappings of the traditional disciplines: journalists, situationologists, or leading academics. The first two groups have provided *débroussaillages*, guided somewhat by social-scientific frameworks but not trapped in it. As for the prominent senior academics, freed to some extent from the need to abide by the rules of the discipline, they would appear to adopt a style and a form of analysis that is not without reminding those adopted by journalists and situationologists. An example of the journalistic pieces might be Blouin (1986) or McLean (1986). For a very lucid piece by a prominent academic economist, see Lipsey (1986); for a good piece by a situationologist, see Doern (1986) and on the notion of situationologist, see Paquet (1982) or Chapter 2 in this volume.

6. Laxer (1986) argues that a market-driven approach is not appropriate; he suggests that a business–government partnership is required to rebuild Canada's socioeconomy. See also Rotstein (1984).

7. This phenomenon has been known for quite some time, but it was analyzed carefully only in the postwar period. James Meade (1955), the Nobel laureate, coined the phrase. The fact that a best solution is ruled out by the existence of imperfections in one sector means that a second-best solution has to be found. Such a solution has to be derived from an examination of the particulars of the case. It cannot be inferred from the use of a general rule like the equalization of marginal costs and benefits. Obviously such a line of reasoning may be used to justify the existence of trade restrictions.

8. In Canada, the debates at the time of the Quebec referendum of 1980 and in the years preceding it, together with those that have been going on about free trade in the 1980s, have provided numerous examples of such apparently contradictory statements. In fact, most of the time there is no inherent contradiction: as soon as they stray away from tautologies or truisms, practitioners can hardly answer any question pertaining to the world of facts (as perceived by the citizenry) except by saying "it depends," and many of the conclusions that follow are simply an echo effect of the assumptions on which they have built their argument.

9. This is the view upheld by neoclassical economists, and their policy advice is anchored in the assumption that the standard rules in force in the ideal competitive world should be used whatever their inappropriateness. For a critique of this view and some suggested alternative approaches to the gauging of performance, see Paquet 1978b).

10. Lancaster (1973) presents capitalism as a differential game and demonstrates the sub-optimality of this regime because of its built-in coordination failures. Social waste ensues. In the face of such inefficiency, it is futile to argue for a return to competition (and therefore freer trade) as a way out. Such a focus on efficiency criteria is not only unwarranted but assumes away too many of the complexities, uncertainties, and strategic dimensions of the real game that underpins the human economy.

11. In Paquet (1977) an argument is developed showing that to the extent that federalism fragments a socioeconomy, it may improve its capacity to adapt. To the extent that regulation and other nonmarket mechanisms balkanize the socioeconomy, the same argument may be made that regulation promotes multistability.

12. Such attempts to persuade the population that *the technical has replaced the moral* have been dubbed "a methodological or epistemological coup" (Wiley in Paquet 1977: 296) perpetrated by social scientists on the population. It has proved effective but only in the short run. Questions of *sovereignty* or *culture*, for instance, would appear to be almost *ultra vires* for traditional social sciences. It is easier for some, like Westell (1984: 22), simply to occlude such dimensions from their analysis or to transmogrify them: "To be a Canadian citizen does not signify a way of life, or a set of values beyond attachment to the community and loyalty to the national state. So the fear that closer association with the United States will erode a Canadian identity in the making or abort a Canadian culture about to be born is unfounded." In the same spirit, he argues that free trade would entail "no sovereignty loss"; it is simply that "both governments would have to look very carefully before implementing domestic policies" (Westell 1984: 18).

13. Given the publication lag and the insensitivity of much of the academic community to current issues, it has been important to sample journals and magazines with a stronger interest in current policy issues. We have scanned a number of publications without any intention of being exhaustive. In alphabetical order they are: *Alberta Report, The Business Quarterly, Canadian Business, The Canadian Business Review, Canadian Dimension, Canadian Forum, Canadian Labour, Canadian Public Policy, International Perspectives, Queen's Quarterly, Policy Options,* and *The Idler*.

14. McCloskey (1985: 83) has analyzed the prose of Robert Solow and others and shown that figures of speech have played a great role in "scientific" arguments.

15. For a more realistic look at the fabric of real economies, see Williamson (1985).

16. Harris (1985) has underlined the fact that the comparative advantages are not inherited from nature but made largely through institutional build-ups and structures. Even though he underlines the limitations of the classical approach to international trade,

his entry barriers approach still focuses unduly on the trade side of the economy and ignores the institutional fabric except as it generates barriers to trade.

17. The 100 million market as a necessary basis for achieving economies of scale is an argument one finds everywhere in the free-traders' prose. It was already there in the 1982 report of the Senate's Standing Committee on Foreign Affairs (Vol. III). It is repeated by Sarna (1985: 302), but also by Lipsey (1986: 225), and by a large number of participants in the free trade debate.

18. There have been many challenges to this representation of free trade as a necessary/sufficient condition to ensure efficiency and of the suggestion that efficiency is a necessary/sufficient condition for increased welfare. Some have argued that free trade is not sufficient (Harris 1985; Proulx 1986). Others have challenged the link between efficiency and welfare, claiming that other goals are more clearly correlated with the welfare of the population. The priorities may differ among those opponents to free trade — the need to preserve our independent use of policy instruments (J. Laxer), the need to design an industrial strategy (S. Smith), the need to combat unemployment and poverty (E. Kierans), cultural objectives (B. Anthony) — but they agree that efficiency considerations cannot be regarded as sufficient to lead to increased welfare.

19. Economic history provides ample evidence of both imperialism through protection *and* through free trade. Hirschman (1945) has shown how Nazi Germany used trade relations and protection to dominate and penetrate southeastern Europe and elsewhere. Gallagher and Robinson (1953) have shown how one of the most common political techniques of British expansion in the 19th century was "the treaty of free trade and friendship made with or imposed upon a weaker state." Therefore, one cannot necessarily associate free trade with benefits and protection with costs. Each country must design the mix of free trade and protection that suits its priorities. In the free trade debate of the last few years, this simple truth has seemingly been forgotten.

20. For a critical examination of this sort of economic sophistry conveniently putting aside the well-known principle that reducing the tariff on an input increases effective protection, see Johnson (1963).

21. This document was published in the *Toronto Star* on 20 Sep. 1985. Excerpts are telling: "The popular interpretation of free trade appears to be keyed to the word 'free.' It is something for nothing — a short cut — to economic prosperity. It is bigger markets for Canadian products, more jobs, more of everything. It is, as Terrence Wills of the Gazette puts it, having your cake and eating it too.... The strategy should rely less on educating the general public than on getting across the message that the trade initiative is a good idea. In other words, a selling job." Late in 1986, this document was reprinted in a book of readings attempting to collect a representative sample of the documents generated by the free trade debate (Cameron 1986). Varzeliotis (1985: 296) has described the strategy document as an invitation to "keep the people ignorant, impact upon them false impressions, prevent the opposition from exposing myths, encourage apathy and rule the society."

22. Some of the material in this section has been developed more fully in Paquet (1987b: sections 4 and 5).

23. For a simple introduction to hermeneutics and a sketch of the manner in which Jurgen Habermas has used it in a manner parallel to Freudian analysis, see Anderson et al. (1986: 76–81). We have drawn from their presentation in the next few paragraphs.

24. For a lucid analysis of the parallel between neurosis and schizophrenia in the individual and ideology and false consciousness at the social level, see Gabel (1962).

25. For a sense of what these concepts refer to see Friedmann (1979) and Kolm (1984). Any major departure from those norms would constitute a "deformation of social space" (Lachmann 1971: 83). One may regard in this context policymaking as elimination of misfits or the search for a good fit (Alexander 1971).

26. One might make the same argument about social policy or social change in general. A case in point of a fundamental change in which social scientists played little or no role is the civil rights movement in the United States (King 1968).

27. The "paradigm of social practice" is stylized as a process of intercreation between the following four subprocesses: theory of reality, political strategy, social values, social action. "These processes come to life only in the context of a concrete situation, and they are so connected that a change in any one of them will necessarily affect all others, either producing a substantive change or confirming the existing practice" (Friedmann and Abonyi 1976).

28. For those schooled in positivism, such a statement may appear rather vague and all encompassing. It should be clear, however, that the exploration of those dimensions is more apt to generate useful knowledge than the attitude that leads one to declare not answerable and, therefore, irrelevant the questions intractable with their disciplinary tools.

29. This is a policy that imposes a sort of market test on the funding of research by the federal government. The granting councils will get additional money only to match funding by the private sector. This should put the demand for social science research through a market test from which social scientists should emerge somewhat humbled. For the details of that policy, see *Strengthening the Private Sector/University Research Partnership — The Matching Policy Rules* (Canada 1986).

CHAPTER 4

SCIENCE AND TECHNOLOGY POLICY UNDER FREE TRADE*

We should not be swayed by our theories
to give up common sense too easily.

– *Karl Popper*

The structure of the national output of advanced economies has changed dramatically since the Second World War: it has shifted more and more away from the production of material goods toward the production of services and information. Knowledge and information have become both a dominant form of output and a separate factor of production: knowledge differentials have come to be regarded as the new basis of comparative advantage and speciali-zation in the world economy (Perroux 1970; Jussawalla and Cheah 1984).

This new knowledge/information economy as an instituted process is substantially different from the previous incarnations of our economy. When *land* was its centre of gravity, the network of institutions used to coordinate economic activities had much to do with bargaining over *rent*; with the growth of commercial capitalism, the *market* became the core institution and the key bargain was over *price*; and with the emergence of the *industrial* world bargain-ing focused on *wages*. Now that the central feature of our socioeconomy is information/knowledge, the key bargain between the different stakeholders is over the control of the *forum* (Tussman 1977; Paquet 1987a). The whole architecture of our coordinating institution has been or is in the process of being reshaped to deal with this new central reality.

The notion of forum is used here not to refer to a particular place, but in a more general way — as we speak of "the market" — to refer to a "whole range of institutions and situations of public communication... [a] system of oppor-tunities and protections" (Tussman 1977). These institutions have to do with the production, allocation, distribution, and regulation of awareness, cognitive energy, symbolic resources, research, knowledge, and information.

In the forum, research, science, and technology raise the question of the production of new knowledge. But knowledge and information are not simple

* This paper also appeared in *Technology in Society* 1989, 11(2), 221–234. The assistance of Denis Jubinville and Marc Racette has been invaluable.

private commodities, and this poses a problem to the private enterprise system. Knowledge is costly to produce and the production of new knowledge (which is the outcome of research) is a high-risk activity, often with only a long-term payoff. Yet new knowledge, once produced, is in the nature of a public good. It can be used by one person without precluding use by others. Consequently, it appears beneficial to make it widely available at a nominal cost. But, if this is done, there will be little incentive for anyone to invest important and scarce resources in the production of new knowledge (Paquet and Taylor 1986).

To resolve this problem, governments have designed many techniques (from temporary monopoly on new knowledge by its private producer, to public subsidy and tax breaks for private producers, to government-managed research). All these techniques are meant to alleviate the chronic problem of underinvestment in the production of new knowledge in a market economy.

SCIENCE AND TECHNOLOGY POLICY

Science is defined in the *Concise Oxford Dictionary* as systematic and formulated knowledge, and technology as the science of the industrial arts (Tisdell 1981). One can imagine a continuum of overlapping domains ranging from pure science, to applied science, to technology. However, it is important to realize that this continuum is not a one-way street: pure science may never give rise to technical advance; technical advance may on the other hand occur by trial and error without science, and new scientific knowledge may also be triggered by questions raised at the technology and practice level (Feibleman 1961; Schon 1983; Paquet 1988b).

The sort of *questions* that an economist is likely to pose about science and technology (S&T) are simple: Who ought to conduct research? How should they be compensated for their effort? What problems should they work on? How many and what kinds of strategies should be pursued in tackling these problems? And how should resources be allocated among research strategies and problems? The key challenge has to do with the setting up of coordinating mechanisms to answer these questions.

One solution readily suggested by economists is that the market should provide the answers to these questions. But there are reasons to believe that the market solution is likely to be incorrect. Knowledge as a commodity has characteristics that make it rather special:

- It is a public good.
- There are strong economies of scale in its production and use.
- Uncertainty is acute in its use and production (Dasgupta and Stoneman 1987).
- Waste results from duplication of search efforts in a simple competitive system.
- Social failures occur in the transmission and diffusion of technical knowledge.

- External industry-wide economies of development exist that individual and isolated decision-making might be led to ignore (Tisdell 1981; Kahn 1966).

An additional complication can be ascribed to the fact that the production of new scientific and technological knowledge is the work of social communities and organizations that have quite distinct attitudes toward the output of research. At one end of the spectrum, science views knowledge as a good for public consumption, while at the other end, technology regards it as a private capital good (Dasgupta and Stoneman 1987). This triggers different ethos and different norms and rules of conduct: the scientist's reward comes from being the first to come up with and fully disclose new results, while the technologist's reward comes from capturing rents from new findings on which proprietary rights are exercised (Dasgupta and David 1987). In both cases, however, the premium on being first is such that it may lead to undue haste, duplication of efforts, and waste.

A final complication comes from the fact that the notion of knowledge in the whole range from science to technology is often presented in simplistic terms, as a blueprint or a recipe. Tacit skill, training, and communication are also involved in acquiring new knowledge or in implementing a technology. Individual traits and idiosyncrasies are also significant. In all likelihood, these elements of the tacit and of the idiosyncratic mean that there is no one best way always and for everyone. "Knowing how to produce a product is as much experienced tacit skill as articulable knowledge. And contrary to the implicit general theory, the tacit skills of one 'skilled in the art' are not interchangeable; who works with the recipe makes a difference" (Rosenberg 1982; Murnane and Nelson 1984; Dosi et al. 1988; Paquet 1989d).

From this cluster of arguments flows the presumption that the market system may not automatically produce the optimal amount of new knowledge in the forum and may not produce it optimally. One possibility is that *too little* may be invested in such activities because of the fact that the costs are largely internal to the firm, whereas a substantial portion of the benefits are external to the firm; or because myopic decisions may not lead to taking full advantage of intertemporal scale economies or industry-wide external economies; or because the high degree of uncertainty may discourage a sufficient research effort because of imperfect capital markets. A second possibility is that *too much* may be invested in R&D because of fixation on the reward mechanism of being first: this inevitably leads to duplication, overcrowding of promising paths, and often neglect of long shots as a valuable hedge from society's viewpoint (Dasgupta and Stiglitz 1980). A third possibility is that the new knowledge produced may be generated ineffectively, inefficiently, and uneconomically both because of excessive competition triggered by the winner-takes-all reward system and because of a lack of understanding and concern for the tacit and the idiosyncratic in the diffusion and implementation of this new knowledge.

All these factors point to the need for government intervention, for a S&T policy. But such a policy should not be simply couched in terms of additional funding for R&D in the hope that technical advance will ensue. Although popular in government circles, this sort of strategy is unlikely to solve the problem and may even lead to instances of "government failures" that would not necessarily correct the existing "market failures" (Dosi et al. 1988). What is needed is an answer to the five economic questions posed above: who? what? how? etc. This in turn requires a politics of cognitive energy and a better forum: experimentation with quick feedback is the only way to learn if one is concerned about guiding the evolution of the socio-technologic-economic system through good use of the forum and government as a learning system (Schon 1971).

In general, most governments (in large or small economies) have taken note of the challenges posed by S&T. Each country has at least an implicit science policy (concerned with education, the stock of knowledge, its availability and use, and R&D) and a de facto technology policy (concerned with the adoption and use of techniques — innovation, diffusion of techniques, and their replacement) (Tisdell 1981). Although this de facto policy is often nothing more than ritualized adhocery, it represents some basic choices: more or less relative emphasis on the science end or on the technology end of the spectrum, more emphasis on production of new knowledge as opposed to the diffusion of existing knowledge, greater reliance on public or private production, more or less competitive or complementary routes in the production of knowledge, etc. For instance, some countries like the United States, the United Kingdom, and France have focused relatively more on the science end to realize certain radical innovations needed to reach goals of national importance. Other countries like Germany, Switzerland, and Sweden have focused on the diffusion of technology at the other end of the spectrum to facilitate the ongoing and incremental adaptation of their economies to change (Dasgupta and Stoneman 1987).

But there have been broad trends in the action of governments on this front over the last decades. First, S&T policy has become more explicit. Second, it has evolved more or less in step in the various countries: in general, S&T policy in the post Second World War period was geared to economic growth; in the 1960s to the mid-1970s, quality of life and environmental concerns generated a series of questions about S&T and the emergence of a defensive policy stand; more recently, concerns about national competitiveness in the international arena and about international spillovers of development based on S&T have generated a renewed interest in a proactive S&T policy.

In general, governments now have a sense that they should intervene in the forum to ensure a leadership "that enlightens, teaches, and forces us to attend to the necessary agenda" (Tussman 1977). However — and this is a third trend — vast amounts of resources have been spent in pursuit of creation of new knowledge, much less for the dissemination of existing knowledge — a strategy that would appear especially well suited for small countries.

Fourth, governments have generally based their policy actions on a rather ill-founded model of the innovative process: it is not sufficient to spend more money on R&D to generate innovation. There is much that is tacit and idiosyncratic about innovation and about the diffusion of new technology. Transfer of new instrumentalities between sectors depends much on these factors. Yet governments have made little effort to develop such a knowledge base (Cairncross 1972; Bonin and Desranleau 1988; Paquet 1989d).

Finally, it appears clear that experimentation with government policy designed to identify who should do what in what manner and with what public support has not generated any golden rule readily applicable everywhere; indeed some have expressed skepticism about the possibility of eliciting such general guiding principles (Pavitt and Soete 1981).

These modest accomplishments do not suggest that government action is not warranted to ensure that additional resources are allocated to the production of new knowledge or to facilitate the diffusion of this new knowledge among sectors or to design a better fit between S&T and the national sociocultural underground. Structural features may also be in need of repair: government laboratories may have taken on too large a share of research in certain countries, transfer of new knowledge may be unduly difficult from government laboratories to industrial plants, and formulation of explicit priorities without rigid commitments may increase flexibility and speed of reaction to new circumstances. But it would be unwise to expect that, in this evolutionary process of change where goals are complex and ambiguous and where means–end relationships are highly uncertain and poorly understood, government policy will be able to do anything more than ensure that the requisite variety of experimentation is conducted, that feedback information becomes available a bit faster, and that the unintended consequences of S&T developments are assessed more vigilantly.

SCIENCE AND TECHNOLOGY POLICY IN THE INTERNATIONAL CONTEXT

The technical literature on the interface between S&T, on one hand, and international trade, on the other, suggests that international differences in technological levels and innovative capabilities are beginning to be the major forces shaping trade flows and the international division of labour.

Three thrusts of forces are at work in three interlocking subsystems: an evolutionary technological system dominated by the logic of science and technique in the sense of Jacques Ellul (1954); an evolving system of multinational enterprises covering the world with a number of managerial nets and internal trading systems; and a mosaic of nation states intent on designing policies maximizing benefits to nationals via subsidies and regulation of the forum.

The Technological Paradigm

S&T constitute a techno-economic system that has a dynamic of its own: a "technological paradigm" defining contextually "the needs that are meant to be fulfilled, the scientific principles utilized for the task, the material technology to be used" (Dosi et al. 1988). This paradigm exists at the transnational level and from it evolve technological trajectories: progress along the technological and economic trade-offs defined by the paradigm. The combustion engine or microelectronics are examples of such paradigms gridlocking firms and industries throughout the world economic system. For the behaviour of firms and industries is influenced by the macro-technological regime that defines the rules of the game. This regime shapes the focusing devices or guideposts used by firms to organize their search for better technologies.

The technological paradigm is based on public knowledge shared by all actors involved in a family of activities — publications, etc. — and a structured set of technological externalities or synergies among sectors, technologies, and firms. This driving force often has unintended and irreversible outcomes, as in Silicon Valley. By following the path, industries enjoy dynamic increasing returns and are in some way locked into particular technologies.

There remains a tacit firm-specific or country-specific form of knowledge that will explain why some firms, some countries, or some firms in some countries have more or less success, and their choice of techniques may be influenced through inducement mechanisms (emerging either from autonomous changes in relative prices or from some manipulation of policy variables), but all this develops *within the boundary* defined by the technological paradigm (Dosi et al. 1988). For Dosi and colleagues, the technology establishes "untraded interdependencies" or "synergies" between sectors, technologies, and firms. Even those who have been critical of the evolutionary paradigm expounded by Dosi and others have acknowledged the importance of this nexus of technological forces (De Bresson 1987).

Multinational Enterprises and Technology Transfer

The race to be in the lead technologically has been based on the belief that the control of new technology entails the control of markets for new products and progressive industries. Indeed, it has been shown that large U.S. companies expect to draw close to one-third of the returns on their R&D projects from overseas markets via all marketing channels — subsidiaries, licensing, and export of innovative goods (Caves 1982). But this technological lead is always precarious, and there is imitation after a lag period. Therefore, the innovative firm is always torn between two temptations: trying to maintain a monopoly on existing knowledge in the country of origin to control lucrative export markets; or transferring the technology and profiting via licensing or foreign investment. The shareholders demand that the right trade-offs be struck.

The futility of efforts to prevent the transfer of technology in the long run has led to the development of increasingly effective modes of international technology transfer to take advantage of the lead while it lasts. The most effective vehicle in this process has turned out to be the multinational enterprise — not only because of the difficulty of trading information and knowledge on markets, but also because of the tacit and the idiosyncratic elements attached to technology. Both transfer costs that are more significant when the transfer is at arm's length than when it is through a firm. After a detailed examination of technology transfer in the electrical industry, Harold Crookell (1973) concludes that

> The transmission of technology within an administrative unit is more efficient — in terms of speed, cost and scope — than transmission across the open market.... Managing the transmission process is an extraordinarily complex and sensitive affair. Insecurity, risk and rapid change abound, and demand an adaptive system with major constraints aimed at controlling relevance.

Multinational enterprises have become so important that a substantial portion of international trade is now intrafirm trade, i.e., via nonmarket or quasi-market channels. Moreover, the multinational enterprise has not only been used to transfer technology from the home country to the host country, but also to tap inventiveness and innovative activities there. In fact, in many cases, multinational enterprises have become vehicles of "reverse technology transfer" from the host country to the home of the multinational enterprises (Cheng 1984).

National Government Policies

National governments have their own priorities, and they differ from those of the shareholders in the multinationals: they wish to maximize benefits to nationals. At first, regulatory strategies were designed to prevent technology from flowing out, but they proved futile except in the short run. The quasi-rents earned from gaining the lead are quickly eroded by international diffusion of the technology. Consequently, governments have come to realize that a successful policy would have to interfere with the whole innovation process and implement rules that are likely to generate a larger continuous stream of new ideas, to ensure that such ideas are transmitted more quickly to potential users, and to encourage domestic firms to exploit more fully their technological lead internationally.

Governments have chosen different strategies depending on the size of the country and the degree of technological sophistication of their socioeconomies. Large countries like the United States have emphasized the production side or new knowledge, through procurement and subsidies; smaller ones like Sweden have emphasized the diffusion side. Advanced countries have exploited their advantage through foreign investment, licensing, and exports; less advanced host countries have attempted to encourage the transfer of laboratories overseas by offering various tax holidays or simply protection and subsidies for certain segments of their industries with the hope of limiting their technological dependence or even altering the existing technological leadership (Cheng 1984).

The effectiveness of these policy initiatives has been limited, but they have had a steering effect. Segments of the forum have been strengthened and expertise has been built up in certain fields, whereas other areas have been allowed to deteriorate. Deliberate policies designed to spread knowledge have entailed a redistribution of resources that so-called centres of excellence have complained about. The result has been an allocation of cognitive energy in various countries according to very different patterns; more important, maybe, has been the politics of awareness and the mobilization of the citizenry in support of such choices. Almost every country can boast of slogans like "*virage technologique*" or "*innovaction*" — to use Canadian labels — as marketing devices for some brand of S&T policy.

As a result of the relative inefficiency of the market in this domain, the major players are likely to be governments and multinationals trying to take advantage of the evolutionary inertia of *technique*: the governments through subsidies, procurement, discrimination, regulations, and controls, and the multinationals by building on synergies and "untraded interdependencies." Those nonmarket hierarchies may not act entirely without constraints, as the technological paradigm constrains them, but their action is bound to affect the paradigm in an evolutionary way.

As a result of these strong nonmarket forces dominating the weak price–quantity adjustments between sectors and between countries, the major adjustment mechanism in the world economy has been *world market shares*: the gains in market shares ascribable to country-specific absolute advantages, i.e., country-specific conditions of technological learning based on degree of innovativeness related to "[i] science-related opportunities, [ii] country-specific and technology-specific institutions which foster/hinder the emergence of new technological paradigms, and [iii] the nature and intensity of economic stimuli" (Dosi et al. 1988). Technological leadership has replaced factor endowment as the main force shaping trade flows.

SCIENCE AND TECHNOLOGY POLICY UNDER FREE TRADE

The establishment of a free-trade area first entails tariff reductions and increased trade in finished products, i.e., in *embodied technology*, and less transfer of technology per se. Existing firms are more likely to bet on economies of scale at existing plants and less likely to need to license technology when there is no incentive to overcome tariff barriers (Bell and Vickery 1988). But multinationals are not only tariff-jumpers. They often seek proximity to markets, market niches, and cost advantages that a host country can offer. To the extent that these other forces are at work, tariff reduction will be a less-powerful trade creator.

In a world dominated by the three sets of nonmarket forces identified above (technological, multinational, government), the elimination of tariff barriers will not make a great deal of difference. The technological paradigm is still evolving, the multinationals are still active, and governments have not lost their rationale for supporting R&D (i.e., underinvestment because of market failures and externalities) and crafting a S&T strategy. Therefore, the impact of any free-trade arrangement will only have a major impact to the extent that nontariff barriers are overhauled and the rules of the "economic war" between nations are altered.

The objective of developing a *level playing field* may be invoked, but governments do not readily agree to abandon national privileges or pretend to legislate away particularly apt synergies generating absolute advantages. Therefore, S&T policies will continue to be built on a structure of government subsidies, on various property laws, on limited access to government-sponsored research by foreign firms, on discriminatory public procurement, and on various overt and covert devices for taking advantage of national circumstances and synergies.

For example, Canada's decision to eliminate intellectual property from free-trade discussions with the United States can be interpreted as a decision either to impose a nonmarket coordinating mechanism for dealing with such issues in the national interest or to reserve judgment in this area for future policymaking. In either case, the challenge remains clear: the need to define the optimal S&T policy in the face of free trade (i.e., the one promoting competitiveness and larger market shares in strategic sectors). And even though some people are very pessimistic about the possibility of ever developing general principles for the design of such policies (Pavitt and Soete 1981), this should not be construed as an invitation for governments to abandon the instruments at their disposal to craft such policies. We are simply in the beautiful world of the second-best.

In a world of increasing returns to scale, unaided markets cannot be expected to regulate world trade effectively. Normally when demand falls, output is reduced, average costs fall, and prices decrease. Lower output leads to more efficiency and lower prices. However, with increasing returns to scale, a decline in demand leads to a reduction in the level of output with consequent *increases* in average costs and prices. The price increase triggers a further decline in demand and a cumulative self-reinforcing downward movement in economic activity. Thus an increasing-returns-to-scale economy is much more unstable and much more sensitive to disturbance.

In a knowledge-based economy subject to accelerating change, new technologies generate increasing returns to scale and this has costs as well as benefits: the central cost is that it reduces the ability of the economy to adjust smoothly to a changing environment. Under these circumstances, free trade and its implicit reliance on markets is no panacea. What is needed, instead, is an aid to the market, i.e., *managed trade*. "In an international economy with increasing returns situations, all the gains from free trade may accrue to just one trading partner, with the others possibly even being net losers. Active management of trade may be required to ensure market clearing and Pareto efficiency" (Chichilnisky and Heal 1986). Managed trade is, therefore, necessary on the grounds of both efficiency and distribution.

In these circumstances, any S&T policy based on substantive but carefully selected trade restrictions geared to support, build, or bolster some national advantages may indeed generate more trade than no restriction at all. Japan provides such a case. The central question is to determine what sort of *planned objectives* are being pursued and how they can be reached at minimal social cost. This is the purpose of an industrial policy: "cherry pick" (Harris 1985).

How can one arrive at a definition of such a useful S&T policy well rooted in Canadian circumstances and values? It cannot be done unilaterally from the centre by technocrats. They have only a small amount of the necessary information. Consequently, this sort of approach is bound to fail as it has many times, in many places. In the information socioeconomy, participatory design of such a policy is the only path likely to be successful (Masuda 1982).

This suggestion does not flow from any ideological fix: it is a consequence of the ill-structured nature of the question at hand. In case of ill-structured problems, analysts must *learn on the job* about both the configuration of facts and the configuration of values, but they must also manage to learn from the stakeholders in the policy game and from the many groups at the periphery who are in possession of important *local knowledge*, for without their participation no meaningful policy can be implemented.

Friedmann and Abonyi (1976) propose a social learning model of policy research to deal with these problems. It combines a detailed analysis of four subprocesses: (1) the construction of appropriate theories of reality, (2) the formation of social values, (3) the gaming that leads to the design of political strategies, and (4) the carrying out of collective action. These four interconnected subprocesses are components of a *social learning process*: any change in one affects the others. This paradigm of social practice in policy research is depicted in a graph by Friedmann and Abonyi that is reproduced in Figure 5 (Chapter 2).

The social learning paradigm is built on reflection-in-action, dialogue, mutual learning by experts and clients, *i.e.*, on an *interactive or transactive style of planning*: "The paradigm makes the important epistemological assumption that *action hypotheses* are verified as "correct" knowledge only in the course of a social practice that includes the four components of theory (of reality), values, strategy, and action. A further epistemological commitment is to the *creation of a new reality*, and hence to a new knowledge, rather than in establishing the truth-value of propositions in abstraction from the social context to which they are applied" (Friedmann and Abonyi 1976; Schon 1983; Paquet, this volume, Chapter 3).

This is a way to develop an S&T policy that suits national circumstances, values, and synergies, a way to launch a major social experiment that would elicit the appropriate role of government in the affairs of the mind in any country that would care to embark on such an experiment. This is an occasion to reflect on the stock of knowledge available, on the uses made of it, on the education system, on the pattern of research effort, on the idiosyncratic nature of the innovative process, and on the diffusion of innovation, but also more broadly on awareness, symbolic resources, and cognitive energy.

Free trade does not mean that national governments should forego important levers and freedom of action to manage trade to the national advantage; it only means that such actions are now somewhat constrained. If a government were forced to forego the possibility of crafting an S&T strategy as a result of a free-trade agreement, it could only be regarded as an immense price to pay for the arrangement.

It has been argued that such is the case with the Canada–United States Free-Trade Agreement. By progressively raising the threshold on direct acquisitions from $5 million to $150 million, articles 1602 and 1607 supposedly exempt such acquisitions from investment review and, thus, from R&D performance requirements. On the other hand, the United States retains the policy power on this front on both their mammoth defense budget and the provisions for a small-business component of government expenditures (McCurdy 1988; McCurdy and Lenihan 1988; Steed 1988). Such a loss of margin of maneuverability is obviously of significance on the S&T front.

So free trade does not make S&T policy less important but gives it greater valence. In an information economy, knowledge is a central input and the production of knowledge, a pivotal activity. Governments are responsible for ensuring that cognitive energies are effectively deployed in the pursuit of knowledge. Such policies at this time are the equivalent of railroad construction and other transportation ventures in the 19th century.

There is no reason to believe that the "natural" outcome of the technological paradigm and of multinationals' activities will correspond to the optimal situation for nationals. Indeed, there is a possibility that just as free trade was an instrument of economic conquest for Britain in the 19th century — some have labeled that strategy "the imperialism of free trade" — it might be the same for large efficient economies in the 20th century. Managing our trade might be a way out but it can only be done if powerful instruments can be mustered.

During the debate on the free-trade arrangement between Canada and the United States, there was a claim that sectors overtly protected by nontariff barriers amounted to 34% of the market for American manufacturers; the comparable figure for Canada appeared to be 10% (Science Council of Canada 1986). Given these figures, some people wonder why the Canadian government appears to have abandoned so many levers on the S&T front: they would appear to be most important in crafting an effective strategy. But governments only echo, however inadequately, the sentiments of the citizenry. A 1985 survey of senior executives in many countries revealed that "43% of Canadian managers see innovation as an important management issue — an astoundingly low figure compared to the world average of 90%" (Science Council of Canada 1986). It would appear that Canadians who have received their technology as "manna" from the multinationals for a long period — two-thirds of Canadian manufacturing is foreign controlled — do not yet see the central importance of this variable and the need to explore alternatives. On this count, the government appears to be in tune with the country's senior executives. I know of no single fact that underlines better the need to design a S&T policy in the manner suggested above, i.e., though awareness-raising and transactive planning. Canadá may be an extreme case but it is far from unique.

CONCLUSION

There is not likely to be a major change in the attitudes of Canadians vis-à-vis S&T in the next while, unless something is done to raise their awareness. But the existence of this blind spot reveals something more serious: a lack of sensitivity to and concern for the new realm of policy areas that have become central in a knowledge-based economy. The whole range of issues from education, to the stock of knowledge, to innovation are only some aspects of the workings of the forum. An information policy would provide a framework on which to graft specific strategies on matters pertaining to education, science, innovation, and the like.

The simple parachuting in of such a policy through some sort of epistemological *coup d'état* would be futile, because the citizens of most Western countries have not yet fully understood the importance of such issues in the new economy. S&T policy is simply a policy about the production and distribution of certain types of knowledge. It is only a part of a broader domain of knowledge ranging from the artistic and the cultural to the political and the technical. Without a national information policy (Nanus 1982) spelling out the way in which the forum should be managed to be fair and adequate, it is not possible to know what importance should be assigned to scientific and technological knowledge or to determine what should be produced, by whom, and in what manner.

"The community has a great stake in the condition of its knowledge-creating and transmitting institutions, in its institutions for informing, discussing, deliberating, deciding" (Tussman 1977). Yet citizens are not persuaded that matters of the mind are important in a managerial sense for the public household. To the extent that debates for freer trade succeed in revealing the limits of market liberalization in a knowledge-based economy, it might be a unique occasion to renew the multilogue on S&T policy that has been somewhat muted for the last decade.

Part II

Social Learning in Action

B – National Perspectives

A SOCIAL LEARNING FRAMEWORK FOR A WICKED PROBLEM: THE CASE OF ENERGY*

> The way to regulate well in times of great uncertainty is by learning rather than controlling. Not learning the answers to known questions that serve the intent to control but learning what questions about balancing and optimizing now merit asking and then learning how those questions might be answered provisionally — until the present moment emerges into a new context of questions.
>
> *– Donald N. Michael (1983)*

Mathematics and dogma often "serve as a substitute for the usually arduous task of coming to grips with the actual phenomena" (Kapp 1960; Georgescu-Roegen 1975). In the world of energy, there has been a flurry of dogma and mathematical models, most often built on mechanical definitions of crises — limited stocks of resources failing to meet unbounded wants. As might be expected, this sort of analysis has triggered simplistic responses.

In Canada, energy issues have been styled in somewhat schizophrenic terms. A dominant version of the problem has been perpetrated by economists: it is couched in terms of shortages, pricing issues, supply/demand vagaries, and efficiency losses when the market solution does not prevail. A parallel and subsidiary sociopolitical version is also popular: it is couched in terms of needs, rights, rent-sharing, etc.

Energy policy is both broader in scope and more complex than those two interpretations suggest. It poses what has been called a wicked problem (Rittel and Webber 1973). Wicked problems have two characteristics: the goals are not known or are ambiguous, and the means–ends relationships are highly uncertain and poorly understood. Solutions are not true-or-false but good-or-bad. A meaningful response to the concerns raised by energy policy entails the definition of legitimate and widely accepted rules capable of dealing effectively (in physical, economic, social, and cultural senses) with future energy problems. This in turn requires a fuller understanding of what makes energy so different as a commodity and of why it should require special rules.

---

* This paper also appeared in *Energy Studies Review* 1989, 1(1), 55–69.

In the spring of 1987, the Energy Options Process (EOP) — initiated by Marcel Masse, the federal minister of energy, mines, and resources — tried to take an imaginative look at energy policy. Under the stewardship of Thomas Kierans, this process culminated in a report tabled in Parliament in the summer of 1988 (Kierans et al. 1988). The report was based on broad consultation with the Canadian population; efforts were made to take into account Canadian values, Canadian institutions, and even dimensions of the Canadian psyche in the analysis. The resulting report made many specific recommendations, but, more important, it put forward seven basic principles that were meant to provide the foundation for a Canadian guidance system in energy matters.

Many have disagreed with the outcome of this process and with the recommendations that have emerged from it, but few would deny that the process itself held promise of a new style of policy research adapted to wicked problems. Some have labeled this new approach a social learning framework (Friedmann and Abonyi 1976); it stresses learning and a transactive style of planning.

In this chapter, the foundations of this social learning approach are examined, and the four components of the social learning paradigm are scrutinized, within the energy context, to show how easily one component might come to dominate the policy analysis entirely, but also how well the four components fit into an integrated framework. The extent to which the EOP may be said to have been patterned on the sort of strategy suggested by that integrated framework is discussed, and in conclusion, it is suggested that the social learning approach might be applicable to a whole family of wicked problems haunting policymakers and policy researchers.

TOWARD A SOCIAL LEARNING APPROACH

Construction of a Meta-rule

Defining a policy means establishing the basis for selecting certain procedures or adopting certain strategies in the face of various plausible sets of environmental circumstances. These procedures or strategies may be aimed at modifying reality, perceptions, or preferences.

Defining an energy policy for Canada amounts to defining a meta-rule likely to be useful in dealing with a variety of *"futurs possibles"* or futuribles. This is akin to the development of guiding principles in the management of projects. For instance, in the case of a major project like the construction of the Trans-Manche Link — the tunnel between France and England — the key guiding principles are contained in a 44-page project manual. Most firms managing large projects have such simple compendia of meta-rules meant to help in the crafting of the required rules of the game as the game unfolds. What is needed in the energy field is something equivalent to a project manual.

The policy research underpinning the design of such a manual is particularly challenging in cases like energy: the problem is wicked, i.e., ill-structured (Ansoff 1960) and, therefore, standard policy research does not provide much help. Friedmann and Abonyi (1976) have proposed an approach to deal with these wicked problems. It is based on the analysis of four subprocesses (Figure 5 in Chapter 2): the construction of appropriate theories of reality (block A), the formation of social values (block B), the gaming that leads to the design of political strategies (block C), and the carrying out of collective action (block D). These four interconnected subprocesses are components of social learning; any change in one affects the others (Friedmann 1979).

Energy as Révélateur

Energy, some have argued, has a special importance in a northern country like Canada because of its cold climate. For others, the federal–provincial quagmire of rent-sharing and conflict resolution mechanisms, and the no-risk proclivities of Canadians and their reluctance to accept costly adjustments in the face of unstable markets have much to do with the priority given to energy on the political agenda (Courchene 1980; Aharoni 1981; Trebilcock 1985).

Fundamentally, energy is creating a social risk in Canada or at least it is perceived as such. As a result, it acts as a *révélateur* of Canadian culture. For risk is a cultural concept: existing institutions select problems and risks worth taking, they do the recognizing and the classifying (Douglas and Wildavsky 1982; Douglas 1986). Thus, energy cannot simply be analyzed within a market context (in Friedmann and Abonyi's (1976) block-A-style) occluding other dimensions buried in values, strategy, and action: all these dimensions must be processed through an all-encompassing issue-machine. However, existing institutions may be unwilling to recognize problems that threaten accepted values or that might deconstruct hegemonic institutions. This explains their structural amnesia (Clark and Munn 1986).

Nexus of Interconnected Problems

Energy raises many problems:

- allocative efficiency (pricing, finances, substitutability between energy types/sources/uses and technologies, choices between domestic and foreign consumption, market failures);

- equity (regionally for consumers and governments, between nationals and foreigners, on the upside and the downside of fluctuating prices, distributional impact on social groups);

- sociopolitical context (treaty obligations, constitutional and regulation-induced constraints, differential adjustment costs and consequent differential social burdens, security of supply, organizational failures, global competition);

- environment (broad and restricted contexts, secondary and tertiary use of energy, exergy);

- industrial strategy (use of natural resources, including energy, as an instrument of economic development and industrial location);

- public acceptance (sense of fairness, paranoias, learning, framing of decisions).

The role of a framework is to impose some order on this nexus of problems, to suggest institutional armistices between the world of physical realities and constraints and the world of values, social concerns, political constraints, and priorities. The meta-rules are a guide in this exercise of social architecture. The framework sorts out what dimensions should play a leading role in the definition of meta-rules. But no framework can be chosen on the basis of objective criteria: the policymaker may either craft his own strategy (Mintzberg 1987) or defer to the stakeholders with their interest-based frameworks or to the scientists with their disciplinary dogmas. In any case, the governance of the policy research process is fundamentally dependent on some normative input.

What may be expected from a meaningful consultation process is a dialectic between the various stakeholders and the social architects (Perlmutter 1965). Under ideal circumstances, such dialectics should affect the emergence of an integrative framework, the one that has the greatest heuristic power, that generates the most social learning.

Useable Ignorance

When dealing with broad policy issues like energy, one cannot hope to produce anything but incomplete answers. In the words of Alvin Weinberg (1972), in policy research we are confronted with trans-scientific questions that cannot be answered by science, they transcend science. Engineering and much of policy science are plagued with such questions: answers may be impractically expensive, the subject matter too variable for scientific canons to apply, moral and esthetic judgment may be involved (Weinberg 1972). What is required is a new understanding built on "useable ignorance" for "by being aware of our ignorance, we do not encounter disastrous pitfalls in our supposedly secure knowledge or supposedly effective technique... institutions should be designed with the ignorance factor in mind, so that they can respond and adapt in good time" (Collingridge 1982; Ravetz 1986).

Coping with ignorance requires a more transactive and transparent policy process and, therefore, a change in the way in which policy research is carried out. It has been argued that the transaction costs of running such a system are high. This is true but unavoidable. Moreover, when compared with the costs of inappropriate responses based on inappropriate policies, these transaction costs may not appear unduly high.

ALTERNATIVE FRAMEWORKS

The selection rule for a framework is simple: the one chosen should have the maximum heuristic and learning power. This is the least objectionable way to choose normatively in the policy field. Yet, it is not a criterion that prevails in most academic discussions on energy. Economists have hijacked the energy problem. If energy is an ordinary commodity, one may count on the market, so the argument goes, to allocate it as efficiently as possible, and there is no need for an energy policy. However, to the extent that energy is not an ordinary commodity, that it has external and asymmetric effects on the rest of the socioeconomy of such a magnitude that it has to be regulated for socioeconomic reasons, then frameworks other than strict allocative efficiency schemes have to be used.

In our socioeconomies, efficiency is not a widely accepted goal: there are other values that society holds in higher esteem, and the political system responds much better to the strongly held viewpoint of powerful interest groups than to the anonymous and diffuse unease of the masses. This is the key to re-election. Any meaningful policy research must, therefore, be rooted in an integrated approach capable of accommodating to a great extent these other dimensions to be politically effective and widely accepted socially.

Efficiency Frameworks

To economists, energy is a commodity that, despite particular characteristics, may be analyzed through the usual market framework (Gordon 1981). Suppliers and demanders are operating in a matrix of markets for different forms of energy. It is argued that these markets, left to themselves, would allocate energy efficiently between competing uses. As supporting evidence, it is argued that price increases in the 1970s have generated a drop in consumption directly, but also through the switch to energy-economizing technologies. All scenarios indicate that this is to continue into the 1990s (Barney et al. 1981: 98–121; CEPII, 1984: Chapter 6). On the production side, scale economies and fixed costs arguments have been used to argue that some regulation may be necessary. But these arguments have been shown to be not as powerful and as easily generalizable as had been first suggested. Consequently, many have argued that the competitive system is working and that whatever problems there are can often be ascribed to ill-inspired government policy interventions.

The only legitimate challenges in this context are the identification of market failures, and the only legitimate energy policies are those crafted to attenuate them or compensate for them. These policies have been directed at production rates (directly through public ownership, regulation, or decrees, or indirectly through tax benefits), the control of imports, regulation of prices (either directly or through subsidies), and energy consumption patterns (either directly through rationing or through moral or financial incentives).

Issues like self-sufficiency, public acceptance, long-run global change, province-building, etc., are characterized as aberrations and styled as impediments to the smooth working of the allocative efficiency machine. Policy analysis in this context recedes to the level of advanced plumbing.

Dominant Value Frameworks

Here, energy is a very special commodity: an ingredient in the socioeconomic system that contributes significantly to the pursuit of some value-based objectives — equity, environmental imperatives, regional/sectional pursuits, etc. The dominant values, whatever they are, frame the energy problem: energy-related issues are reordered in a manner derived from them.

No dominant value framework can claim to be a guidance system in studying energy issues, or in sorting out energy policy options unless one can persuasively argue that there is a clearly demonstrable link between energy and the dominant value, but also that such a value is of primary importance for the population, that there is a close link between the dominant value or values and the energy welfare of individuals, and that there are some needs that have to be met. The concept of needs is not easy to use in policy analysis. It always appears tainted by some paternalism because needs are often defined by experts, externally. They are also fluid, clumsy, difficult to ascertain. But it is a central concept in dominant value frameworks, and the practical use of needs appears to be possible (Friedmann 1979; Ignatieff 1985; Braybrooke 1987).

Such externally defined needs provide a guidance system both for a research program and for the design of policy. They replace the free-wheeling crafting forces of money-backed preferences registered by the market as a list of priorities to be met at a minimum standard before preferences are allowed to have their way. To allow needs to be satisfied, policy instruments and institutions have to be set up, for there is a presumption that the market will not do the job automatically in a satisfactory manner (Willson 1980; Robinson 1982).

A common data set (from Friedmann and Abonyi's [1976] block A) can yield quite different political strategies (block C) and programs (block D) if interpreted through different value filters (block B).

It has been argued that, in a northern climate, within a balkanized polity where many governments have explicit development strategies and in a society that has a strong taste for security, there are energy needs that should be considered as a priority. This is tantamount to calling for meta-rules of a distributional sort when scarcity occurs. Because the energy-producing endowment is spread over the territory in a whimsical manner, and the energy needs (not only for immediate consumption but also for economic development) are located very differently, reallocation and redistribution are necessary.

The dominant value frameworks call for a broadening of the concept of property rights: from rights to material things (that markets handle well) to rights to "a certain quality of life, certain liberties to develop and enjoy the use of our capacities" (Macpherson 1985). The research program would originate with a clarification of the dominant values that are to act as guiding forces. This can be achieved first through some historical analyses illustrating the way in which Canadians have chosen to socialize risk, how the sense of shared parsimony and mutual obligation within the Canadian community has been instituted (Hardin 1974). Second, one might also identify values revealed to be important to Canadians by some mental experiments that have received wide public support like the conserver society or the sustainable development programs (Science Council of Canada 1977; Clark and Munn 1986; Robinson 1987). These values (environmental protection, increased wisdom in resource use, socioenvironmental diversity/flexibility/responsibility, importance of sociopolitical values as equity, cooperation, participation, etc.) could be the starting point for developing scenarios to be evaluated for acceptability.

Such a research program would have a long-run bias. Block B variables (social values) would play the leading role: in the final analysis, markets would be allowed to operate only to the extent that they would serve the genesis of some fair outcome, however defined. Yet, intolerably expensive values would have to be discarded because of the constraints they would impose on any feasible scheme.

Gaming Frameworks

Another family of frameworks focus on the political choice processes of stakeholders, the design of the mechanisms for dialogue or struggle. Even in the simplest case, when it is assumed by all that government should manage the "commons" — however defined — to meet certain needs and that regulated markets should take care of the rest, a key question remains: how should the design for state institutions (to perform these jobs) be arrived at? Such frameworks focus on process, on the definition of the public administration/regulation schemes and the design of feasible regulatory forms (Mitnick 1980).

In such schemes, energy is identified as "something" that cannot be entrusted fully to the unregulated market because sociopolitical groups have said so: unlike the dominant value frameworks where energy is singled out because of its social importance, here it is singled out because of its political features. A research program based on such frameworks starts with the prevailing rules of the politico-administrative game to understand who the stakeholders are, what form of pluralist political choice mechanism is viable, and what administrative arrangements are likely to get the agreement of the community. These arrangements define a "collective game which exists independently of the individual games played by each of the organizations" (Crozier and Thoenig 1976).

This administrative game is not contractual, democratic, or simply hierarchical. It is a political/bureaucratic game built on simplified notions of efficiency and effectiveness and on the very sketchy account of basic social values recorded by the political/bureaucratic agents. It is not geared to pursue objectives or purposes, but rather to accommodate all forces into a game of dispute settlement or spoils-sharing. This regulatory game is played at many levels. The gaming research framework focuses on ways to

> ...understand the games which are played at the bottom of the system. Then it proceeds to discover and reconstruct the more general mode of regulation through which these games are articulated to one another. Finally, it tries to ascertain the basic mode of government and the values that make it possible for the system to exist by legitimizing these rules. [Crozier and Thoenig 1976]

These frameworks are rooted in block C variables, i.e., the family of interacting public agencies harmonizing variables of blocks A and B: from international and interprovincial accords to regulate transborder flows of energy and ensure security of supply; to rules on the ownership or management of the energy resources; to rent-sharing, symmetric obligation, and equalization rules between the federal and provincial governments and other stakeholders; to energy conservation programs.

The overall energy game (with its cross-controls and exceptions) acquires a momentum of its own that has little bearing on or connection with what is physically at stake. This is the world of lobbying. Energy is no longer seen as just a resource: it is an entitlement, an idea — both in the sense of a futurible, like the development of oil sands, and in the sense of a lottery prize. The game becomes a game of bluff — very much like some operations on futures markets. A research program focused only on fiscal principles, studies of concepts like level-playing-field, models of rent-sharing, etc., would allow political/administrative gimmickry to take precedence over substantial issues. The discussion would degenerate into plumbing, albeit plumbing of a more complex variety than the sort highlighted by efficiency frameworks.

Collective Action Frameworks

Although political strategies and stratagems are elaborated from above or from the centre, much is happening at the periphery. Individuals, groups, and clubs experiment with ways to cope with their natural and manufactured environment. The logic of this experimentation is learning, and its outcome is collective action, i.e., purposive action by groups.

These groups may be large or small, woven by meaningful dialogues or by the challenge of common struggles. They make up the fabric of civil society. This multicentric or reticular social fabric is occluded in the stylizations proposed by administrative or market-centred models: life at the periphery is branded marginal or christened "alternative life style" to be conveniently written off the main record. These conceptual and political blinders have been exposed (Ramos 1981), but few social scientists have paid any attention to the critiques.

In the energy world, this peripheral reality is extraordinarily rich: ecologists, sustainable development specialists, those interested in community development, survival, convivial relations, grants economy theorists, etc. For those defending the conventional wisdom, these groups represent a "lunatic fringe" to the "real" political economy. The revival of wood stoves, wind power, and solar energy, experiments with less energy-intensive life styles, etc., are phenomena that do not find their way into the mainstream of the process of social learning.

The differences between political/administrative gaming frameworks and collective action frameworks are important. The output of the former is a policy or plan fanned out from the centre and armed with monitoring devices and enforcement mechanisms. The latter's output is experimentation through "a network of related processes of local public learning" and the derivation of policy themes by induction. In the political/administrative framework, performance is measured by the degree of conformity of the periphery; the collective action scheme is built on local knowledge, public learning, and the diffusion of innovation (Schon 1971; Geertz 1983).

An Integrated Framework

These four families of frameworks are partial maps of the world of interest to policy analysts. If a research exercise is to be a form of social action or social learning, it has to ensure that its research framework casts a very wide net over the whole *terrain des opérations*. It is the only way in which the research program can produce a sense of direction (Gastil 1972). This comprehensive program must take fully into account allocative efficiency, social values, political stratagems, and collective action in a general integrative scheme if an energy system with a high degree of goodness of fit with its circumstances is to ensue.

Policy analysts should not embalm or mummify the problem at hand through an orgy of unrealistic assumptions. Policy research in the social learning paradigm is reflection-in-action (Schon 1983), its intent is to invent the right institutional form by eliminating incongruities between institution and circumstances. This is the way the potter crafts his work, the way medical doctors pursue negatively the maintenance of health through elimination of illnesses (Alexander 1964). Policy is very much in the nature of design: in the words of Christopher Alexander (1964: 26–27),

> We are searching for some kind of harmony between two intangibles: a form which we have not yet designed, and a context which we cannot properly describe. The only reason we have for thinking that there must be some kind of fit to be achieved between them is that we can detect incongruities, or negative instances of it.

Policy research, like design research, is intent on producing a different kind of knowledge — delta knowledge — the sort of knowledge acquired through learning by doing (Gilles and Paquet 1991).

Henry Mintzberg (1987) has borrowed from potters the apt metaphor "crafting strategy." "Formulation and implementation merge into a fluid process of learning": the need to maintain a continuous feedback between analysis and problem-formulation is central in both design and policy work.

This sort of social experimentation is not a new *outillage mental*; it was propounded by John Dewey (1935) under the general labels of "experimental intelligence" and "socially organized intelligence." Others have referred to this learning process as transduction (Lefebvre 1961). Still others propose such an approach to deal with ill-structured problems (Ansoff 1960; Paquet 1971). But it was a path abandoned by social scientists when they became totally seduced by positivism.

THE ENERGY OPTIONS PROCESS

An initiative like the energy options process (EOP) was not a *sui generis* phenomenon. It followed an era of centralization of the design of energy policy under the Trudeau government (Doern and Toner 1985) and corresponded to the philosophy of openness and consultation propounded by the Mulroney government after the 1984 election and evidenced by the process that led to the three accords (the Atlantic Accord, the Western Accord and the Agreement on Natural Gas Markets and Prices in 1985). This Tory energy program had clearly indicated a commitment to nonintervention in the market — a central feature of the Western Accord (Toner 1986). Moreover, in 1987, there was a clear sense that consultation could be carried out without major risks — that it was a controllable process — after the "happy policy" of 1985.

Yet, much in the design of the EOP held the promise of introducing a new style of policy research and national dialogue akin to the social learning approach. The advisory committee and the advisory groups selected for the EOP were not made up entirely of narrow specialists on physical energy questions; environmental groups, interest groups, and critical individuals were offered an opportunity to air their views, and the process of consultation was orchestrated in such a way as to allow a major forum for interaction among all the stakeholders in December 1987 in Montreal. Even the final report could have broken new ground: it was structured on the basis of an explicit energy policy framework that, we were told, had effectively been used to frame the recommendations.

Yet, the final report leaves any reader who expected a major policy breakthrough with a sense of disappointment. The EOP was a controlled exercise in policy that was unwilling to delve much beyond block A issues, to be attentive to local knowledge, to listen carefully enough to what Canadians said and to draw inferences from it. Indeed the central weakness of the report was a refusal to acknowledge the fundamental contradiction between the commitment to the market and the commitment to sustainable development. For this latter commitment can only translate into an expanded role for the state.

The final report developed a framework of principles that represents a sanitized version of the discourse of Canadians: it ensured the hegemony of efficiency considerations. Cognitive dissonance loomed large. People not only have preferences but beliefs, and preferences about their beliefs. Consequently, they are often led to choose their beliefs subconsciously (despite evidence suggesting that the contrary view is warranted) by choosing sources of information likely to confirm their "desired" beliefs and shutting out information challenging these beliefs (Akerlof and Dickens 1982). In a way, the EOP has "chosen to believe" that efficiency considerations were the hegemonic ones.

The EOP report was dominated by efficiency considerations to the point of occluding other perspectives or of minimizing unduly the importance of the concerns they raised. The broader integrated policy research framework that one had hoped might be used has not been, and the interactive planning that one might legitimately have expected to emerge from this experiment, has not materialized. Finally, the proposed meta-rules turned out not to provide the sort of guidance system likely to be of use in meeting the challenges of the next "energy crisis."

Eliciting Inadequate Meta-rules

The EOP was meant to be an "opportunity for a dialogue," for a multilogue, "among Canadians about our common energy future" (Kierans et al. 1988: 1). Indeed, "A Canadian Dialogue" was the subtitle of the whole EOP. So, from the very first page of the report, there was an effort to summarize what Canadians said (WCS). This can be synthesized as follows:

- WCS 1: Energy "cannot be treated just like any other market commodity" (p. 1).

- WCS 2: "Energy policy must be founded on Canadian values" (p. 2).

- WCS 3: Energy efficiency is important and markets are "invaluable instruments" to achieve efficiency and "governments should intervene in the allocation process only to correct serious market imperfections or failures" (p. 6).

- WCS 4: Instruments used to achieve an appropriate degree of equity or fairness in income distribution should be developed but they should be as nondiscriminatory as possible, be based on federal–provincial cooperation, and be such as to keep as much as possible the rules of the game stable (pp. 7–8).

- WCS 5: Energy policy should be developed on the basis of the general objective of "sustainable development" (pp. 8–9).

- WCS 6: Development and implementation of new technologies should be factored in (pp. 9–10).

As the report itself acknowledges (p. 10), such a summary of views cannot do justice to the wealth of information presented to the EOP. Yet, on what basis can one challenge the validity of this sort of perilous exercise? Would it be warranted to do so on the basis of one's impression of the cathartic December 1987 synthesis meeting? Yet, this is the ground on which my counter-impressions are based: the official summary of "what Canadians said" does not convey as fully as one might have wished the array of concerns heard at the final Montreal meeting.

Concerns over energy needs, over redistribution rules in times of crisis, and over security of supply were prominent; debates over notions of fairness, over acceptable forms of regulation, and over an acceptable degree of socialization of risks were very much present. Conservation as a supply option ("a unit of energy saved is a unit of energy found") and the need to mobilize the population to conserve were important messages conveyed in December 1987. The "time myopia of the price mechanism" and "free trade as a blind tyrant" were also central concerns. Little of this can be found in the summary of what Canadians said. Cognitive dissonance has been at work.

From this partly muted message from Canadians, the EOP attempted to construct "a report on the direction of future energy policy in Canada that would reflect the best of all that had been written and said throughout the Energy Options Process" (p. 10). This is the source of the seven principles or meta-rules (MRs), each one being the central topic of a subsequent chapter in the report. It is worth restating these seven principles:

- MR 1: "Canada's energy should be developed and used to its economic potential to provide growth and prosperity for Canadians today and in the future."

- MR 2: "Energy security is best sought in ways that increase energy choices and enhance adaptability to change rather than by hoarding or by government forcing uneconomic development. At the same time, Canada should cooperate internationally and maintain domestic emergency measures against possible oil supply disruptions."

- MR 3: "Environmental goals should be accorded the same importance as other economic and social goals in the planning, development and use of energy."

- MR 4: "To achieve efficient allocation of energy resources, market mechanisms should be relied upon wherever possible and enhanced where necessary."

- MR 5: "The fiscal system, as it applied to energy, should raise and spend revenues in ways that are nondiscriminatory, neutral, stable and predictable, and that promote harmony among governments."

- MR 6: "Enhancing the economic efficiency with which energy is used should be an essential component of energy policy, both to make the best use of energy and to reduce environmental impact."

- MR 7: "Commitment to research and development and management of technology is critical to enhancing Canada's energy choices and environmental quality into the 21st century."

One cannot fail to detect a narrowing of perspective when the meta-rules are compared with "what Canadians said." In the meta-rules list,

- The efficiency framework is raised to a higher level of prominence.

- Concern for relevant dominant values is almost exclusively limited to the recognition of environmental values on a par with other economic and social values; yet the extent to which such other values would appear to raise fundamental questions for the proposed market solution is occluded.

- The political gaming and public administration aspects of energy policy are handled without much depth: government intervention in general is played down; moreover, a technical rationality model of policy (from the centre down) appears to prevail if and when state activities are allowed.

- Concerns about local knowledge, learning, collective action, and implementation are virtually obliterated; the dialogue stops short of the implementation phase.

The overriding concern for efficiency, and the consequent reliance on markets as the main instrument to ensure efficiency, are the foundation of these meta-rules. This raises serious questions. It is difficult to see how these meta-rules could be of use as a project manual in times of crisis: nowhere does one get a sense that they could guide an effective dynamic monitoring or provide anything but rather inert leadership in times of crisis.

Four Components Out of Kilter

Why have block A (theory of reality) issues come to dominate the scene so completely? Fundamentally, because of the fact that the EOP did not emerge from a policy vacuum. It was constrained by the Tory policy framework. As a result, the EOP has refused to accept WCS 1 as a meaningful statement; whatever the rhetoric, the EOP regards energy as a market commodity like any other. Consequently, markets are seen as well adjusted to handling it, and the burden of proof is shifted entirely onto those who claim that the market is unlikely to do an adequate job overall.

Dominant values are almost completely overshadowed by the many references to *choice*. The word "choice" is used, throughout the report (Kierans et al. 1988), both as a dominant value — let people choose — and as a synonym for "market" (p. 43), for markets are seen as the best way, if not the only way, to operationalize choice. Moreover, "market" and "economy" become almost interchangeable notions and "non-market economy" appears somewhat suspect: MRs 1, 2, 4, 5, and 6 end up hinting at the market institution as the solution. This is not only the case for "normal times": little emphasis is put on emergency preparedness and vigilance, environmental concerns, research needs. These are mentioned, but they are handled by marginal exhortations in the whole script. These exhortations are made in connection with elusive times of crisis, improbable eventualities when market mechanisms might lead to excessive exports, cases where markets might be blind to environmental points-of-no-return or to research needs.

What emerges is a sense that social values and collective action are bound to be handled adequately by the market and that there is simply a need for minimal and nondisturbing government intervention of a traditional market-failure variety. Such action is, in any case, seen as a lower priority adequately dealt with by a refurbished National Energy Board.

The little time spent on spelling out exactly what a refurbished National Energy Board might be asked to do is symptomatic of the philosophy underpinning the EOP report. There is little in the report that would appear to indicate what new role the board might undertake, no hint that such a role might entail a radically different type of regulatory operation. There is no indication of any awareness in the report that regulation has taken a new turn over the last decades and that a refurbished energy board might have to become a negotiating tribunal not simply an administrative ruler (Paquet 1978b). There is also little sensitivity to the central role of norms and values in this new sort of gaming: no awareness that the negotiating will have to be conducted over more than efficiency concerns, that it will have to be done over values and not only environmental values.

Finally, there is no effort to root any of this process in basic local knowledge and civil society; no need is felt for anything but the market as an institutional contraption to gather information and coordinate activities at the periphery. The market model flattens this rich underlying social reality. There is no need to encourage local experimentation as the market mops up all the information worth having in this commodity world. Indeed, the most depressing aspect of the EOP report is that, after having posited in the very first pages the necessity of building an energy policy on Canadian values and a Canadian dialogue (p. 2), the outcome might be said to have evacuated concern for values and dialogue.

Much of the reductionism of the EOP is ascribable to an emphasis on energy output. A focus on production processes (exploration, transformation), which have multiphase and multidimensional impacts, would have led to a shift away from the fixation on *choice* to a larger concern for *design intervention*. Moreover, there seems to be little awareness in the report, as it espouses economic deregulation, of the interplay between economic and social regulatory dynamics: as economic deregulation proceeds, there is a strong push for some social regulation to ensure that the social costs of the market coordinating mechanism are prevented from growing unduly (Doern 1989).

Implementation Vacuum

The poor coverage of blocks B, C, and D issues — or rather the virtual suppression of these dimensions in the EOP report — sanctions the hegemony of the market as the response to the energy issue. This explains the lack of emphasis on implementation: there is no need to worry about implementation as there is no policy to be implemented. Quasi-laissez-faire has become the norm and it absolves the policy research scheme from any responsibility in attending to the implementation agenda, because the automatic pilot will take care of most of the problems, and the rest of the agenda, to which government must attend, is so dramatically reduced that no extensive discussion is necessary.

This is an energy policy by immaculate conception and one that requests little in the form of fanning from the centre. The reciprocal is also true: because the market mechanism adequately takes into account the wishes, desires, wants, and values of citizens, there is no need to experiment, to design mechanisms to promote learning from local experiments, or to organize public learning.

The EOP has not sketched a process of dynamic interaction between the stakeholders (and between planners and plannees) likely to continue the dialogue it was meant to initiate, and it has not suggested a mechanism for such a dialogue. Neither do the recommendations propose a process of dynamic monitoring allowing strong feedback from the periphery. Yet, without a strong feedback mechanism, there is little possibility of learning or of ever dealing reasonably with wicked problems: social experimentation is stunted and, if and when it does occur, there is little chance of fanning its results over the system. There is no socially organized intelligence to guide the process of norm holding and implementation (Paquet 1971).

A Provisional Evaluation

A standard way of looking at policymaking has identified four areas of concern: goal setting, control, innovation, and intelligence (Wilensky 1967). The traditional approach to policymaking has largely emphasized the first two components because the problems being dealt with were rather well-structured: goals could be defined and means–ends relationships ascertained. In dealing with ill-structured or wicked problems, an alternative approach is called for — one that puts the emphasis on the last two components: intelligence as the basis for an innovative learning process.

Those promoting the EOP knew that they were tackling a wicked problem and that such problems cannot be effectively addressed using a traditional approach. One might reasonably expect that an alternative approach would have been used:

> Since the problem formulation itself is open, the evaluative function involves designing an information system to provide the medium for effective feedback between analysis and problem formulation. The interplay between norm-setting, goal-setting, course-holding, control on functioning, and organizational and institutional innovations becomes fundamentally dependent on organizational intelligence. [Paquet 1971: 54]

The EOP has produced an incomplete statement on energy issues. It has done much to launch a process of policymaking by defining guiding principles — and for this EOP must be praised — but those principles have been too narrowly defined to provide adequate guidance for navigation in turbulent times. Moreover, little has been done to ensure that the sort of dialogue that EOP has originated will continue. As a result, it is unlikely that this report will have much impact. Cut from an implementation phase likely to bring with it new learning, it will dry up very much like any tree cut off from its roots.

EOP has failed. It has not set up the organizational intelligence likely to generate a genuine learning process. It may have held hopes that it would do so, but it has not delivered the goods. A wicked problem has been approached as if it were a well-structured problem: simple norms have been declared goals and a simple control mechanism — the market — (sometime aided by the National Energy Board) has been declared sufficient to guide the policy in the right direction. This choice of research strategy may be regarded as hardly surprising by some cynics: it was predictable given the thrust of the Tory energy policy. But because of great early expectations that EOP might adopt an alternative approach and set up the basis for a continuous dialogue with Canadians, disappointment has been all the greater in the end.

Some have suggested that, through the dual channels of ongoing consultation among federal and provincial energy ministers and a follow-up on the EOP report by the Standing Committee of the House of Commons on Energy, Mines and Resources, the EOP might get its second wind. This is unduly optimistic. The EOP report is unlikely to fuel a sustained and fruitful debate in either forum for the very reasons we mention above.

CONCLUSION

It is not sufficient for the wise owl to tell the grasshopper that to avoid the severe pains of winter, he simply has to turn himself into a cricket and hibernate. The client might legitimately ask how one goes about performing that metamorphosis (Bennis et al. 1961). Thus, one might ask about the likely contours of a research program and of an energy policy designed along the lines suggested above. On the other hand, as social learning can only come with practice and action, it is not possible to spell out completely ex ante a design for policy-in-the-making.

Therefore, we cannot sketch what problem formulation might have been generated by a learning process that has not been set in motion nor what policy outcome might have ensued. The history of most policies over time is a sort of ongoing dialogue between planners and plannees. The great limitation of a policy framework that does not build on this and provide a forum for such exchanges is that it is bound to become dated very quickly and that the best features of this arrested plan are likely to be lost in the process of evolution.

Some of the great successes in policymaking have come out of a liberation from the fixation on goals and controls and from a gamble on process and a well-managed forum. Geoffrey Vickers (1965) has taken the lead in the analysis of policymaking in this way, but there have also been interesting initiatives in Canada (Law Reform Commission). However, this view is not yet widely held.

Problems are often wicked, and the design of a learning system is the only way to break the artificial barrier between problem formulation and the process of implementation. In the alternative approach, both components merge smoothly into each other and an evolutionary way of handling issues becomes the norm. The same process has been shown to work in private decision-making (Schon 1983). It may not be as tidy as dogma or mathematics would edict, but it has the definite advantage of dealing with actual phenomena.

CHAPTER 6

THE ENVIRONMENT–ENERGY INTERFACE: SOCIAL LEARNING VERSUS THE INVISIBLE FOOT*

Despite all the pleasant rhetoric at the last Houston Summit and the formal negotiations between the United States and Canada regarding acid rain, neither government is resolved to taking a strong stand on the energy and environment issues they face. Both governments welcome additional studies, and negotiated agreements between the two countries are welcome as a progressive approach to the solution of current environmental problems — mainly in response to the intense public concern and media attention — but these issues are not very high on the political agenda of either government.

The lack of congruence between rhetoric and action is attributable to the acute economic problems experienced by both countries and, in particular, to the shadow their huge budget deficits cast on any initiative likely to be costly in terms of public funds. In addition, there is still an immense amount of ignorance and uncertainty about both the *real* energy challenges facing North America and the *real* costs of "green-type" initiatives suggested by environmentalists. Not only is there no precise measure of the price Canadians and Americans are willing to pay to achieve energy sovereignty and to meet the environmental standards they purport to defend, but there has also been little evidence to indicate that they are willing to accept important sacrifices. Finally, much of the inertia on the policy front is also a result of the extraordinary tension between the natural myopia of politicians (whose time horizon rarely extends beyond four years) and corporate leaders (whose loyalty is to quarterly earnings and sound bottom lines) and the essentially long-term nature of energy and environment issues.

The recent period of intense negotiations between Canada and the United States leading to the Free Trade Agreement has focused the attention of officials of both countries on the long term and on strategies for sharing their energy and environmental resources. This continental solidarity might be expected to increase concern over the prudent use of resources, but this has proved too optimistic a forecast. The only commitments emanating from the

---

* This paper also appeared in J. Lemco (editor). *The Canada–United States Relationship*. Westport, CT: Praeger, 1992, pp. 129–151.

Free Trade Agreement discussions on the energy/environment front pertain to a continental sharing of energy in what is still regarded by both parties as the unlikely event of a crisis (risk-sharing amounting to little more than a minimal insurance policy) and to a continuing interest in educating their citizens about the realities and costs of environmental problems.

While policy discussions flounder, political choices are still being made daily by governments, corporations, and citizens to effectively craft an overall policy stance. This de facto policy on both sides of the border puts priority on market mechanisms as the appropriate means for handling energy production and for ensuring viable environmental quality. Experts have argued repeatedly that national policies of a more ambitious sort are unwarranted and would be counterproductive for the problems are ill-structured, the policy goals are unclear, the technological future is less than transparent, and governments in both countries are still too ignorant about energy and environmental issues to experiment effectively with various policies. Only a substantial deterioration in environmental quality or an increase in energy prices appears likely to force both countries to question their total reliance on markets and lead them to craft the necessary international and intersectoral arrangements capable of reflecting critical trade-offs on the energy/environment front. In the meantime, there is a policy vacuum.

A POLICY VACUUM

Despite the lack of explicit environment/energy policies on both sides of the border, the casual reader of the popular press probably has the impression that the United States did not craft an energy policy in the 1980s while Canada did. This is a result of the attention that accompanied Canada's National Energy Program (NEP) in 1980. In fact, after the world oil price shock of 1973–74, both the United States and Canada developed temporary policies to cushion their citizens from spiraling prices. Only in 1981 did the United States move away from such arrangements toward deregulation; Canada did not follow suit until 1985 when a change in government occurred (Watkins 1987). On the environmental policy front, the two countries have been somewhat out of sync, but they are drifting in the same general direction. In the United States, a concerted effort to promote environmental policy strategies was developed in the 1970s, but was relaxed in the 1980s. In Canada, the policy thrust was much weaker in the 1970s and today remains largely unfocused.

There are many reasons for these choices and the same underlying forces are likely to continue to influence policies in the 1990s. Taking them into account is crucial if one is to attempt to gauge future policy trends.

Energy

There are a number of reasons why the United States has no effective energy policy: the lack of a stable focus for energy concerns in the American legislative system; the sharp ideological infighting between advocates of public power and the free marketeers; the absence of a strong, coordinated leadership on the issues; and so on. But perhaps the most convincing explanation is that throughout the 1970s and 80s, there was a lack of consensus among the American population as to "what ought to be done on energy" (Uslaner 1987). In the absence of government intervention in the pursuit of explicit goals, officials have simply allowed the market to become the main referee. Thus, a de facto market-based energy policy evolved in the United States.

In Canada, the NEP was crafted in 1980 following decades of explicit government intervention on the energy front (Doern and Phidd 1983). Energy had become a vital issue to government officials during the 1980 election, and, from that campaign, one could infer the existence of a clear "national division" on this issue. The newly elected Trudeau government, which received almost all of its support from the eastern and central provinces, imposed a number of important constraints on energy producers in the western provinces (Doern and Toner 1985). This policy was not the result of a national consensus, but rather of a *coup de force* by one of the two national coalitions of interests. However, when Jean Chrétien replaced Marc Lalonde as minister of energy in 1983, the policy climate had shifted as a result of the disastrous consequences of the NEP on investment in the energy sector. A greater willingness to consult and bargain with western energy interests evolved. By the time the Mulroney government ended its first term of office in 1988, any lingering effect of the NEP had evaporated.

In fact, by 1988, government officials in both Canada and the United States had built up a rationale for nonintervention in the energy field. In the spring of 1987, Canada's federal minister of energy, mines, and resources, Marcel Masse, all but admitted that there was a policy void when he charged a special committee with responsibility for consulting the Canadian population to determine appropriate directions for Canadian energy policy. This task force, under the stewardship of Thomas Kierans, submitted its report in 1988 (Kierans et al. 1988; Paquet, this volume, Chapter 5). The report urged, in a general way, the adoption of a market approach and the continuation of a policy of nonintervention. There was understandably no follow-up to the Kierans report, for it called for no real public action. "No explicit policy" had become the policy on the energy front in both Canada and the United States.

It would be hard, therefore, to predict what strategies Canada or the United States would adopt in the event of a new energy crunch, especially given the fact that their recent Free Trade Agreement has further reduced the real possibility and, therefore, the likelihood of unilateral efforts to promote a national energy policy on either side of the border.

Environment

Officials in Canada and the United States, as in many other countries, have been conscious of environmental issues for quite a long time. Between 1968 and 1978, some 150 governments created departments of the environment or their equivalent (Roots 1988). Canada and the United States were leaders in this pack: the United States created the Environmental Protection Agency (EPA) in 1970 and Canada created its Department of Environment (DOE) the following year.

This early interest did not fare well through the second oil price shock and the recession of the early 1980s which influenced a systematic decrease in spending on environmental protection (Regens and Rycroft 1989). However, environmental issues have become prominent again since 1987, due mainly to increased awareness generated by the report of the World Commission on Environment and Development (the Brundtland Commission), which outlined the necessary steps to environmentally sustainable economic development for the planet by the year 2000 and beyond (Brundtland 1987). However, this awareness has not yet been translated into meaningful policy proposals.

The reasons for such inertia are simple: there is a substantial amount of soft grassroots support for environmental policies, but the political costs of action in the face of much ignorance and great uncertainty appear to be much higher than the economic costs of inaction. Political decision-making is concerned with short-term cost–benefit analysis, and, in the short term, tough environmental regulation is bound to hurt many polluting industries and, therefore, to affect the employment and income of voters. Yet in the longer haul, the losses attributable to environment degradation affecting crops, soils, aquatic ecosystems, forests, and human and animal life are seemingly catastrophic. At this point, the short-term time horizon of politicians has stacked the deck against longer-term environmental policies.

In Canada, the creation of a department of environment could be regarded as a package of "positional policies" to "signal to affected groups and the attentive public that emerging problems have been recognized and are being dealt with" (Adie and Thomas 1982). But during the subsequent periods of economic difficulties, environmental concerns were displaced by priorities such as budget deficit cutting and international competitiveness imperatives. Although the DOE retains its symbolic value, there is little room for substantial and meaningful action in the current system despite the strong statements of Lucien Bouchard, who was minister of the environment until his resignation in 1990.

Indeed, the fact that the environment portfolio has been handed, albeit temporarily, to the minister responsible for the Treasury Board, Robert de Cotret, appears to confirm that it no longer represents an autonomous generative policy locus. A "framework for discussion on the environment" has been issued — the so-called *Green Plan* (Bouchard 1990) — and a truncated and unsatisfactory national consultation has been hurried through the government. Yet the political and economic resources allocated to environmental protection continue to diminish, and whatever momentum might have been injected into the policymaking process by the former minister has all but evaporated with his departure.

In the United States, the terms of the environmental debate have been more explicit as the confrontation between ecologists and certain environmentally-unfriendly industries developed earlier. A measure of ethical environmentalism has even emerged (Schwartz 1989) as well as a widespread belief that citizen action should be the primary force in the protection of the environment. It has also become clear that it will not be acceptable to rely almost exclusively on bureaucratic efforts to solve environmental problems. This dual approach of public and private action has evolved slowly, but in the 1980s there was a shift toward a greater reliance on private protection of the environment as government-initiated environmental protection measures proved less effective than expected. Public sector policies were sharply criticized as being often motivated more by populist sentiment and pork-barrel politics than by actual environmental concern (Caldwell 1988; Fraas and Munley 1989; Stroup and Shaw 1989). As a result, "the new breeze blowing in Washington" has tended to promote a myriad of market-based mechanisms to supplement the existing policy framework (Stavins 1989).

THREE ISSUES

These energy and environment dossiers raise complex questions; uncertainty and potential surprises become possible. The issues are not dealt with adequately by economic theory, for they include the complexity of economy–society–environment interactions where resources are not divisible, property rights are nonexistent, market failures are prevalent, and other problems such as uncertainty, public goods, external effects, and irreversibility are omnipresent (Paquet 1990d).

Charles Perrings (1987) has shown that because of the complexity of ill-understood direct and indirect interdependencies, external effects in the socioeconomy are neither anticipated nor taken into account by the price mechanism. This incompleteness of the price mechanism results in the market not being able to detect intertemporal environmental deterioration even though it is physically observable. A great potential for surprises ensues. Without a time perspective that perfectly discounts these surprises or a price mechanism that anticipates them perfectly, the efficiency of the market mechanism in solving environmental problems is suspect.

Three issues are central to the current problems in effectively addressing environmental concerns: a lack of appreciation of the complexities underpinning the notion of sustainable development, a fundamental myopia about the politico-economic system in dealing with energy and environment issues, and the need for some innovative theory-building if appropriate institutions are to be established.

Sustainability as Resilience

Sustainable development is a difficult concept for economists to deal with. It amounts to development with nondeclining natural wealth (Pearce et al. 1989). This concept is not a static notion: it is not only a process of natural capital conservation and of maintenance of productivity, but also a matter of maintaining the stability (a certain constancy) and the resilience (a capacity for the system to maintain its integrity) of *the overall ecological system*. Both energy and environment issues challenge the stability and the resilience of the system.

Market-based strategies cannot deal effectively with certain irreversible problems. As a result, even though market-type approaches may serve to improve the incentive-reward system in some ways and, thereby, extend the time horizon of economic agents somewhat, it is unlikely that this will suffice to ensure resilience.

Research by animal ecologists has shed some light on the strategies developed by animals for acquiring system resilience. Vertinsky (1987) has noted the uncanny parallel between the successful behaviour of animals in the face of uncertainty (the balance and capacity to switch during crisis between a competitive myopic individual search for efficiency and a collective search for resilience) and the behaviour of Japanese companies that are operating in an environment where the market prevails, but are capable of subjecting themselves to a cooperative framework (through radical state intervention) in a crisis "to secure the collective survival." This duality of private competition in general, coupled with the possibility of switching to cooperation and guidance by collective norms during a crisis, ensures resilience.

This model can also be applied on the environmental front. The source of system resilience may be manifold. A variety of sources may elicit cooperation in crisis — ethics, "deep ecology," hierarchies of rights and obligations in the context of social norms, and conventions are all more or less effective ways to trigger a switch to different sets of rules during a crisis. But successful switches require a well-developed and operating sociocultural underground within which the market mechanism is nested. Some sort of "social capital" that supports individual actions at normal times but constrains them in critical circumstances is necessary (Coleman 1987). But one cannot expect such social capital to emerge organically, and resilience is unlikely to crystallize without the institutional prerequisites for a smooth co-evolution of the economic, social, and environmental systems being put into place (Norgaard and Dixon 1986).

Discounting the Future

The myopia of the price mechanism condemns all evaluations of energy and environment dimensions as somewhat truncated. Energy and environment issues raise questions of long-run collective needs, whereas the market mechanism effectively monitors only short-run individual preferences. Moreover, sustainable development, i.e., development with nondeclining natural wealth, raises questions about intergenerational comparisons: how should the fate of future generations be factored in when we make current decisions?

Questions of intergenerational equity are bothersome for economists, for they expose incontrovertibly the fundamental incompatibility between intergenerational equality as an objective and any positive rate of discount that dramatically shrinks the present value of future flows of benefits and costs (Diamond 1965). As soon as the rate of discount is positive, this entails a certain myopia and a bias against the future state of the ecological system. This has led many to point to the social discount rate — the socially agreed on positive rate of discount — as the culprit, because it enforces a certain degree of myopia.

A suggested solution has been to reduce the rate of discount and, thereby, increase the time horizon of decision-makers. This may not be the right approach. Artificially reducing the discount rate can only introduce yet more distortions as the new rate would ignore time preference and opportunity costs. It would most certainly extend the time horizon and force decision-makers to take into account more fully some long-run environmental costs, but it would also modify the rate of harvesting of renewable resources and of depletion of nonrenewable resources in ways that may turn out to be both surprising and deplorable.

Tinkering with the discount rate is hardly sufficient. A lower discount rate would not only make long-run costs more relevant to current decisions, but it would also give more valence to future benefits in present decisions. Consequently, it is not clear in what way the energy/environment interface would be modified. A more reasonable way to respond to the concerns raised by high social discount rates is to work harder at identifying all the costs and benefits in matters dealing with energy and environmental resources (Pearce et al. 1989).

Institutional Carpentry

In both the United States and Canada, the tools used to identify costs and benefits have mainly been of two sorts: impact analysis and market tests.

Environmental impact analysis is now used worldwide. It requires agencies to take into account the effects of their policy decisions on the quality of the environment in the hope that assessing even nonquantified damage before the fact will lead to a change in values and generate more attention to environmental costs even though they may be external to the agency. The concept has now been accepted in more than 30 countries including Canada and the United States. These analyses have served as "an informing and testing of policy," but it is fair to say that it has been much more effective and pervasive in the United States where it is more firmly, if imperfectly, embedded in the normal process of planning and decision-making (Caldwell 1988). However, recent judicial decisions in Canada (in the case of huge dams in Saskatchewan and Alberta) indicate that this is becoming a more potent tool in Canada.

This being said, the main tendency in both Canada and the United States has been to rely more and more on market-based environmental policies, even if the pace at which both countries have proceeded is quite different. In the United States, the actions of citizen-enforcers have created enough pressure (even though they were not always productive in environmental terms) to allow questions to emerge concerning the best mix of permissible "bounty hunting" and tolerable bureaucratic foot dragging (Greve 1989). In Canada, the move toward market-based environmental policies was much slower: it has been defended on intellectual grounds since the 1960s (Dales 1968), but much of the Canadian economic decision-making structure maintains a preference for public enterprise in these matters (Hardin 1974), and the present government has had to proceed more carefully. But there has been a recent wave of publications in Canada emphasizing the importance of understanding the environment *in* the economy, i.e., the centrality of market-oriented approaches to environmental problems (Block 1990; Doern 1990). This would appear to indicate that Canada is now rapidly catching up with the United States on this front.

Still the following cautious statement by the Canadian minister of the environment to a Standing Committee on Environment of the Canadian House of Commons (Bouchard 1989: 18–12) indicates that indecisiveness and prudence are still prevalent:

> Energy is a big industry in Canada; energy is almost Canada. It is almost in terms of energy that this country has been built. The modern country of Canada is so blended with energy preoccupations that it is very difficult for us when the time comes to establish a plan for environment, because environment could be perceived as the enemy of energy programs. It is not, and the Minister of Environment is not the arch-enemy of the Minister of Energy. We are not, because we know now that energy consumption must be renewable, sustainable, and protect the atmosphere.

Despite much agitation at the task force and committee level, *valse-hésitation* is the style of the day in government and there remains a policy void in both countries. Not much work has been done on the construction of either an alternative paradigm to look at energy and environment or refurbished institutions and attitudinal changes that are likely to foster the needed adjustments to policymaking on these fronts (Daly and Cobb 1989).

In the meantime, citizens in the United States and Canada, indecisive as they may be, have become restive. Although, in early 1988, only 4% of Canadians thought of environment as the country's highest priority, by mid 1989, 94% placed the environment at or near the top of their list of concerns (Dyer 1990). The impatience of some Canadians was also evident in the emergence of Earth First members who were willing to use civil disobedience and even ecological terrorism in pursuit of their environmental goals. In the United States the same tendencies on the environmental front are present, but with a higher degree of impatience and radicalism emanating from deep-rooted environmental ethics. In Canada, frustration is still in the incubation phase, but growing quickly.

THE INVISIBLE FOOT AT WORK

Although Canadians and Americans may share a soft consensus in favour of effective environmental protection, there is no agreement on how to construct the appropriate private–public action mix to create the sort of resilient system that is desired. There is a great cacophony of voices of various groups and factions on both sides of the border. However, each of these coalitions is slowly being transformed into an action group expending much time and resources to ensure that its point of view is registered. On the energy front, one notes an even higher level of rent-seeking activity in Canada than in the United States. It is ascribable to the greater dependence on energy in Canada's northern climate, but also to the relative importance of energy-related activities — both economic and symbolic — for regions of the country (Hydro Québec, for instance) (Paquet 1989e).

On both the energy and environment fronts, the voices are as volatile as they are vehement. One is not sure that either government has fairly represented the points of view of its constituents. In many cases, governments have added to the already high degree of false consciousness and anomie. For instance, at the beginning of the 1980s, Canadians regarded energy as a very special commodity and supported a national policy for the sector. By the end of the decade, officials wanted to believe that such a policy was no longer necessary and that the market could be relied on to alleviate all problems on this front. This "new" Canadian view was promulgated in the final report of the Energy Options Process (Kierans et al. 1988) and embraced by the Mulroney government officials.

But what was said to the Kierans task force by Canadians and what was finally reported was not the same thing. Much *cognitive dissonance* was injected in the task force process. Canadians still do not feel that energy is a commodity like others and the "new" Canadian view propounded by the Mulroney government — that there is no need for a national policy — is not widely shared by the citizenry. Polls indicate that Canadian citizens have a much greater concern for conservation and for environmental issues than does their government. They are not necessarily swayed by government officials in the energy field in Ottawa who repeat constantly that "hoarding is not good economics" or that conservation is not critical. For the Canadian public, "energy saved is energy found." Consequently, there has been concern over the fact that government-initiated energy conservation projects have all but disappeared and it has become apparent that Canada's energy policy is not to have a policy at all (see Chapter 5).

Indeed, the same sort of concern about "officials" misreading the concerns of the population may be seen in the United States where, despite the fact that one high-efficiency light bulb over its lifetime eliminates the need for nearly one barrel of oil, energy efficiency and conservation programs continue to be canceled or downsized (Hirst 1990).

Because of energy misinformation disseminated in Canada and the United States, there have been negative consequences of environmental action. A hands-off policy on energy limits the possibility of public involvement in environmental policies that might constrain the energy industry. Government policymaking on both sides of the border is fragmented. In the United States, cohesive pressure groups already best articulate what environmental policy should be. Yet such groups have not been powerful enough to reinvigorate the conservation movement that would lead North Americans to consume 30% less energy than they now do (Stobaugh and Yergin 1983). Nor have they been able to reverse the environmentally malignant energy strategy based on fossil fuels.

However, the progress made on the acid rain front in 1990 suggests that one should not discount too readily the power of environmental groups in the United States: at times, the EPA has been the largest regulatory agency both in terms of budget and personnel (Rosenbaum 1985). After a period of softening environmental drive, Canada may also give encouraging signs of some strengthening of the tonus of environmental policy in spite of all the equivocation and federal–provincial squabbles.

The popular attention focused on, and the extent of the litigation associated with, environmentalism does not provide the best conditions for energy competition and cooperation (Vertinsky 1987). There is much waste of resources in the energy and environment fields (Buchanan et al. 1980). The invisible foot marches in.

> Adam Smith's invisible hand symbolizes the unseen benefits that economic competition confers on the coordination of economic activity. The 'invisible foot'... symbolizes the unseen costs... the negative welfare effects of competition over distributive shares. [Magee et al. 1989]

The important lobbying activities of sectors threatened by environmental policies have led to an increased politicization of the EPA context in the United States and of the DOE in Canada. This has had a great impact on the effectiveness of these agencies. Current efforts to neutralize the emergence of a strong environmental policy in Canada owe much to the lessons that energy producers have learned from the United States record over the last decade.

Energy-related projects create jobs, regional development, and growth-producing megaprojects within relatively short periods. These features imply a focus on well-identified beneficiaries. On the other hand, environmental losses are diffuse and likely to hurt only in the long run. It is not difficult to see why the "invisible foot" may operate effectively: redistributing from environment to energy may not be right in terms of long-term societal opportunity cost, but it is quite attractive in the short run.

In the United States, the energy and energy-related sectors took some time to realize the dangers presented by developing environmental concerns: the energy crisis blinded them in the 1970s. In Canada, the energy players are intent on ensuring that current environmental policymaking is not defined in threatening terms. The present reactive approach of the DOE — emphasizing the broad responsibility of all citizens for pollution control — is bound to generate more paralysis than progress in government policymaking in Canada. As Lucien Bouchard (1989: 18) insisted before the Standing Committee on Environment, environmental questions challenge "the current life style of our society.... We must tap the creativity of Canadians in designing acceptable solutions. Better informed and educated citizens will be better able to make intelligent decisions."

Such cautiousness does not reveal a weakness of will on the part of the Canadian government, but rather the depth of the issues raised by the energy/environment interface. The Canadian government does not feel either compelled or able to propose a proactive environmental policy that would amount to a modification of Canadian life style.

The continental integration of economic forces in terms of energy-based resources leads one to believe that there will be coordinated efforts on both sides of the border to neutralize attempts to promote environmental policies likely to impose high costs on the energy and energy-related sectors. Consequently, one should not be too optimistic in examining the environmental agenda for the next decade. There have been many promises made by many countries. Scenarios call for 20% and 50% reductions in carbon dioxide emissions by 2005 and by 2025, respectively. But this will not be possible without massive progress in energy efficiency and, perhaps, without greater reliance on nuclear energy. Yet neither front is very promising at this time in view of the withdrawal of resources from both. Moreover, as energy prices will continue to rise and energy crunches will thus become more probable, energy lobbies will likely grow in both power and persuasiveness. When faced with a trade-off between energy and environmental concerns, the Canadian and American public and politicians will probably choose to support the energy sector.

SOCIAL LEARNING

An alternative to the litigious chaos of the rent-seeking society is the design of a democratically rooted policy capable of effecting the necessary switch from competition to cooperation when necessary. This is possible only if governments become learning organizations and if policymaking is reframed in terms of social learning.

Governments as Learning Organizations

Defining a policy requires establishing the basis for selecting certain procedures or adopting certain strategies in the face of different plausible sets of circumstances. This cannot be done by presuming that experts already have all the necessary information, and that it is only a matter of negotiating the technically adapted policy. The information is widely spread through the population and scattered among many expert subgroups. A reasonable policymaking process must be based on social learning — on mutual learning by experts and clients, on interaction likely to generate a more complete picture of what measures are feasible, acceptable, and implementable.

Attempting to solve the energy/environment problems by using a research organization (Garratt 1987) might appear to be a roundabout and ineffective strategy, but this is not so. The development of a policy stance in the environment/energy field requires policymakers and policy analysts to recognize a central problem: the goals of the policy are either unknown or very ambiguous *and* the means–ends relationships are highly uncertain and poorly understood (Rittel and Webber 1973; Paquet, this volume, Chapter 5).

As we saw in Chapter 5, a standard way of looking at policymaking à la Wilensky (1967) is based on four elements: goal setting, control, innovation, and intelligence. When the problem is well-structured, policymaking emphasizing the first two elements is quite adequate. But when dealing with ill-structured and elusive problems, one must use an alternative approach that focuses on innovation and intelligence.

Friedmann and Abonyi's (1976) approach to such problems is again applicable in the energy/environment context (see Figure 5 and discussion in Chapter 2). Social values (block B) provide normative guidance in either the transformation of reality or the selection of strategies for action; they define what is acceptable. Theory of reality (block A) is a symbolic representation and explanation of the policy environment; it depicts what is feasible. Political strategy (block C) refers to the political action chosen; it identifies the stable and implementable options. Social action (block D) deals with the practical measures taken to ensure an effective policy outcome.

A Joint North American Task Force

The long-term costs of the scenario of the invisible foot are very high, but there is no hope that social learning will proceed unless one can force the debate outside the present framework, which emphasizes short-run technical and economic efficiency while excluding other considerations. The time may be ripe for a first Joint North American Task Force on Environmental and Energy Resources to reframe the basic questions. If the Free Trade Agreement has made clear that the United States and Canada are now to share energy and environmental resources to a greater degree than in the past, a coordinated policy on such matters as environment and energy should be sought.

This sort of new regional learning organization is akin to what was recommended by the Advisory Panel on Energy of the Brundtland Commission in 1986 (Iglesias 1987). Such agencies were meant to provide:

> Needed capability to identify and seize opportunities for regional cooperation in financing, developing and exploiting new technologies for energy supply, energy saving, and environmental regeneration.

Both Canada and the United States appear to be converging toward related environmental policies, yet in neither country is there a crisis of great immediacy. Therefore, current conditions provide an opportunity to create a North American forum to discuss issues that are continental in scope. Presumably, the presence of both Canadian and American environmentalists and energy industry representatives on this task force would ensure that the right questions would be asked and that various aspects of the issue would be explored. Moreover, one might count on such a first continental effort to ensure a degree of social learning for all interested parties and the public in general, and for the effort to have enough moral authority — as a result of the wide coverage of its surveying and the extensive amount of knowledge contributed by all the stakeholders to its ultimate recommendations — to be considered seriously by the governments on both sides of the border. Such an initiative would echo the separate initiatives of the Resources for the Future (United States) and Resources for Tomorrow (Canada) undertaken some 30 years ago as major efforts at stock-taking on the state of national resources and to develop natural resources policies.

A Joint North American Task Force on Environmental and Energy Resources would provide the basis for some harmonization of policies at the continent level on issues that are already commanding some world-level attention. Such an initiative would not only foster a higher degree of North American awareness and due concern in the aftermath of the Brundtland report but might also enable much of the good work that has begun in Canada and in the United States to find an outlet likely to result in refurbished rules of the game on both sides of the border. For instance, much use might be made of the work done for the National Task Force on Environment and Economy (Canada) — made up of ministers from seven governments, federal and provincial, and the CEOs of seven of Canada's top corporations — in adapting the Brundtland report to the Canadian arena. This has already generated a landmark report (National Task Force on Environment and Economy 1987).

In the same spirit, United States senators John Heinz (Republican, Pennsylvania) and Timothy Wirth (Democrat, Colorado) initiated and sponsored Project 88, "a bipartisan effort to find innovative solutions to major environmental and natural resources problems." Also in the United States, 50 people from industry, government, academia, and the environmental community worked on the final report *Harnessing Market Forces to Protect Our Environment — Initiatives for the New President* produced in 1988 (Stavins 1989). Indeed, if a meeting of some 100 senior representatives of corporate and political strategists from both Canada and the United States in New York in December 1989 is a harbinger of things possible, battles of words may be soon replaced by calls to link arms at the North American level (Howard 1989).

POSSIBLE STEPS

Social learning cannot occur *ex nihilo*. It must evolve from a set of basic principles and build on bets on certain promising directions. In the energy/environment world, certain key principles have been put forward as guidelines for any exercise in social architecture (Perrings 1987): the principle of intergenerational equity, the principle of collective property, and the principle of individual accountability. These may serve as prime movers in the learning process.

Three Principles

The principle of intergenerational equity points to the contradiction between the criteria of intergenerational egalitarianism and a positive social rate of discount. It forces the debate onto a field where means have to be found to extend the time horizon of the present generation if the common inheritance is to be preserved.

A small step in this general direction might be taken through the *collective property* of natural resources — energy and environment — and through the astute use of contracts governing such resources. This has been accomplished effectively in the world of mines and forestry. Such contracts could prohibit practices with proven deleterious effects and institute mechanisms resembling both royalties on depletable resources and taxes on polluters.

To enforce such contracts, *individual accountability* would need to become an effective norm and mechanisms would need to be designed to ensure that those not meeting contractual obligations would be effectively charged for the damage they have caused. Given the possibility of escaping such charges through bankruptcy or the like, the idea of natural resources bonds — reimbursable deposits equal to the maximum possible damage in the event of violation of the rules of the contract — might be used (Solow 1971). The conjectured value of the bond could always be revised upward or downward as experience reveals that more or less destructive methods have been used.

New Norms

These three principles may be put into effect in a variety of ways depending on basic current values. To the extent that intergenerational solidarity prevails, there may be little cause for the establishment of priorities within the present generation to emphasize the importance of longer-term objectives like the resilience of the system. Some (Daly and Cobb 1989) have chosen to bet on the construction of new solidarities. Others, who are either more cynical or averse to risks, would prefer the state to accept responsibility for sanctioning some priorities in the choices made by the present generation: the precedence of needs over preferences for instance (Frankfurt 1984a). Such norms or rules would direct traffic in the forum and ensure, like traffic lights in large cities, a way to orchestrate the actions of all agents. (Who would claim that the market would do this job better than coercive traffic lights?)

Such norms or rules may vary with normal or abnormal times, very much as instinct guides animals to changes in the rules in critical times. Conventions may be changed according to certain meta-rules, and one of the central roles of the Joint North American Task Force would be to hammer out such meta-rules (Orgogozo and Sérieyx 1989; Paquet, this volume, Chapter 5).

However, there is little hope that such developments will occur organically in Canada or the United States on the environment and energy fronts. A reframing of the issues is necessary. This, in turn, requires a revolution in the mind of the citizens of both countries. This new consciousness might begin in the year of the 200th anniversary of the death of Adam Smith with a recognition of a forgotten portion of his message: competition and markets cannot do everything, and governments should provide "certain public works and certain public institutions, which it can never be for the interest of any individual, or small number of individuals, to erect and maintain" (Smith 1776). The world of energy and environment calls for such public institutions, and until such a time as this is widely recognized, there is little hope that the requisite social architecture and carpentry will be allowed to proceed.

CONCLUSION

Canada and the United States have been groping for market-oriented energy and environmental policies. Recent reports may serve as a basis for a promising process of social learning on this front (Stavins 1989). However, the market cannot be a panacea. To political and economic actors who focus on energy and environment policy, public goods loom large and, unfortunately, market-place decisions and calculations do not take into account public goods to an appropriate extent (Kash and Rycroft 1984). Social learning will have to lead both governments to return somewhat to some interventionist form of policy-making.

Moreover, what is acceptable, what is feasible, what is stability-generating, and what is effectively implementable need not be the same all across North America. Much of the existing diversity may not be rooted so much in fundamental differences or in poor understanding of the issues as in historical circumstances and differing values. An occasion to take stock of the knowledge and values of the energy/environment players in Canada and the United States may be useful even if it does not lead to a unified policy, but only to critical appraisal of current policies and to the elaboration of different but coherent strategies. For example, there may be advantages for both Canada and the United States in developing joint policies on matters of binational concern such as acid rain, where the spillover effects from one country to the other are important, but this need not be the case across the board. It should become clearer to each nation (as social learning proceeds) why and to what extent values and priorities differ and why explicitly different policies may be desirable.

Some may regard the social learning approach as futile or at least as likely to generate more heat than light. F. Scott Fitzgerald (1945) may have been right in saying that no grand idea was ever born in a conference, but "a lot of foolish ideas have died there" (Fitzgerald 1945). A Joint North American Task Force might be expected to slaughter foolish ideas in good currency. While the United States and Canada determine their own policy options, such a task force could effectively evaluate their potential for success. As Canadian humorist Stephen Leacock has reminded us, Canadians can only be passionate about moderation, one may reckon that any slaughter of foolish ideas and sacred cows at such a conference would likely be civil and humane.

Part II

Social Learning in Action:

C – Social Perspectives

CHAPTER 7

MULTICULTURALISM
AS NATIONAL POLICY*

> Valorisons les obstacles entre les hommes...
> non pour qu'ils communiquent moins, mais
> pour qu'ils communiquent mieux.
>
> – *Jean-Pierre Dupuy*

Multiculturalism is a label for many things in Canada: our multi-ethnic cultural mosaic, a policy of the federal government, and an ideology of cultural pluralism (Kallen 1982a). As a Canadian policy, it is one of the most daring initiatives of the last 25 years, but it has been assessed in varying ways, ranging from "enlightened" (Jaenen 1986), to a "manipulative device used to perpetuate control over ethnic groups" (DeFaveri 1986), to a policy that "undermines the foundation for national unity" (Kallen 1982a). These differences of opinion stem, to a large extent, from the vagueness of the language in good currency, and the Rorschach-type interpretations this vagueness nurtures, but also from the difficulty inherent in the assessment of such a bold policy move.

Our purpose is to deal with this complex question from the point of view of policy research and cultural economics: what is sought is some *clarification* of the underlying issues, for there is much confusion about this policy domain *and* some provisional *conjectural evaluation* of the Canadian multiculturalism policy of the last two decades. We have to be satisfied with conjectures because such a policy may not be amenable to meaningful evaluation except in the very long run.

Our approach emphasizes two major points. First, multiculturalism poses an ill-structured problem to policy analysts, a *wicked problem* (see Chapter 2) — the goals are not known or are ambiguous and the means–ends relationships are highly uncertain and poorly understood. Second, the central feature of the multiculturalism policy has to do with *symbolic resources* and the reallocation of those sorts of resources with a view to generating equality of recognition and status; economists have little experience with the analysis of the economics of symbols and of the sociocultural underground — truth, trust, acceptance, restraint, obligation — social virtues that are the underground of the economic

* This chapter is based on a paper with the same title which appeared in the *Journal of Cultural Economics* (1989, 13(1), 17–34). The help of A. Burgess and M. Racette is gratefully acknowledged.

game (Hirsch 1976). We will argue that multiculturalism as an exercise in production and redistribution of symbolic resources may have had positive impacts on ethnocultural pride (and, therefore, on the efficiency of the economic system), but such a policy has also a dark side that has been occluded and may be of importance.

Consequently, any provisional and conjectural evaluation of this policy must be prudent because of the wickedness of the problem *and* somewhat inconclusive because of the limited development of the economics of symbolic resources. When dealing with such issues, one finds oneself in what might have been the predicament of Alfred Marshall (1907) when he was presenting his disquisition on the social possibilities of economic chivalry.

Traditional approaches to policy research focus on attempts to falsify hypotheses about an objective reality. This is too narrow a focus for policy research when the ground is in motion. This is the reason why the social learning model is helpful. It focuses on learning on the job about both the configuration of facts and the configuration of values, but it emphasizes also the importance of learning from the stakeholders in the policy game and from the many groups at the periphery who are in possession of important local knowledge. In this transactive style of planning action, hypotheses are verified as "correct" only in the process of creating a new reality. This approach à la Friedmann-Abonyi (1976) — more fully described in chapters 2 and 5 — is based on a sharp awareness of the limits of our policy research tools: one cannot hope to produce anything more than incomplete answers.

In this chapter, we present two major characterizations of the policy of multiculturalism in Canada — as *containment policy* and as *symbolic policy*; look at the dynamic this policy has triggered; give some reasons for the necessary unfinishedness of the current policy; and mention some of the pitfalls and challenges lying ahead.

The rationale for initiating such a policy thrust may have been narrowly electoralist, as some cynics claim, but an evolutionary process has been un-leashed that will not be easily reversed or slowed down. Given the very limited knowledge base on which such a policy initiative is based, unintended conse-quences will loom large in a final evaluation. This explains why we have allowed our preliminary evaluation to be somewhat speculative; because we are in the process of learning how to be multicultural, concerns about possible perverse consequences should not be ignored even though hard evidence may still be slim or lacking. Indeed, as Schumacher (1977) wisely suggests, even though the prevailing philosophy of cartography is "if in doubt, leave it out," naviga-tion is much safer in these turbulent times if we adopt the opposite approach "if in doubt, show it prominently."

MULTICULTURALISM: A CONTAINMENT POLICY

The social fabric of Canada has been polyethnic and multicultural since the very beginnings of the country. The native population was displaced by French and English invasions, and the new ethnic groups occupied the whole of the territory. Despite efforts in the 19th century to stimulate immigration from other countries, in 1881 the population of non-British, non-French extraction was a shade less than half a million and represented only about 11% of the Canadian population. After the 1967 change in the Canadian immigration laws, the process of visible multiculturalization accelerated: before 1970, 12–13% of immigrants were Asian; now the figure is 50%. In 1981, more than 8 million people or 31% of the population were members of non-British, non-French ethnic groups (Sheridan 1987), and by 1986, the proportion was 38% (Cardozo 1988).

But multiculturalism is more than a reality in Canada. It is a set of social values, an ideal type. It has been said of Canadians in the 19th century that they only had "limited identities," i.e., that they did not define themselves entirely or even primarily as Canadians. Rather, they identified first with their region or province, and only in a limited way with the nation (Paquet and Wallot 1987). This reality of "limited identities" has made it easier to accept and even to promote the legitimization of multiple identities: from a country lacking a global identity and being loyal first and foremost to regions or sections of the country, we have drifted toward a celebration of ethnocentrism and to the development of a *mosaic* model of Canada, in which distinctive ethnic collectivities make up the country. Collective cultural rights making all of us *hyphenated Canadians*, with "equal weights on each side of the hyphen" would ensue (Kallen 1982a). The positive valuation of ethnic segmentation, which necessarily follows from these assumptions, is not shared by all Canadians. But it is most certainly defended with lesser or greater vehemence by many stakeholders.

A soft version of this mosaic model became government policy in the early 1970s. Faced with a growing electorate from ethnic communities that were neither French nor British, the Trudeau strategy was to recognize symbolically both the right of ethnic groups to choose to maintain their distinctiveness, *and* a protection of individual rights of members of ethnic groups to choose whether to maintain their ties and loyalties to their ethnic community.

The objectives of the 1971 policy were fourfold: (1) support of ethnocultural diversity for cultural communities that choose this option; (2) assistance to people to overcome cultural barriers; (3) promotion of creative interchanges between ethnic groups; and (4) assistance to immigrants in acquiring one of Canada's official languages. On items (2) and (3), there was little disagreement. On item (1) — the encouragement of cultural diversity — there were two schools of thought: some supporting the promotion of ethnic identity as of value per se (Burnet 1976), and others suggesting that this would make Canada into "some kind of ethnic zoo" (Brotz 1980). There was also strong disagreement on item (4) between those for whom living cultures and languages are "inextricably linked," who argued that linguistic rights of ethnic communities and immigrants should also be recognized and guaranteed, and those for whom assimilation into one of the two official language groups was essential and the egalitarian mosaic model on this front had to be subjected to the overriding official languages constraint.

If one had to find a label for this Canadian model, an apt description might be "contained pluralism" (Arnal 1986), for our pluralism is constrained in a variety of ways by a number of core Canadian values (bilingualism, democracy, nonviolence, etc.). Multiculturalism is only one of many core values and one that is limited by all the others.

Such important constraints imposed on the pure mosaic model have led many to argue that the policy of multiculturalism within a bilingual framework is nothing but a policy of appeasement and containment designed to accommodate the demands of non-French/non-British groups and those of French and English Canadians (Peter 1978). The limited efforts to implement this new policy in the 1970s lent some support to this view (Lupul 1982). In 1972, a minister of state for multiculturalism was appointed and, in 1973, an advisory body was established (later to become the Canadian Multiculturalism Council) to help the minister implement the policy.

It was only in the 1980s that institutionalization of this policy began: in 1982, multiculturalism was mentioned in the *Canadian Charter of Rights and Freedoms*; in 1985, a Standing Committee of the House of Commons on Multiculturalism was created. In its June 1987 report (Mitges 1987), it recommended the creation of a separate department. In 1988, new legislation — *The Multicultural Act* — was passed, and a full-fledged ministry to deal with multiculturalism was created. Recently, efforts to help fund nonofficial-language training have been acknowledged, and some work has been done on the issue of confronting racism (Stasiulis 1988). If the total budget of this sector remains minuscule — approximately $1 per Canadian per year — there are clear signs that additional financial resources will be forthcoming. The construction of new infrastructure (ministry, research institute) is bound to make multicultural issues more visible and create a channel through which interest groups might be able to communicate their concerns.

If progress has been slow and no all-out effort to move Canadian society toward the ideal cultural mosaic template has been attempted, this is due to a situation in which power and opportunities are still largely shared by the two founding nations. However, opposition is not restricted to this group; Canadians as a whole are only "mildly positive toward the idea of cultural diversity" (Berry 1977). The political strategy of containment and accommodation by Canadian governments through most of the period since 1971 appears to reflect fairly accurately the state of mind of the nation.

Some cynics would go so far as to say that the objective of the multiculturalism policy has always been for the state to regulate the collective interests and goals of minority groups. In this sense, the political strategy may be said to have worked rather well (Stasiulis 1980) and, if this is correct, one might regard it as unlikely that the institutionalization of the department will do much in material terms to effect dramatic changes under the circumstances. But this conclusion stems from an interpretation of multiculturalism that is too narrowly focused on the concept as a *social policy* designed to eliminate discrimination and reduce income and employment inequities in a social system that is not free of cultural barriers. Progress on these fronts has clearly been very slow, even though this was most certainly one of the objectives of the 1971 policy. But it would be unwise to reduce multiculturalism policy to this dimension.

MULTICULTURALISM: A SYMBOLIC POLICY

The true significance of the multiculturalism policy is to be found at another level, and at that level it is truly revolutionary for it corresponds to some of the new roles of the state in the affairs of the mind in modern society (Tussman 1977; Lowi 1975). It is a contribution "to the reconstruction of the symbolic system and to the redistribution of social status among linguistic and ethnocultural groups in Canadian society" (Breton 1984). As Breton has shown rather well, multiculturalism is "largely an instrument for re-structuring society's identity system and for managing cultural tensions that arise in the process," for it may be hypothesized that people are less interested in their ethnic cultures and organizations than in maintaining their ethnic identity, finding ways to express it in suitable ways, and gaining recognition for their status (Breton 1984; Gans 1979).

Multiculturalism is an effort "to regenerate the cultural-symbolic capital of society: to restructure the collective identity and the associated symbolic contents," and such efforts may be analyzed in terms of production and distribution of symbolic resources (Breton 1984).

The Canadian policy on multiculturalism has been interpreted in many ways: (1) as a social policy, designed to eliminate inequalities between ethnic groups and remove barriers to entry into the mainstream of Canadian life; (2) as the purposeful construction of a mosaic of institutionally complete ethnic communities; (3) as an effort to produce "symbolic ethnicity" as a psychological benefit. On the whole, reactions to these partial versions of the multicultural policy have been skeptical. If the first objective is sought, this policy was *unnecessary*, for the *Charter of Rights* and other instruments could well take care of the problem. In terms of the second objective, the policy is simply an *unrealistic* exercise in social architecture. If "symbolic ethnicity" is the name of the game, some have argued that it is an *unwarranted* activity on the part of the state, for the state has no business in the affairs of the mind nor in the symbolic order.

These partial characterizations have not fully captured the import of the Canadian multiculturalism policy and most certainly have not recognized the central importance of *symbolic ethnicity*. This is much more than simple psychological gratification. Changes in the symbolic order often have fundamental impacts on the framing of decisions and on the dynamics of society; the slow process of status-enhancing of ethnic minorities in Canada has acquired a logic of its own which has blown away the containment of the 1970s.

Culture is a "shared symbolic blueprint which guides action on an ideal course or gives life meaning" (Roberts and Clifton 1982). Cultural identity formation is the result of a progressive crystallization of a new ethos: the sum of characteristic usages, ideas, norms, standards, and codes by which a group is differentiated and individualized in character from other groups (Banfield 1958). In a sense, identity formation occurs very much like capital formation: only if a new social contrivance proves to be "profitable" for some will it emerge and persist.

It would be naive to expect a cultural identity to evolve in a vacuum: there are public goods and social overhead capital attached to this production process, as there are in other sectors. One cannot expect that such overhead capital (meta-rules) will evolve organically: the state may have a role to play, and the optimal amount of coercion may not be zero. In the same way that the state is seen as legitimately involved in the creation and sustenance of a monetary system and a political order, it is quite legitimate for the state to "sustain the appropriate state of mind" (Tussman 1977), and in fact the state is involved in many ways in shaping the institutions of awareness, in politics of cognition, and in managing the forum — "the whole range of institutions and situations of public communication."

Breton (1984) has argued that public policy in our socioeconomies attempts to shape or modify the symbolic order — "the shaping and protecting of awareness" (Tussman 1977) — by producing and allocating symbolic resources. These interventions amount to a *bricolage* of the underlying ethos and translate into the reranking of status groups and the redistribution of recognition.

Multiculturalism as a national policy is such a granting of status and recognition to various ethnic communities. Although this production and redistribution of symbolic resources may not translate into big budgets, one would be unwise to presume that they are unimportant. Multiculturalism is redrawing mental maps and redefining levels of aspirations. This in turn modifies the frame of mind of those groups, but not always in a positive way.

It is true that status enhancement through multiculturalism might be presumed to have a positive impact. By providing primary securities for the ethnic communities and by helping to develop collective pride and redefining higher levels of aspiration, multiculturalism might be expected to modify the framing of decisions by members of those communities and to engender an outburst of *entrepreneurship* (Light 1972; Paquet 1986, 1989f). This is a process that has been noted elsewhere. Some have even argued that the ethnocultural communities might take advantage of their intimate awareness and appreciation of cultural nuances to become go-betweens with our foreign trading partners and thus enhance Canada's trade potential (Passaris 1985).

But there is also the possibility that the multiculturalism policy might have the opposite effect. For this form of psychological self-poisoning is maximal in societies where more-or-less egalitarian rights coexist with considerable differences in the power, wealth, culture, etc., of the various groups (Scheler

1958). It was Nietzsche who understood the importance of spite and rancor in modern societies. Multiculturalism policy may generate *ressentiment* in the very population it was meant to upgrade. A French word is necessary here as

> Ressentiment is to resentment what climate is to weather... *ressentiment* is a free-floating disposition to visit upon others the bitterness that accumulates from one's own subordination and existential guilt at allowing oneself to be used by other people for their own purposes, while one's life rusts away unnoticed. [Friedenberg 1975]

Canadian multicultural policy has had an impact of this sort. An illustration of this outcome is provided by Bharati Mukherjee (1985) in the introduction to *Darkness*. Mukherjee, who was born in Calcutta, lived in Toronto and Montreal, and became a writer here before moving to the United States. Her words are rather harsh.

> In the years that I spent in Canada — 1966 to 1980 — I discovered that the country is hostile to its citizens who had been born in hot, moist continents like Asia, that the country proudly boasts of its opposition to the whole concept of cultural assimilation.... With the act of immigration to the United States, suddenly I was no longer aggrieved, except as an habit of mind. I had moved from being a 'visible minority,' against whom the nation had officially incited its less-visible citizens to react, to being just another immigrant.... For me, it is a movement away from the aloofness of expatriation, to the exuberance of immigration. I have joined imaginative forces with an anonymous, driven, underclass of semi-assimilated Indians with sentimental attachments to a distant homeland but no real desire for permanent return... instead of seeing my Indianness as a fragile identity to be preserved against obliteration (or worse, a 'visible' disfigurement to be hidden), I see it now as a set of fluid identities to be celebrated.... Indianness is now a metaphor.

Mukherjee has not found in the celebration of a fragile cultural identity a basis for cultural equality; yet one of the objectives of the multicultural policy was to respond to the status anxieties that had been voiced. Far from breaking down "cultural jealousies" as the prime minister announced in 1971, the policy of multiculturalism has led to some dissatisfaction in the ethnocultural communities, to interethnic competition, and to heightened demands for more symbolic capital (Breton 1986). Moreover, given the expectations created by the policy, there has been much frustration at the slowness of the process of "realization" of the cultural equality that had been promised. Political leaders responded to these growing pressures, especially in the 1980s, by legislating ethnicity as a feature of Canadian life and by raising again the level of multicultural promises: from the preservation of cultural heritage to the enhancement of ethnocultural communities.

THE DYNAMICS OF MULTICULTURALISM

One cannot predict unambiguously the future of the daring multicultural experiment Canada has embarked on. Nothing less than a research program paralleling this experiment, tapping continually into the local knowledge at the periphery — in the ethnocultural communities — taking fully into account the values of the stakeholders, their *Weltanschauungen* or theories of reality, and the dynamics of political gaming can offer any hope of leading to a plausible scenario. But even in these quasi-ideal circumstances, the amount of ignorance would remain great: the action hypothesis on which the multicultural gambit is based can only be verified in the course of its unfolding.

Yet, a few unintended consequences are emerging from the experiment and might be worth noting if only to ensure vigilance. As we said earlier, our norm is if in doubt, show it prominently.

The first of these consequences is *a growth of ethnocentrism* in Canada. Some have referred to it as a tribalization of Canadian society (Spicer 1988). As Claude Lévi-Strauss has put it, "loyalty to a certain set of values inevitably makes people partially or totally insensitive to other values... a profound indifference to other cultures [is]... a guarantee that they would exist in their own manner and on their own terms" (quoted in Geertz 1986). Such *imperméabilité* does not authorize the oppression of anyone, but it leads to a *growing segmentation* and to a drift away from unhyphenated Canadianism into ethnic bloc-action. This has already led to the ugly confrontations noted in recent nomination meetings (Spicer 1988). For even if segmentation is somewhat idealized in the mosaic model, most experts would agree that it leads to ethnic particularism and impedes national unity (Kallen 1982a).

The second notable factor is a *resurgence of racism under a different name*. As a result of the growth of ethnocentrism, a new rhetoric, based on *the right for each culture or ethnoculture to be different*, has emerged. This rhetoric has led in turn to a sort of juxtaposition of ethnocultures, each claiming its right to be different but also to be equal. This claim that groups can be equal but different is an illusion: a whole literature from de Tocqueville to Louis Dumont (1983) has clearly shown that in any society, a difference can only mean a value difference, i.e., some explicit or implicit hierarchy (Taguieff 1987). In Canada, "intentionally or not, the multicultural policy preserves the reality of Canadian ethnic hierarchy" (Kallen 1982b). A new differentialist neo-racism is germinating here, as it flourishes in other polyethnic societies that have consecrated this illusory search for equality/difference (Taguieff 1987).

The third negative force at work is the *permeating influence of envy in inter-ethnic relations*. It is well known since de Tocqueville that egalitarian societies, or societies claiming to decree equality are more prone to envy. The equality among ethnocultural groups decreed by multiculturalism has provoked a heightened degree of inter-ethnic group competition and animosity. Indeed, the sort of *ressentiment* described above by Mukherjee is at the very root of envy as symbolic behaviour (Foster 1972). This in turn poisons inter-ethnic relations, as the success of group A is perceived by group B as a sign that the latter group has been injured or maligned. The zero-sum syndrome looms large.

Multiculturalism may claim to try to break down cultural jealousies (a rather innocuous zeal in the preservation of something possessed — as any dictionary indicates) but it has been the source of envy (displeasure and ill-will at the superiority of another person in happiness, success, reputation, or the possession of anything desirable) (Foster 1972). In his study of envy as symbolic behaviour, Foster examines the socioeconomic and psychological conditions that breed envy and the cultural forms used by those who fear the envy of others (concealment, denial, symbolic sharing, and true sharing) and the institutional forms used to reduce envy. One of the latter is a system of encapsulation — a device making use of the egalitarian principle to produce subsocieties "marked off from each other by social, psychological, cultural and at times geographical boundaries" (Foster 1972: 185). However, the balancing act between ethnocentrism/encapsulation as institutional forms and envy/resentment as a state of mind may become a vicious circle with a violent outcome, if they were ever to begin reinforcing each other in our society (Dumouchel and Dupuy 1979).

In parallel, one might tally growing evidence of tolerance, of a shift from juxtaposition to integration, and some signs of the emergence of a new modern concept of *citizenship* to replace old nationalities. But, at this time, one can see only the harbingers of this new *citizenship* based on collaboration and achievement rather than status. In any case, these features do not appear to have been fostered by Canada's multiculturalism policy. Proximity and closer personal contacts have eroded barriers as they do in the melting pot world and have led to some appreciation of other ethnocultures. Although it is difficult to apportion success or failure to the restructuring of the symbolic order undertaken by the multiculturalism policy as such, some have argued that, if anything, this policy might have generated on balance *more* emotionally-charged conflicts ascribable to status anxieties for those at the top of the vertical mosaic and to rising expectations and relative deprivation at the bottom.

CONCLUSION

Canada has faced the challenge of its polyethnic society by defining a multicultural philosophy within a bilingual framework. The national policy of multiculturalism that has ensued has been translated slowly, but more and more importantly, it has developed into a set of institutions that have performed two very different sets of functions.

On one hand, these institutions and policies have helped cultural groups to overcome cultural barriers, and they have promoted some interchange between cultural groups. But these efforts have been much less important than those that fostered, on the other hand, their ethnocultural consciousness and encouraged institutions and organizations that appeal to such consciousness.

As a result, it cannot be said that the multicultural policy has done as much as it might have to nurture an ethnic or race-relations policy in Canada. Rather, it has emphasized ethnocentrism and segmentation with unintended consequences of some import.

At this point, when important new resources appear to be likely to be channeled toward the implementation of the policy on multiculturalism, it might be useful to repeat a statement often made by Jean Burnet (1976) —

one of the pioneers in ethnic studies in Canada — about the need for more research (research of a different sort, i.e., action research) likely to help in the redefinition of our multicultural policy in line with directions that are feasible, acceptable, implementable, and effective. Such directions cannot be elicited from the centre, but need to tap into local knowledge. There is little point in encouraging specific consciousness among groups who have seemed dormant or largely assimilated for the sole reason that they are there.

Continuing redefinition of policy directions is essential in any ongoing policy domain, but if this bold gamble of Canada on multiculturalism is to succeed, such a refocusing is essential now.

And if in the midst of this complex investigation, policy analysts were ever in need of a sextant to guide them toward what might be a sense of Canadian identity in the making, they could do worse than to reread an old classic — a book of essays edited by Malcolm Ross (1954) — for Ross' introduction is a gem.

> We kick against the pricks of our necessity. Yet strangely, we are in love with this necessity. Our natural mode is not compromise but 'irony' — the inescapable response to the presence and pressures of opposites in tension. Irony is the key to our identity.... Our Canadianism, from the very moment of its real birth, is a baffling, illogical but compulsive athleticism — a fence-leaping which is also, and necessarily, a fence-keeping.... Ours is not, can never be, the 'one hundred per cent' kind of nationalism. We have always had to think in terms of 50-50. No 'melting pot.' Rather the open irony of the multi-dimensional structure, an openness to the 'larger mosaic'... we can see vividly the actual movement from the dual irony to the multiple irony, from the expansive open thrust of the French-English tension to the many-coloured but miraculously coherent, if restless, pattern of the authentically Canadian nationhood.

As a popular philosopher used to say, "It is that simple, and that complex."

Some might be tempted to reject outright these conjectures in the name of the old cartographic orthodoxy — if in doubt, leave it out. To them, I can only suggest a rereading of Ionesco's *Rhinoceros*, in which the characters are turned into rhinoceroses for mysterious reasons. Yet, there is always an unmistakable clue that a character is about to be transformed into a rhinoceros: this character has just stated that he or she feels completely immune.

CHAPTER 8

LIBERAL EDUCATION AS SYNECDOCHE*

> May God us keep from single vision
> and Newton's sleep.
> – *William Blake*

The conference "Who's Afraid of Liberal Education?"** was inspired by a wave of concern in Canada and the United States about the decay of cultural literacy, the suggestion that a change in postsecondary curricula might be the answer, and some recognition that the postsecondary enterprise was not doing much to address the problem. It was natural, under the circumstances, to inquire about the occult forces that might stand in the way of the implementation of a curative program; for there is some agreement on the seriousness of the concern, even though there is no agreement about the sort of liberal education curriculum, if any, capable of dealing with the problem.

There is a danger that the current crusade for a new classicism, if defined too narrowly, might lead well-intentioned higher education reformers in the wrong direction, and allow the real challenges facing higher education to be occluded. There is undoubtedly a case for curriculum reform, but it must be approached from a broader and more global perspective than it has been by some defenders of the new classicism.

A FEW SIGNPOSTS

The Saskatoon Forum

In October 1987, the National Forum on Post Secondary Education staged true *états-généraux* on higher education in Canada. One would have expected from these a comprehensive *cahier de doléances*. It did not materialize. A careful reading of the *Forum Papers* (NFPE 1987a), the *Proceedings* (NFPE 1987b), the workshop reports, and the final recommendations reveals that the sensitivities

* This chapter is taken from *Who's Afraid of Liberal Education?* edited by C. Andrew and S.B. Esbensen (Ottawa: University of Ottawa Press, 1989, pp. 1–20).

** Organized by the Social Science Federation of Canada in Ottawa, 30 September to 1 October 1988.

of all parties in this first national chautauqua on higher education have stood in the way of fruitful discussion. Debates were rendered aseptic by an excessive civility in the dialogue between lay persons and academics, and by the chronic Canadian obsession with federal–provincial sensitivities.

An unfortunate consequence has been the level of generality of the discussions and the weasel nature of the consensus arrived at. It was hoped that *l'esprit de Saskatoon* would guide educational reforms in Canada, but it was too feeble-hearted to do the job: it could not march on, it had to tiptoe all the time.

As a result, most of the contentious issues: the crisis of confidence in higher education, the management of postsecondary, the inadequacy of the curricula, and the need for a national strategy — all issues that had been well documented in the *Proceedings of the Standing Senate Committee on National Finance* (Leblanc 1987) — were carefully avoided. On the other hand, noncontentious issues, like promoting accessibility for marginal groups and providing additional public financial resources to the postsecondary enterprise, became the foci of discussion.

The very generality of the discussions and recommendations allowed observers to use them as a Rorschach test, and to extract for special attention idiosyncratic themes — however fleetingly recurring. At the midpoint of the National Forum, Lise Bissonnette (1987: 81–82) took advantage of her breakfast address to underline what she saw as "a renaissance of the concept of general education... a yearning for a new kind of classicism." This perception caught on. Given the fact that there was little of real substance on which the participants had developed a consensual view; that Bloom's (1987) *The Closing of the American Mind* was a best-seller at the time (as was Hirsch's [1987] *Cultural Literacy*), liberal education became a safe discussion item because it allowed everyone to address a truly academic issue, without the need for close scrutiny of the performance of the higher education enterprise.

It is important to note that this "yearning" did not find a place in the concluding remarks of the chairperson of the National Forum. Flexibility, adaptability, accessibility, federal–provincial cooperation, a better statistical database, and a call for leadership were *les cris de ralliement* supposed to give a momentum to these *états généraux* and ensure that *l'esprit de Saskatoon* would live on. For obvious reasons, it did not.

Le Non-dit à Saskatoon et à Ottawa

The most surprising feature of the Saskatoon meeting was the implicit agreement of participants to exclude a variety of central institutional issues already well documented in an extensive literature on the crisis in Canadian higher education: excessive provincialization, the rigidity and protected nature of higher education institutions, and the poverty of their management had been singled out repeatedly. Epistemological entrapments that stood in the way of reform were also ignored: the so-called (and so mistakenly labeled)

Rousseau–Dewey type of perception of education as content-free; the disciplinarization of knowledge production that triggered the emergence of methodism; a naive characterization of the way in which knowledge is acquired; the dominion of technical rationality, etc. (Emery 1980; Schon 1983; Neilson and Gaffield 1986; Hirsch 1987; Paquet and von Zur-Muehlen 1987; Watson 1987; Laplante 1988).

These issues might have been raised in the follow-up that many anticipated after the National Forum, but that now seems unlikely. They were also excluded from the subsequent Ottawa conference, and this was especially true for the epistemological issues. Yet the epistemological questions are the truly revolutionary ones, because they are about fundamental aspects of knowledge acquisition and can threaten existing arrangements more dramatically than mere institutional tinkering. It is understandable, therefore, that the vested interests in the postsecondary enterprise have ensured that they would not be raised in an open forum.

Liberal education is such an epistemological issue: it has to do with the sort of knowledge that needs to be acquired, given certain educational goals, and how it should be acquired. It represents a stratagem recommended by some educational reformers to accomplish objectives they regard as fundamental, yet the desirability of such a strategy can only be gauged by showing how it would make the postsecondary system more effective. This in turn requires that the whole process of education and education policy be clearly understood. This nexus of issues was hardly discussed.

Entrapments Highlighted

Lise Bissonnette (1989) indicates clearly that she is very pessimistic about the implementation of this "new classicism" curriculum for which there was supposedly such a "yearning" in Saskatoon. She ascribes this phenomenon to institutional obstacles standing in the way of the new curriculum (organizational sclerosis, pedagogical incapabilities, diversity of the clienteles, demands from the marketplace, and strong differences of opinion about the content of this new classicism).

Howard Clark (1989) of Dalhousie University appears to support Bissonnette's diagnosis: there is at present both a phenomenal pressure to promote specialization at the postsecondary level, and an equally phenomenal incapacity in the universities to do more than just cope. For Clark, the debate on curriculum is a symptom of the fundamental problems that postsecondary education institutions face.

Among other things, Grant's (1989) puzzling testimony in response to Bissonnette's paper urges postsecondary institutions to resist private-sector pressures to educate for utilitarian ends. But, more important, he reveals the basic puzzlement of the business community when dealing with the higher education issue. As George Bernard Shaw diagnosed a long time ago, "every profession is a conspiracy against the laity"; so it is hardly surprising that lay people find it so difficult to come to terms with the crisis facing universities. In this case, both institutional and epistemological entrapments are ignored and simplistic suggestions ensue.

Karelis's (1989) analysis of the American scene helps to put things in perspective. The central question, he states, is "about the ends of general education and about the kind and type of general education that will best serve those ends." Karelis refers to studies identifying many different purposes for education, all equally valid. From there, one may derive a wide range of recipes to reach these different sets of objectives, yet none of these broad goals commands a core curriculum as a *sine qua non*. Indeed, experiments at Harvard and Miami show a high degree of dissonance about these issues in the higher education system. Some have even argued that an enlightened education in a small number of typical concrete instances might provide an opportunity for a wide-ranging appreciation of historical, technological, and social concerns.

What is striking in Karelis's paper is evidence that the "public" and the "academy" appear to be at odds. Some parents in the United States want their children to be taught the traditional content or knowledge base they themselves were exposed to in their youth, while the academy would appear willing to supply only what its professoriate knows, i.e., disciplinary knowledge. The romantically nostalgic public or the self-interested professoriate: who should decide what is needed?

Experiments: A Very Small Sample

Canadians have performed only a few experiments in search of a third way with the result that the variety of available programs is much narrower in Canada than in the United States. One such experiment sketches a strategy that is both timid and successful: the Arts One curriculum of the University of British Columbia — 60% of the freshman year is especially designed. It has worked well for over 20 years for a very small cadre of students.

The second strategy is broader in scope: the liberal arts program proposed by the University of Toronto. This Unity of Knowledge program is intriguing; perhaps for that reason, it has not yet been implemented.

The third summarizes a more ambitious strategy. It does not deal with liberal education directly; rather, it is an attempt to break down the monolithic structure of the university and to create a quasi-market *within the university*: a separate entity — *le module* — (including professors, students, and socioeconomic agents) responsible for assessing the demand for courses making up programs and another — *la famille* — (made up of the professoriate) responsible for supplying the courses. This is the system in place at the Université du Québec.

The first two strategies address the narrow question of what a liberal education curriculum might look like; the third is a strategy designed to shake loose the producer-dominated structure of universities, a factor that many observers believe is responsible for the rigidity and inadequacy of university programs.

Although other examples exist, by and large, epistemological issues are not high on the agenda, and the range of institutional variables remains relatively narrow. This stems from two sets of implicit premises:

- *The equation between cultural literacy as needed currency and liberal education as the only way to provide it.* In fact, one might defend the importance of cultural literacy without any commitment to core curriculum or other paraphernalia of liberal education as a strategy (Hirsch 1987).

- *The presumed existence of a strong demand for liberal education.* In fact, evidence for such a demand is difficult to gauge and largely anecdotal. On the other hand, there is strong evidence of a growing demand for training and personal development activities, and massive sums of money have been spent on such activities by the public and private sectors. In Canada, we spend some $9 billion dollars for postsecondary education through our universities and colleges, but at least another $3 billion is spent by business, trade associations, and public and private agencies to produce postsecondary education privately. Indeed, some have argued, on the basis of extensive interviews with firms and public agencies, that a much higher proportion of postsecondary education is produced by this shadow higher education system. To a certain extent, these activities are complementary to the postsecondary education publicly produced, but much of it is a substitute — a focused, practical, vocationally-oriented substitute for what the public regards as unsatisfactory output by postsecondary educational institutions (Paquet 1988c). This sort of massive investment raises questions about the view that postsecondary education should drift toward a new classicism.

EDUCATION POLICY: A WICKED PROBLEM

Education has always had a variety of functions in society: to produce literate, responsible citizens; to acculturate a heterogeneous citizenry; to develop the human capital necessary for the maintenance and improvement of economic growth, competitiveness, and living standards; to allow individuals to develop character, self-awareness, interpersonal communication capabilities, and competence; to develop mind and ability to reason (Peterfreund 1976). This is a complex task, and over time a variety of groups have crafted different strategies to realize diverse parts of this ambitious agenda.

Yet there is no indisputable notion of what the goals should be in a pluralistic society. Education policy poses an ill-structured problem to policy analysts, what Rittel and Webber have labeled a *wicked problem* (Rittel and Webber 1973). As we saw in Chapter 2, such problems have two characteristics: the goals are not known or are very ambiguous and the means–ends relationships are highly uncertain and poorly understood. Rittel and Webber (1973) have spelled out some basic characteristics of wicked problems: they lack definitive formulation and a stopping rule as in a chess problem. In addition, solutions are not true-or-false but good-or-bad; every attempt at solving the problem counts significantly; and the planner has no right to be wrong.

Problématique

Educators, trainers, and developers defend different approaches. For *educators*, operating in the mislabeled "Rousseau-Dewey tradition," the shaping of the mind and the ability to reason is somewhat content-neutral and focused on general principles, on general knowledge; this is the way to learn how to think critically. For *trainers*, knowledge is skill and skill is knowledge, and there is no way to develop general transferable abilities without focusing on procedural and substantive schemata that are highly specific to the task at hand. For *developers*, the cornerstone might be loosely called an anthropological theory of education: knowledge and skills can be developed only on the basis of a capacity to grow as a human being within a human community to which one is acculturated (Hirsch 1987).

These three notions are ideals in most discussions. In fact, much of what is done under any of these labels turns out to have educational, training, and developmental components. Any curriculum, course, or seminar may be represented as existing somewhere within a triangle of human capital formation (Figure 6), where each apex is an ideal representation of each of these valuable types of human capital formation (Paquet 1988c).

The centre of gravity of the traditional Canadian postsecondary enterprise (PSE) — and of any other national system for that matter — should be mappable as a point or as a zone within this triangle. It is the result of a variety of private and public initiatives and policies that have favoured one or another component. Moreover, all such systems have evolved through time, and their drift should be traceable within the triangle. Indeed, ideally any PSE should, through a diversity of institutions, cater to the diversity of private demands and public needs, for there are important differences in the strategies pro-

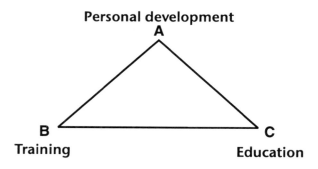

Figure 6. The Human Capital Formation Triangle.

posed by educators, trainers, and developers: educators bet on C as the baseline, trainers on B, and developers on A.

In the 19th and early 20th centuries in Canada, the mix of education, training, and development in traditional postsecondary education was probably more balanced than it is now. Much importance was given to each component of human capital formation, through a diversity of institutions and arrangements. During the first half of the 20th century, however, a formal philosophy of education, mistakenly ascribed to Jean-Jacques Rousseau and John Dewey, came to be in good currency. This so-called Rousseau–Dewey tradition emphasized education as a formal process, shaping mind and reason, that could be effected through content-neutral curricula. Education, as apex C, became the linchpin of the PSE. Segments of the PSE became more specialized, and a division of labour crystallized more sharply between the different institutions — universities, colleges, technical schools, etc. — with a higher or lower status depending on the mix of components they provided. Personal development ceased to be a central variable in the PSE.

Technical schools, colleges, and polytechnics developed a different brand of curriculum (more practical and more training intensive) but the social status of these programs remained relatively low, and the training they purported to give became more and more "tainted" by the ruling educational philosophy. Within universities, training-intensive activities have also been given lower status and are starved for resources. A recent report by the Canadian Chamber of Commerce was quite harsh in evaluating these institutions: the students are being trained on outdated equipment, and the quality of instruction is so low that "students graduate without sufficient skills or ability to pursue their chosen careers effectively" (Basken et al. 1988). Frank Stronach of Magna Corporation (in a personal interview) offered this very rationale for setting up his own training school.

Goals Not Known or Ambiguous

This problématique does not suggest that postsecondary education should adopt a particular contour or should emphasize, as a matter of course, one of the three components. The education system must fit within the broader appreciative system that a society elects. Particular societies with quite different appreciative systems and norms may select quite different patterns of educational institutions located in different portions of the triangle of human capital formation. Identifying the underlying norms and specifying the required directions for curriculum reform are very difficult tasks, for the basic goals are not agreed on or even unambiguous in a pluralistic society.

For instance, the directions of curriculum policy will be quite different if postsecondary education is considered as *closed* (i.e., independent of its social context) as opposed to seeing its survival as dependent on its capacity to adapt. In the same way, policy directions will be quite different if the postsecondary institution perceives its main goal as *training* individuals as opposed to *educating* them or to *developing* them into better human beings.

This leads to six quite different philosophies of postsecondary education as can be seen in Table 2 (Paquet and von Zur-Muehlen 1987: Chapter VI).

Table 2. Six Philosophies of Postsecondary Education.

		...depending on whether they are:	
		CLOSED SYSTEMS	OPEN SYSTEMS
with the main objective of	TRAINING	A science	B technology
	EDUCATION	C tradition	D culture
	DEVELOPING	E perception	F creativity

Institutions in position A wish to train people in the scientific method. Position C corresponds to institutions whose vocation is to train students to act in life in the light of a tradition used as an instrument to decode and make sense of the world. Position E institutions start from the individual and provide opportunities for fulfillment and self-improvement through improved perception. Those in position B train individuals in a way best suited to economic development. In this case science is no longer sufficient; the institution must also take into account the technical needs of society, and the institution becomes a location for the development of highly skilled manpower. Position D corresponds to a situation where it is felt that specialized and technical training does not suffice to ensure that individuals adapt well to an ever-changing scene: the institution then attempts to be the locus for the production of culture in the sense of Clifford Geertz (1965) — a set of control mechanisms, of approaches and ways of defining problems, of "programs" in the sense that the computer scientist uses the term. Position F institutions emphasize creativity and the development of innovative power as a way to cope with a changing environment.

This is only a preliminary and somewhat simplistic stylization of possible goals and environmental conditions, but it illustrates how the general strategy of postsecondary institutions depends fundamentally on the definition of such parameters.

Institutional Entrapments

The history of educational reform is replete with failed attempts to direct the education system in different directions by means of institutional repairs. Traditional educational practice has accommodated these innovations easily, particularly in times of affluence, when efficiency mattered little or when educational goals were overridden by other purposes: for example, keeping the baby boomers off the street and out of the job market. When resources became scarce, postsecondary education institutions felt threatened and reacted to pressure for change by making use of defense mechanisms to protect existing ways. They evolved into a dynamically conservative system, i.e., the system as a whole developed a tendency to remain the same and a capacity to resist change through a variety of means like unionization (Paquet 1988a). At present, the PSE is not unlike the building industry — "a coalition of shared interests built on prevailing technologies" (Schon 1971).

For education is a social system and, as with all social systems, it contains a *structure*, a *technology*, and a *theory*. "The structure is a set of roles and relations among individual members. The theory consists of the views held within the social system about its purposes, its operations, its environment, and its future. Both reflect, and in turn influence, the prevailing technology of the system" (Schon 1971). The best way to initiate change is to create a disequilibrium among these three components.

Changes in technology and structure are easily neutralized by the existing institutions' "dynamic conservatism"; viz. the numerous attempts to change the PSE by computerizing it or by imposing standardized curricula. The PSE has a capacity to repress such threats in much the same manner as bees in a beehive neutralize the danger when a mouse invades the beehive in winter. The bees sting the mouse to death, then encapsulate it in wax; it looks alive, but it has become innocuous. The PSE finds it easy to prevent change by opposing or delaying it, or through continuous chanting that there is no existing problem in the PSE that more public money could not cure. On the other hand, it finds it difficult to initiate real change because of the fact that the very technical and structural devices it might mobilize for change in its so-called collegial way are easily frustrated by internal systems (guilds, etc.) with their traditional conservatism.

It can be argued that it is quite different in the case of theory. Tampering with the way in which educationists perceive the world and themselves and the way in which they answer the question — what should we be doing? — is very potent. It may appear more difficult to effect, but the likelihood of generating a truly creative disequilibrium and cumulative causation is much higher from that angle. Although it is true that theorizing may be a tool for rationalizing away any alternative procedure as unsound, it is also a most powerful channel of attack when it can be shown that the whole knowledge production operation is wrongheaded.

Epistemology as Lever

The positivist revolution, together with the so-called Rousseau-Dewey tradition, shifted the centre of gravity of the PSE by imposing a certain formalism on it: there was more and more emphasis on theory, general principles, and "methodism" and less and less on matters pertaining to the "oral," the "particular," the "local," and the "timely" (Paquet 1988a; Toulmin 1988). What has evolved in universities is a curriculum made up of a variety of general principles and broad surveys, providing the necessary elements for the educated person to learn to think critically. The idea of a true vocationally-oriented higher education system has disappeared (Gunderson 1978) and the ruling philosophy of education has percolated down to the secondary level: even there, the skill component has dwindled and general content-free curricula prospered (Adams 1980).

But there has been a revival of practical philosophy in recent years (Toulmin 1988), and the ruling philosophy of education has been challenged by recent work on cognition. Critical thinking, it would appear, evolves not from general content-free principles or methodologies, but from schemata that are highly specific to the task at hand and that are not easily transferable from one task to the next. Developing a human being is, therefore, ensuring that he or she acquires a fair number of such schemata, shared by others in the community, so as to be able to communicate competently and effectively with them — providing the person with a sort of "cultural currency" in the sense that economists give to existing national currencies (Hirsch 1987).

The development of this basic currency — capacious and vague, but fundamental to communicative competence and competitiveness — cannot be ensured either through general disembodied principles, in the manner of the traditional curricula, or simply through skill-building, in the manner one proceeds to coach an athlete to success. Facts and skills are inseparable and *background knowledge* — even that which is specific culturally and nationally — is of great import in the development of critical reason, skills, and personal growth as a competent citizen. Traditionally, universities and colleges have provided through their core curriculum some smattering of background knowledge, but most often this has degenerated into formal general principles built into rigid curricula rather than being closely related to the national community, to the personal circumstances of students, and to schemata likely to be of use.

A revolution at the epistemological level is raising questions about existing structures and technologies in the PSE and is, therefore, creating pressure for change. Indeed, it may be said that one of the reasons why the PSE has chosen to insulate itself from the teachings of its own schools of education or to belittle considerably the significance of what might be learned from them is that such insulation constitutes an apt defense mechanism.

A different image of educating, i.e., of imparting knowledge, flows from the work of Schon (1983) on the epistemology of practice. Schon shows that the dominant model of technical rationality wrongly presumes that knowledge flows from underlying disciplines (basic science) to applied science to actual performance of services to clients and society. For this narrow view of knowledge flow — a sort of one-way street — he substitutes a two-way approach, emphasizing knowing-in-action/reflection-in-action, where knowledge emerges equally well from groping with situations and from surprises leading to on-the-spot experiments and knowledge creation.

The implications of this different approach to the professional education process are significant: an emphasis on the development of skills and a capacity for conversation with the situation though reflective practicum. It translates into a different curriculum (Schon 1987).

How Do We Learn?

One should not presume that there is unanimity on the epistemological front. Research on cognitive skills is buzzing with competing paradigms and is characterized by strong disagreements among critics of the current conventional wisdom.

Herbert Simon and others (Larkin et al. 1980) have been arguing that cognitive skills "depend on procedural and substantive schemata that are highly specific to the task at hand" and cast doubt on the idea that there are general or transferable cognitive skills and on the so-called Rousseau-Dewey tradition that has led us to believe that if students look at a few cases, they will understand general principles and learn how to think critically (Hirsch 1987). This work maintains that much of education is the imparting of a large number of schemata, and that this requires "extensive knowledge of specifics."

In this system, the process of abstraction provides bridges from sensations to higher levels of thought. The ladder of abstraction begins with sensory data from repeated observations; from these, observed replicated associations emerge and are memorized; the knowledge gained by association is generalized by inference to classes of objects and associations between classes of objects, such as those of cause and effect. Knowledge is thus the accumulation of these tried and true associations, and education becomes the distribution of accumulated knowledge (Emery 1980).

This approach departs from tradition and re-introduces specifics (the local, the timely, the oral, the particular) into the process of knowledge acquisition. However, many observers would say that it does not go far enough because this approach remains based on a theory of perception that leaves much to be desired: "to perceive the world one must already have ideas about it. Knowledge of the world is explained by assuming that knowledge of the world exists. Whether the ideas are learned or innate makes no difference; the fallacy lies in circular reasoning" (Gibson 1979: 304).

An alternative paradigm starts from a different theory of perception, a theory of direct perception that has no need for a ladder of abstraction. This Gibsonian (1979) approach may be summarized as follows:

- The act of picking up information is continuous — an activity that is ceaseless and unbroken.

- What is perceived are places, attached objects, detached objects, and substances, together with events that are modifications of these things.

- Information is the specification of the observer's environment.

- The perceptual system is a mode of overt attention: it can explore, investigate, adjust, optimize, extract.
- The perceptual system registers persistence and change.
- The process of information pick-up is susceptible to development and learning: better extracting, exploring, etc.

This new theory of active perception has important educational implications (Emery 1980):

- Because limitless information is available in the environment, access is restricted only by habits of perception.
- The perceptual systems can be improved: this is "an education in *searching* with our own perceptual systems, not an education in how to someday *research* in the cumulated pile of so-called social knowledge" (Emery 1980:29).
- Education is "learning to learn" from our own perceptions.

This foray into cognitive psychology is not an aside: it is central to the main theme of education reform. For these shifts from general principles to schemata, and from schemata to direct perception suggest different conceptions of knowledge and, consequently, different notions of education. The further one moves away from a view of knowledge attributed to Rousseau-Dewey toward a view of knowledge à la Gibson (with the Simon-Hirsch view standing somewhat in the middle), the less persuasive is the case for a standard liberal-education core curriculum.

In place of an educational system based on the accumulation of proven knowledge by memorization of established associations, rules of classification, and logical inference and based on students being taught to distrust their personal experience as a guide to knowledge (the goal is to produce a critical, disciplined, and literate mind), one is led to suggest one starting with the perception and experience of the individual, regarding education as the training of attention and higher studies as providing aided modes of apprehension or extraction of information (by means of instruments to allow metric knowledge; by means of language to make knowing explicit instead of tacit; and by means of pictures to extend perceiving and consolidate the gains of perceiving) (Gibson 1979; Emery 1980).

If one accepts a Gibsonian view of the world, knowledge is only restricted by our habits of perception, and one may and must educate one's perceptual systems. This entails recentring education on the process of searching, on learning to explore and learn, for the weight of evidence is that even literate adults find it difficult to use their own perceptions.

This revolution, in turn, calls for an education process that puts much more emphasis on exploration and playfulness than is usually accepted in the PSE, for this is the way to enhance the capability to extract information from our worlds (March 1976). The usual university insists above all that it must produce "disciplined intelligence... that is trained in logic and logical analysis" (Ross 1961). What is emerging from the new epistemology is a much broader approach that covers a variety of types of thinking — mathematical, logical, lateral, etc. (De Bono 1969) and this does not mesh well with the way in which the PSE perceives its vocation and its task (Paquet 1985b).

Education Reform as Social Learning

At a time when the possibility of designing a liberal education curriculum is examined, it is essential to ascertain in some way what the ends of general education are and what kind or type of curriculum design is likely to lead in this direction in the light of what is known about cognition and learning.

On these questions, there is no clear *a priori* choice one can offer from the policymaker's point of view among mixes of goals, or among theories of knowledge acquisition, or among institutional/curricular arrangements likely to accomplish certain ends. This is the nature of a wicked problem. Policy analysts faced with ill-structured problems must *learn on the job* about both the configuration of facts, and the configuration of values, but they must also manage to learn from the stakeholders in the policy game and from the many groups at the periphery who are in possession of important *local knowledge*, for without their participation no effective policy can be implemented.

Friedmann and Abonyi's (1976) *social learning model of policy research* is a way to deal with these wicked problems (see Chapter 2). In Figure 5, "cognition is linked to the world of events via social action and the result of that action. The adequacy of a theory of reality, and/or the political strategy is therefore dependent on the results of action and the extent to which these results satisfy the given social values" (Friedmann 1978).

CONCLUSION

The challenge put to the PSE by the epistemological revolution underway is bound to entail much more than the reshuffling of a few courses, the development of a core curriculum, or the insertion in the curricula — one way or another — of the 5000 essential names, phrases, dates, and concepts to ensure "cultural literacy," the Hirsch (1987) middle-of-the road solution. It forces a serious rethinking of what education is all about and it emphasizes the need to launch a social learning experiment to learn how "to learn how to learn."

The debate on liberal education has posed the problem of "the ends of general education and about the kind and type of general education that will best serve those ends" (Karelis 1989). In that sense, it has put on the front burner an issue that the PSE has been refusing to face for some time.

Those arguing for liberal education must establish why such a strategy would improve whatever postsecondary education wants to do; and we are back to the more general questions raised above. These more general questions have to be probed if one is to be able to put forward a strategy likely to be effective. Yet, there is no way to learn about these issues except through action hypotheses.

The challenge put forward by the liberal education debate cannot, therefore, be resolved *a priori*. It cannot be resolved in isolation either. What is required is a broad-based social inquiry into the problems of higher education very much on the model of the Energy Options Process launched in 1987 to provide an opportunity for a dialogue among Canadians about the common energy future (see Chapter 5). The resulting report (Kierans et al. 1988), although somewhat biased and unsatisfactory, showed that much had been learned within one year through a process of wide consultation with all interested parties and groups throughout the country.

It may well be that nothing less than such a process can clarify the objectives of our education system and answer questions about the kind of postsecondary education we should design for our grandchildren. The process is difficult to manage and does not always generate unambiguous or satisfactory answers (see Chapter 5); moreover, it is not likely that such a broad consultation can be engineered easily given the federal–provincial quagmire surrounding all issues educational in Canada. But such an inquiry may be the only vehicle likely to generate the sort of debate on postsecondary education that is so urgently needed. The problem of higher education is no easier to tackle than biculturalism or transportation; so, there is no reason to believe that anything short of an inquiry of the sort suggested is likely to bring forth the feasible, acceptable, and implementable solutions we are looking for.

Some may argue that we have shifted the debate from a simple question about liberal education to the broad question of higher education in general. This is undoubtedly true. One of the characteristics of wicked problems is that they are often a symptom of a "higher-order problem." Thus, crime in the street may be a symptom of general moral decay, lack of opportunity, poverty, etc. (Rittel and Webber 1973). In the same manner, the liberal education debate is an echo of a higher-order malaise in the postsecondary education system. The malaise in education may also reflect some still higher-order malaise in our society. The best way to deal with lower-order issues is not to deal with them in a restrictive way if they are only symptoms. One might be more effective by tackling the problem on as high a level as possible.

PART II

SOCIAL LEARNING IN ACTION:
D – ADMINISTRATIVE PERSPECTIVES

CHAPTER 9

HOW TO SCHEME VIRTUOUSLY: THE ROLE OF PUBLIC SERVICE COMMISSIONS IN MEETING THE NEEDS OF CHANGING SOCIETIES*

> There is only one excuse for a lecture:
> to challenge.
>
> – *Karl Popper*

It is presumptuous for a career academic to address practical men and women holding important responsibilities in human affairs on the role of their agencies in meeting the needs of changing societies. This borders on temerity when the group of experts represents a wide array of cultural and national circumstances, especially when the academic in question is known to have traveled widely only in Ottawa. It becomes daredeviltry to do so at a time when the ground is in motion.

Yet there is some merit in listening to the interrogations of a lay person: much merit for *le profane* — a dangerous word used in French to refer to the uninitiated. There is much to be learned by the lay person in the process of tackling such a task; there is also some merit for the initiated to hear the lay person, if only to understand better what lies behind the puzzlement and criticism they face in their rapports with the public.

My only credentials for this task, besides a quarter of a century of casual public service watching, stem from some adventurous comments I made on the Canadian Public Service Commission (Paquet 1985c). The paper was published, but I was also relieved, as a result, of civic duty as a member of the Auditor General's Comprehensive Auditing Task Force charged with an assessment of the PSC. I learned first-hand that criticizing the PSC can be perilous. I hope that, in this second round of critical discussion of the roles of public service commissions (PSCs) and kindred institutions, I will succeed in airing my interrogations, and even in making some suggestions, without encountering the anger of the experts.

* Parts of this material appeared in "Virtuous Scheming." *Policy Options*, 1989, 10(6), 8–12. The assistance of Jeffrey Holmes and Marc Racette is gratefully acknowledged.

Let me start with a few basic propositions:

- despite the contemporary rhetoric about the demise of the state and the downsizing of governments everywhere, the state will not play a lesser role in our socioeconomies in the future;
- the role of the state, however, will be quite different; there will be a shift from a regulatory to a strategic function (Paquet 1978b; Navarre 1986);
- human resource management is likely to be much more complex in this new setting;
- PSCs are bound to be key players in the strategic management of the public household;
- to play this role PSCs will need to be proactive and become more experimental instead of focusing on their traditional functions.

THE CHALLENGES OF GOVERNANCE

Canada is relatively young as a modern administrative entity. Yet, paradoxically, like many other young Commonwealth countries, it is also *an aging socioeconomy*. The last 30 years of relentless rule-making and institution-building have developed in our economies some incapacity to adapt and transform easily. There are only a few prognoses and therapies for such socioeconomies (Kindleberger 1978):

- building up protective barriers against foreign competition and bundling up in blankets;
- searching for a Fountain of Youth under the guidance of an economic Ponce de León; or
- inventing ways to dissolve the social arteriosclerotic structures in the body politic.

This painful third way is unfortunately the only reasonable one to follow. Many countries have crafted a strategy of this sort over the last decade. But, because much of this sclerosis has also been diagnosed as being of the iatrogenetic variety (i.e., generated by ill-inspired policies), many have seized on a philosophy of downsizing the public sector as the only way to make our socioeconomies less sclerotic. This, in turn, has triggered the recent efforts to reverse the vast transfer of material, human, and financial resources from society to state that occurred in the post-World War II period — to replace state regulation by self-regulation in a civil society equipped with a strengthened legal framework (Cohen-Tanugi 1985). These dual objectives (to rejuvenate the socioeconomy and to downsize the public sector) have become confounded.

Those bold enough to attempt to refurbish the state apparatus to invest it with a renewed capacity to deal effectively with the changing needs of society have had to face striking challenges. The *first major challenge* was that whatever might be accomplished would have to be done with fewer rather than more resources.

The *second challenge* has come from growth: from the world population increase and from the new form of knowledge-based development of our socioeconomies. Demographic growth has meant a larger demand for public service, with geometrically expanded personnel management problems, whereas the development of knowledge-based economies has entailed the demand for services that were not necessarily those provided by the state in the heyday of industrial growth. Because information and knowledge are not handled as well by markets as simple commodities, the need for nonmarket coordination has grown considerably with the development of the information economy. Indeed, the very notion of state intervention has experienced a fundamental transformation: in the world of the mass economy, governments built their legitimacy on their roles as agents of protection, stabilization, and redistribution; in the information economy, governments have to become agents of integration, coordination, and networking (Paquet 1985c).

The *third challenge* has come from the growing involvement of states and governments in matters of culture and values. Formerly, governments and their public services were not asked to act as regularly as they are now as referees between stakeholders in these realms. But the growing importance of affairs of the mind in the information economy has led governments to become more and more involved in adjudicating matters of values. This is not only of consequence in the rapports between government and the population, but it is a matter that has become very important internally, in the operations of government, as new norms of equitable treatment of employees and different types of affirmative action in dealing with racial, linguistic, or gender groups, etc., have arisen. These have created new constraints on the mode of delivery of public service. Administration has become philosophy-in-action and is becoming more so all the time (Dlugos and Weiermair 1981; Hodgkinson 1983; Mitroff 1983).

The *fourth challenge* is the world scale of many of the new problems facing public servants: from environmental issues, to urbanization processes, to technological change — issues that cannot either be abandoned to the market forces or be controlled by any national government in isolation, even under the most auspicious circumstances. This calls for new forms of collaboration between national organizations and going concerns, which have traditionally perceived themselves as in conflict but whose fates have become positively correlated in these turbulent times.

Finally, all our public administration apparatuses are frightfully deficient in the face of these new challenges. At the very moment when problems are becoming more difficult to solve, the public bureaucracies are under attack for their inadequacy. Although this is true to different degrees as one roams the continents, the style and procedures of public administration have been, and remain to a great extent

> Legalistic, formalistic, inelastic and authoritarian, with almost unassailable status arrangements... corruption is pervasive; there is no orientation towards goal setting and individual initiative is strangled. Functions are restricted to control and regulation plus a few limited services, with a marked

bias in the direction of overcentralization. There is what amounts to a continuous administrative crisis. [Goldstaub 1981]

This general diagnosis applies to developed and developing countries: the key difference is that the problems do not appear insoluble when resources are abundant; in less wealthy countries, the disproportion between the scale of the problems and the resources available to deal with them is awesome. But this is a difference in scale not in kind.

The situation is clear: more public service of a more complex sort has to be performed with fewer resources by public-sector organizations and personnel who do not appear to be capable of delivering the goods.

THE TASKS GOVERNMENT SHOULD/ SHOULD NOT TAKE ON

The growing complexity, turbulence, and interdependence in the global socioeconomic environment have led to a loss of the stable state and to an evolution in government functions. It is no longer possible to regard the state as a simple policeman enforcing certain rules, acting as protector and provider in a placid environment. Those functions persist but they are no longer the only responsibilities of the state. Governments have had to develop capacities to act as animateurs, facilitators, and negotiators, as accelerating change and growing related uncertainty create circumstances where no simple rules will do, where judgment is called for (Vickers 1965).

The hierarchy of layers of public administration — ranging through politics, policymaking, implementation, administration, operations — still exists, but the need to attend to each of these with sensitivity to their novel particular constraints has been heightened. Over the last 20 years, both industrial countries and underdeveloped economies have seen a dramatic change in the nature of the perception of government and in the way in which government is expected to carry out its duties (Solo 1975; Islam and Hénault 1979): a shift from a Taylorian view of public administration to an *interactive* perception of the process of public management (Friedmann and Abonyi 1976; see also Chapter 5, this volume).

In the Taylorian model, the different layers of the hierarchy are presumed to trigger a cascading of decisions from top to bottom: the political body determining the goals, and the implementation process apparently occurring mechanically through controlled activities of functionaries. In the interactive model, this one-way process of goal-setting-cum-control is replaced by a two-way process putting greater emphasis on different areas of concern — intelligence (i.e., gathering, processing, and interpreting the information needed for policy decisions) *and* innovation (i.e., changes in the design of administrative arrangements). In this context, the problem to be solved is regarded from the start as ill-structured, i.e., the goals are not spelled out and the means-end relationship is blurred. Consequently, the process of public administration and government becomes a *learning process* (Wilensky 1967; Paquet 1971; Schon 1971).

Government is hesitant to accept this second mode of operation and the new sort of policy research it entails. Despite the rhetoric and the language of experimentation that is in good currency, government continues to perceive itself as the centre and to view society as the periphery. Much of what passes for policy and administration are efforts by governments to induce groups at the periphery to conform to central policy. By contrast, social learning entails listening to the periphery, interacting with the periphery in such a way that the centre becomes a party (but only one of many) in identifying, analyzing, and solving society's problems. This in turn calls for policy research, policy-making, and administration to take on a cybernetic flavour: it is no longer a simple delivery system but a continuing process of information-gathering and organization redesign leading to a continuing redefinition of the goals and reassessment of the directions of policy (Paquet 1971).

Such a need for local participation in the design and implementation of policy and for participation in the minding of the public household is a central feature of the public philosophy required to reform the administrative process. It postulates that local knowledge is crucially important in the crafting of policy. Administration becomes a process of *mutual education*. This mutual education leads first to a recognition that the state does not necessarily belong in every aspect of the life of citizens. Second, learning must also reveal where the state needs to play a role as animateur and what structures will be necessary for it to play such a role effectively. Third, learning must show what sort of areas should simply be abandoned to private activities or to community work and what sort of structures might be useful to ensure that such activities will be conducted according to acceptable norms of efficiency and fairness.

PSCs must play a key role in shaping this broad process of mutual learning. Not to do so would be tantamount to allowing the system to evolve as if public services were unconcerned, and accepting a limited technical staffing management role. This would almost condemn PSCs to ineffectiveness. Ignoring its design role would be akin to a central bank being unconcerned about the nature of financial institutions and their regulation.

The allocation of functions (among the private, public, and civic sectors and within the public sector among the local, provincial, regional, and national levels) is not an easy task, and it is unlikely that PSCs will have a final say on such matters. However, as central agencies equipped with a fair sense of what is feasible and implementable, public services might benefit immensely from getting involved in the design of the institutions they will have to staff. Otherwise, they might find themselves relegated to an *ex post* role, on the personnel front, not dissimilar to the one played by the Auditor General on the financial side, while they should legitimately expect to play also an *ex ante* role, very much akin to the role of a Comptroller General on the human resources front.

Each country must design its own brand of allocation of functions among the public, private, and civic households and within the public household. In each case, it will be inspired by ideology and culture, effectiveness concerns, political and sociocultural circumstances. Yet within these country-specific constraints, a few general principles might be used as a basic sextant in designing a starting point for the process of social learning (Kirby 1980; Paquet 1988d):

- the principle of government exiting from routine management of nonessential or nonstrategic sectors;

- the principle of decentralization and devolution and of strengthening or creating intermediary organizations capable of acting as relay stations in this process of mutual education;

- the principle of full costing of public service;

- the principle of revenue dependency for all units where the services have the potential of being marketed;

- the principle of encouraging direct private–public competition;

- the principle that, if a subsidy must be given, it should be given to the consumers;

- the principle of a necessary culture of public service through mission statements, corporate plans, and a legitimate system of status and rewards.

This would amount to a philosophy of public service that might dramatically transform the contours of public service: not less government but a different form of government.

These principles of organization or institution design are meant to be only a starting point in discussions likely to lead to a set of *meta-rules* in the management of the public household. Most project managers define such meta-rules in their project manuals. What is necessary for PSCs is a project manual adapted to their own circumstances.

Completely abandoning these broad concerns to political leaders may be disastrous for PSCs. Given the constraints of values and circumstances, not all possible allocations of tasks between sectors are equally feasible, implementable, and manageable. If PSCs are to ensure that they will be able to do the best they can with reduced resources, it may not be unimportant for them to have a say in shaping the tasks devolved to them. This clearly means a redefinition of the central functions of PSCs: abandoning the security-generating in-basket/out-basket routine management and contracting-out of such services (Kemball 1984), but allocating more of the reduced resources to the intelligence, innovation, and design functions.

These are important *new roles* for PSCs in increasingly organizational states (Laumann and Knoke 1988), roles of an entrepreneurial sort (Giersch 1984). PSCs have neglected this side of their work in the past: as a result, in most countries, policy reviews or royal commissions have been struck, from time to time, reminding them that these concerns would not go away.

PUBLIC SERVICE COMMISSIONS AS DESIGNERS

Once it is decided that an activity should fall under the responsibility of the state in some way and that PSCs will have to overview its organization and staffing, the key job is to determine how this task will be despatched. These decisions are rarely made once and for all. The form of the required organization and institution often evolve in unexpected ways. But there is still a need to work at the architecture of the organization and institution from the start to achieve *effectiveness, efficiency, economy,* and *equity*: doing the right thing, doing the thing right, doing it cheaply, and doing it fairly.

Organizations and institutions are the tools that refurbished PSCs have to design. These are quite different creatures: an organization is, more or less, a technical instrument, an expendable tool; whereas an institution is related to society's requirements, it embodies its norms and values. An institution may be said to be viable if it "creates conditions in which the competencies of its personnel are well utilized, *and* the positive values applied to structures related to its clients are also applied to structures related to its members" (Perlmutter 1965). In many ways, PSCs as designers must get away from the job of organization-building (which is obviously tempting because it is easier) and get involved in the construction of viable institutions. This in turn requires a good understanding of institution-building taking into account people, values, and environments.

Because these parameters are quite different from country to country, one cannot expect to be able to transplant institutions from one setting to another without major adaptations.

This is hardly the place to develop a primer on social architecture but it might be useful to summarize basic principles of institution-building before proceeding to specific recommendations about the way PSCs might design new institutions. Perlmutter (1965) has prepared a textbook for social architects. It both sketches the conceptual requirements and provides a step-by-step description of the working relationship between social architects and their clients in the institution-building process. (A statement of the seven conceptual components of a theory of social architecture as seen by Perlmutter is presented in the appendix at the end of this chapter.)

Conceptually, institution-building is the outcome of *mutual education* of the architect and of the clients and it is based on a sort of intercreation process leading both parties to develop jointly a structure that takes as fully as possible into account the human and technical criteria of effectiveness in a global sense (including positive values such as health, respect for the individual, and acquisition of skills — technical and interpersonal).

But there is more to building an institution than simply the conceptual basis. The practice of institution-building must proceed on the basis of a set of clear assumptions that one must fully realize and steps one must go through. Again Perlmutter (1965) spells this out clearly:

- preliminary mutual exploration of the clients' commitment to build;

- mission of the institution and central objectives of the clients;
- alternative routes to building objectives;
- choice and commitment to a specific strategy;
- implementation process;
- validation and stabilization.

PSCs, as designers of institutions, have to acquire a research capability if they are to perform this sort of task. At present, it is fair to say that, in most countries, no central agency is charged with organizational and institutional design. As a result, much of it is improvised at the local level and PSCs are, then, asked to staff organizations and institutions that often turn out to be unworkable.

This research requirement has to go much beyond the usual studies of remuneration, evaluation, training, and classification which have used much of the time of PSCs in the past. It is not that these requirements have to be ignored or their importance downplayed. But effectiveness cannot be achieved by concentrating on such plumbing issues. The whole process of personnel management has to be put in broader perspective and the PSCs have to be able to contribute in a meaningful way to this broader perspective through an alternative approach to public policy. PSCs would fill a vacuum in so doing and might succeed in developing a higher status within the government apparatus if they were to become not only the locus of expertise on remuneration and classification, but also the place where expertise on organizational and institutional design resides.

The social learning framework suggested by Friedmann and Abonyi (1976) might be an interesting policy framework to help the PSCs develop this new role as designers (Figure 5). It calls for a new sort of policy research developed not on the sole basis of analysis of technical data, but on the basis of a full exploration of values, political gaming and collective action as it evolves in the civil society (see Chapters 2 and 5).

On the basis of such policy research — done nowhere in governments except sometimes through task forces and royal commissions — PSCs might be in a position to suggest organizational/institutional designs that will not only be efficient, but will also likely provide the ongoing intelligence, the innovative capability, the political viability, the sensitivity to evolving values, and the mobilization and commitment necessary for the public organizations/institutions to perform well.

PUBLIC SERVICE COMMISSIONS AS ANIMATEURS

The research function necessary for the PSCs to become effective designers is also necessary if they are to become effective animateurs. The PSCs have to develop a theory of human behaviour if they are to have any impact on the ethos of the public household and the organizational culture of the public service. Professionalism, collective pride, and a sense of civic responsibility have disappeared to a great extent from the public service. In its place, one finds anomie, alienation, corruption, and a fundamental lack of commitment to the organization/institution.

A recent study in Canada has shown that loyalty and commitment in the public service is much lower than in the private sector (Zussman and Jabes 1987). This has been interpreted as resulting from a variety of causes. However, the root cause of this disenchantment is easily summarized under two headings: flawed organization/institution designs and poor understanding of the motivation of public servants.

I suggested above that the flawed designs could be resolved by some architectural repairs or through preventive architecture according to certain principles, and that experimentation with new structures would be a central outcome of new policy research culminating in social learning. But institutional architecture will not suffice. Nothing less than a new concept of *citizenship* needs to be developed and, concomitantly, a new concept of the appropriate way for public servants to deal with the new citizens inside and outside the civil service (see Chapter 7, this volume). Private firms have learned to deal with their employees and customers in new ways over the last few years: the manager in both the private and the public sectors has to become an *anthropologist* (Boisot 1987).

Managing an organization/institution requires a capacity to understand the sociocultural circumstances of the employees. If the employees are not properly trained, if their social responsibilities outpace their income, or if their remuneration is whimsically defined, it is hardly surprising that motivation and competence are wanting. Before one is tempted to engage in elaborate efforts to provide leadership and to stimulate entrepreneurship in the public service, one has to ensure that the *basics* are there. These basic components are somewhat trivial but fundamental:

- a well-established recruitment and selection capability;
- a sound classification/evaluation/compensation system;
- a fair remuneration policy;
- a good performance evaluation scheme;
- a clearly stated human resource development policy;
- good training arrangements and facilities.

None of these basic features can be imported ready-made from other countries: they depend on the dominant values and the sociocultural underground. Some *organizational features* may be importable, but many *institutional features* have to be learned locally and must fit local circumstances. For example, in societies where the central institution is the family, any tacked-on administrative organization is simply going to be milked in the name of family priorities, and no "sermon on the Mount" will do any good.

The role of PSCs as animateurs entails balancing coercion (i.e., external pressure) with effective stimulation (i.e., internal pressure). The simplest way to apply coercion is still competition: it provides a decentralized and omnipresent external pressure to perform according to certain standards. The best way to generate internal pressure is to develop an organizational culture likely to reduce shirking and corruption.

There has been undue reliance on competition as the guiding force. Peter Drucker (1988) has reminded managers that organizations of the year 2000 will look much more like symphony orchestras, hospitals, and universities than like the typical manufacturing concerns of the 1950s. Much of Drucker's argument indicates that private concerns will look more and more like public concerns in the year 2000 and that there will then be a need for mechanisms of motivation more sophisticated than those emanating from simple market competition: new sociocultural institutions creating a unified vision, developing collective pride, building an *esprit de clan*, and getting professionalism to act as a moral bond to complement the commercial and utilitarian pressures (Haworth 1977).

The importance of professionalism as a bond and of professional identification as a way to bring "commitment to assure that action is characterized by excellence" (Haworth 1977) has been underestimated, very much like clan-type relationships within organizations (Ouchi 1980). Indeed the extraordinary wealth of motivational forces contained in the pursuit of excitement and novelty has hardly been tapped (Scitovsky 1976; Servan-Schreiber 1986). Yet these represent a promising basis on which to build commitment, loyalty, creativity.

There has been a *grand malaise* in public services everywhere and the fundamental questions of values, leadership, morale, and motivation have now been put on the agenda. It has reached such a critical level that even the media are taking notice. Yet little has been done to probe these dimensions because the social sciences as currently practised are ill-equipped to deal with them (Paquet 1988a).

It is not clear that the industrialized countries have performed any better than developing socioeconomies in tackling this task: the lack of concern for values and related dimensions in the large bureaucracies of industrialized nations has become so ingrained that it may be even more difficult to get their PSCs to acknowledge the existence of such problems. On the Canadian scene, it is not unfair to say that the artillery of defense mechanisms deployed in response to studies, such as those of Nicole Morgan (1981, 1985) and the Zussman/Jabes (1987) team has been impressive, and the degree of cognitive dissonance that has marred the interpretation of their results extremely high.

However, built into the social learning paradigm (sketched in Chapter 2 and mentioned above), there is the capacity to bring the social sciences back to their original questions, back to mixed positive/normative concerns. Such an approach might entail a long overdue *remise en question* of the methodological naïveté and pretensions of the social sciences (Schrag 1980). The roots of this crisis of the social sciences can be traced back to the 17th century philosophers who have set the research agenda in a theory-centred style bent on framing solutions in timeless universal terms. As a result there has been an unholy shift of what is regarded as interesting from the oral to the written, from the particular to the universal, from the local to the general, and from the timely to the timeless (Toulmin 1988). Yet the practical questions are calling for timely, local, and particular answers.

The social learning paradigm is only one of many new approaches signal-ing a move back to those very things that made social sciences and philosophy "practical," and case studies and case ethics (casuistry) are not maligned as much and as openly as they used to be. There has been a growing concern over the moral dimensions of statecraft in the recent past (Waldo 1980; Dwivedi 1987). The refurbished social sciences that one hopes will ensue from this renewed concern for practical affairs and normative values may pave the way to new policy research into the central issues mentioned above.

IN PRAISE OF SHORTCUTS

The time may be long before PSCs are allowed to transform themselves into the informed and competent designers and animateurs we might wish them to be. In the meantime, there is room for experimentation based on a sound appraisal of where each PSC starts from: a point that is quite different (culturally and administratively) for each. The basic features of any legitimate public service (listed in the previous section) must be in place: for no meaningful reform movement can be built on whimsical remuneration, classification, and evaluation. One must also realize that only 5% of public administrators advise ministers on policy issues, while 95% are involved in routine work. Both groups cannot be motivated by the same techniques: a two-track system will have to be put in place. Studies have already shown where the crucial points are in each case (Montgomery 1986; Glaser 1988).

Betting on New Organizational/Institutional Forms

One of the central weaknesses of public bureaucracies is the overcentralized nature of their operations. Much can be said, therefore, in favour of experi-menting with techniques of *decentralization of decision-making*. This has been a common feature of the newly industrializing countries: they have allowed "key state actors and bureaucracies to perform as economic entrepreneurs" (Luke 1986). This sort of flexibility and freedom cannot be exercised without the appropriate framework of participation and accountability, but there have been many proposals that look promising.

One approach is to experiment on a small scale with *intrapreneurship*, i.e., the development of "profit centres" within larger bureaucracies (Macrae 1982). The decision to separate some portion of the work in public bureauc-racies and to subcontract it to interested groups of employees may appear far-fetched at this time, but it amounts to nothing more than the simple decision to make-or-buy that bureaucracies all around the world are forced to make. The question is simply that what is made internally by a bureaucracy might be produced more efficiently by a "minifirm," either inside or outside the bureaucracy. Peter Kemball (1984) has shown how this can be done quite simply, and he has worked out a scheme through which a standing offer might be extended: anyone inside or outside the bureaucracy "who can deliver a service currently being offered by government at the current quality level and at a saving of 50 percent of current costs will be awarded a multi-year franchise or license to do so, upon submission of a credible plan of action."

Another approach is to go directly to the concept of *franchising* and to carve out of the existing bureaucratic work some portion that could, experimentally but legitimately, be contracted out. On matters like training and auditing, this is already done. The solution is all the more appealing if one is willing to consider the possibility of allowing some local concern to bid on a franchise from a well-organized international network providing instant know-how and quality control. There is no reason to believe that there would be adverse reactions to such experiments any more than there has been when local governments have begun to contract out services like sweeping hospitals or collecting rubbish. One advantage of franchising is that it might provide an ideal vehicle for technology transfer: if an advanced country like Canada that has developed expertise in services like classification were to develop a franchise system open to groups capable of serving other PSCs in the developing world, one might be able to ensure high-quality service by nationals under stringent franchise rules (quality control, standards, etc.) at much lower costs than at present (Bettinger 1978).

Crafting New Public Service Cultures

Tinkering experimentally with institutional forms will not suffice. It might, at best, inspire the top quartile of a bureaucracy to become intrapreneurs or project leaders. To reach down into the other levels, it will be necessary to create *a new public service culture*: as new norms come to be in good currency in public institutions and organizations, rules will become less important. However, the new norms will not be developed without an *acculturation* mechanism. This mechanism is training and development. Private firms have used it extremely well, and there is no reason to believe that public bureaucracies could not do the same.

Training and development are the ideal vehicles in which to send throughout the organization the philosophy, norms, and cultural distinctiveness one wishes to develop and to show how the reward system is linked to this philosophy. Dissemination of information about the goals, strategies, and tactics of the government apparatus may be effected this way, and this message is often much more important that the so-called technical know-how imparted. Yet, it is surprising to find that this is not done by public service training agencies (Dwivedi and Engelbert 1981). Training and development is also the channel through which professional standards and professionalism may be best inculcated. With professionalism comes the basis for the development of self-enforced norms, collective self-reliance, and a lessening of corruption. Nothing less than a *mafia* can be developed in this way: a group having attended the same courses, speaking the same "language," and consequently communicating more effectively across departments (Carmichael 1986; McAllister 1987).

As for the morale and motivation of public servants, there can be no instant fix. A renewed PSC would do much toward solving the morale and motivation problem. Under the present arrangements, with their byzantine rules and regulations, civil servants are becoming impersonal and irresponsible (i.e., incapable of responding effectively) because it is no longer clear to whom they should respond and to whose needs they should attend. Much depends on the development of a home-grown management culture in the public sector. This, in turn, depends much on the role that the PSCs appropriate. Much could be accomplished if PSCs could recast their role away from an ever-interfering hand between management and staff toward a three-pronged function: (1) a recruitment service at the lower level (where large numbers trigger economies of scale), (2) an audit/certifying agent to ensure that proper procedures have been followed in the case of higher appointments, classification, promotion, etc., and (3) an agency of designers and animateurs along the lines suggested above.

One cannot hope to develop an "esprit de corps" (Fayol 1949) and eliminate "soldiering" (Taylor 1911) — a work phenomenon whereby average productivity approximates that of the *least* productive worker — without attacking the principal cause of "soldiering" and low productivity, i.e., the system of compensation. One might experiment with decentralization of fiscal authority at the departmental level and with discretionary authority for unit managers to "increase salaries of their subordinates *but only as a group* and only if the unit meets a predetermined output" (Halpern et al. 1988). This would reintroduce the principle of merit into public service compensation on a broader scale: not at the level of the individual but of the unit. This sort of compensation, based on a consensus or negotiated agreement about fair and meaningful work goals, would encourage functional cooperation and maximum employee input, eliminate soldiering, take full advantage of the informal organization, and help develop "esprit de corps." This sort of system is implementable even in public sector departments providing "complex services to the public requiring interpretation and professional judgment in their normal course of business" (Halpern et al. 1988).

This sort of initiative would encourage participative management and eliminate another major source of morale problems in public bureaucracies — the whimsicality factor in dealing with subordinates in the absence of clear and fair work goals. Managerial accountability, efficiency in the use of resources, and better programs would ensue from joint clarification of work goals and from the reduction of whimsicality in compensation.

CONCLUSION

To propose a social learning framework is to suggest that learning is essential. The necessary unfinishedness of such *ex ante* analysis is one of the costs of the strategy we propose: social learning can only come with practice and action, it is not possible to spell out *ex ante* the design of policy-in-the-making. The problem formulation will evolve with the learning process.

At this point, PSCs everywhere are torn between neo-Taylorian imperatives and the dominant values in their societies, and everywhere rules and regulations are in the end perverted to fit dominant values. The only recourse of political masters, who are anxious about having lost control over the public bureaucracies and are searching for ways to discipline the elusive mass of civil servants, is to decree drastic cuts: if one cannot control the civil service process, one may always scale it down.

The only meaningful response of PSCs wishing to escape the trappings of local dominant sociocultural values is to initiate a social learning process likely to lead to a reasonable balance between what is feasible, acceptable, implementable, and effective. This cannot be done from the centre but requires action hypotheses and interactive planning.

In each country's design of its own brand of PSC, some international collaborative work might be fruitful. It might take the form of franchise-type links or less-formal networking on issues of common concern. It might even be possible to develop better liaison through dissemination of the results of applied research. A good example is the replication in a number of countries of the Zussman and Jabes (1987) study. This would both serve the community of PSCs and be a much-needed basis for the revaluation of the importance of research capabilities within the PSCs. Indeed, the devaluation of the status of research within PSCs is as dangerous and fundamentally wrong-headed as the devaluation of the status of training and development in ministries and departments.

Finally, there may be a case for PSCs that elect, as a matter of strategy, to exit with fanfare the monitoring of a multitude of routine transactions between managers and employees in the public sector, to enter forcefully into activities of organization/institution design, even if it means temporarily scaling down the size of the agency. This might be an astute tactic for PSCs in their efforts to move the public household into a new style of public administration, by showing the way.

APPENDIX: CONCEPTUAL REQUIREMENTS
FOR A THEORY OF SOCIAL ARCHITECTURE

- Concepts concerned with the human dimension of institution-building: at the level of individual personality, interpersonal relations, group behaviour, intergroup behaviour, the total organization, and the social, economic, cultural, and political systems that constitute the environment in which the organization exists.

- Concepts dealing with the objective-reaching process, whereby the mission of an institution is formulated and translated into structural, i.e., sociotechnical and performance objectives; the strategy for reaching these objectives is devised on the basis of alternatives that are realistic in terms of an analysis of the consequences, e.g., to resources, payoffs, and risks; the choice of alternatives leads to implementation; and implementation in turn leads to validation, when the objectives actually reached are tested against desired results, and structures considered necessary for further growth and survival are stabilized (Simon 1960).

- Concepts relating the institution to its environment, especially sponsoring institutions and special interest groups:
  - how the institution being built influences and alters the environment;
  - what the environment in its political, economic, social, and technological aspects seems to demand of the institution;
  - how the institution responds to changing environmental conditions, political instability, prosperity and economic depression, war and peace.

- Concepts relating to the creation of essential organizational structures, either formal or informal: work-process systems, patterns of authority, of reward and punishment, evaluation, communication, identification, perpetuation.

- Concepts that concern the realization of positive values: respect for individual dignity, for physical and mental health, justice, freedom, human growth, authentic relationships, technical excellence, service, productivity, profitability, distribution of wealth and power, and efficiency.

- Concepts regarding changes of feeling, anxieties, and emotions; dealing especially with the reduction of persecutory and depressive anxieties and the promotion of more constructive emotions.

- Concepts related to a general-systems model of the organization; in particular the transformation of inputs, resources (both human and non-human) into results and outputs or performances.

Source: Perlmutter (1965: 17–18).

CHAPTER 10

GRANTING COUNCILS IN SEARCH OF EXCELLENCE: DYNAMIC CONSERVATISM VERSUS SOCIAL LEARNING*

> Précisons de plus que le homard n'aboie pas
> et qu'il a l'expérience de l'abîme des mers,
> ce qui le rend très supérieur au chien.
> – *Alexandre Vialatte*

The great buzzword of the 1980s was excellence. Through a perversion ascribable to illiteracy and self-interest, a comparative — *excellens* — has been transformed into a superlative and used to confer some *nec plus ultra* status on virtuosity in certain types of activities. This idea of excellence is a modern concept; it was foreign to the Greeks (Dumézil 1987).

The word has been used recently in a flurry of policy initiatives designed to create Centres of Excellence: the federal Secretary of State developed such a program in the early 1980s; Quebec has had a similar program; the same approach was used more recently in Ontario; and a major round of competition for Centres of Excellence was carried out by the federal government in 1989.

There are two separate components in the term "centre of excellence" as used in the current debates. The term "centre" refers to a form of organization of research built on synergies and a crossing of disciplinary bounds; "excellence" is based on a rationale for constructing some centres instead of others, i.e., usually the comparative quality of a group of researchers measured in a particular way. Although I have argued forcefully for the creation of a national network of research centres in the humanities and the social sciences in Canada as a strategy of great promise (Paquet 1987c), one does not necessarily have to argue in the same breath for the funding of "centres of excellence," especially if excellence is defined in narrow academic disciplinary terms.

This may appear to be an untenable position: how can one disagree with *excellence* as a criterion for selecting among potential candidates in a competition for funding for research centres? Clearly, there is nothing wrong with this

* This chapter also appeared in Preston, R.J. (editor). *Centres of Excellence: The Potential for Social Sciences and Humanities*, Hamilton: McMaster University, 1992, pp. 113–129. The assistance of A. Burgess is gratefully acknowledged.

criterion per se, as long as one realizes that excellence is a weasel word and that behind this label lies a complex scheme for evaluating competing projects — a scheme that may or may not be reasonable depending on what evaluative social system underpins it.

THE MISGUIDED SEARCH FOR ACADEMIC EXCELLENCE

Human beings have an unlimited capacity for distinguishing and classifying, especially when this serves their interests (Perrenoud 1987). For any strategy of classification corresponds to the fabrication of a hierarchy, and the logics underpinning these ways of classifying are many, often contradictory, and always contentious: it depends fundamentally on what is the norm, the criterion on which the hierarchy is based.

Asking a group to assess excellence is tantamount to authorizing some classification. Any useful debate about choice centres on the legitimacy of the institution charged with the job. On the occasion of recent competitions in Canada, there has been much argument in favour of a classification scheme defined under the agency of the professional academic disciplines. Others have argued that such a classification scheme would produce a hierarchy that is irrelevant to today's context, that professional academics are the worst possible group for such a job as the professionalization of academe has led to a perversion of its notion of excellence.

A Sociology of the Academic Profession

Katouzian (1980) has provided a vivid sketch of the way in which professionalization has transformed scholars into full-time academic mental workers and has led to the emergence of the professional academic, "a complete layman outside his own discipline and a narrow specialist within it." These professional academics are members of narrow disciplines; they communicate through specialized journals, and the more integrated the disciplinary profession, the greater the constraint on intellectual activities. The greater the control over the means of publication and propagation of ideas, the less tolerant the official journals are of ideas that threaten established views. Because promotions and academic reputations are linked to publication in these journals, this becomes the overriding objective of the professional academic, which, in turn, dictates academic cautiousness and a high degree of specialization.

As a result of this sort of development, the following pattern has emerged (Katouzian 1980, Paquet 1988a):

- a tendency to concentrate on the solution of "puzzles" instead of attacking substantial problems;

- a proliferation of printed material that adds comparatively little to knowledge;

- a research agenda for academic work that is set by fashion and the whims of the "invisible college."

This pointed characterization is not unwarranted. The power of the academic professions has grown to the point where they have become a determining force in the allocation of financial support for research through granting councils and such agencies. Professional academics are the driving force in panels defining the priorities and standards in funding agencies. This explains the high degree of cognitive dissonance of these agencies, even when the public communicates its discontent.

For as soon as the notion of excellence is mentioned, professional academics are quick to point out that they are uniquely equipped to determine what is and is not excellent through the social organization of peer evaluation that they have in place, and through certain measures like citation indexes — the number of times a paper or an author has been quoted or cited in journals regarded as appropriately disciplinary. Indeed, a recent appeal in a competition for the funding of centres of excellence at the federal level has been based, in part, on the unsuitability of a peer reviewer because his citation index was not as robust as the pedigree of some of the people whose projects he was evaluating.

Politics of Confirmation

The social organization of the production of academic knowledge has come to be regarded in certain circles as the only source of meaningful standards by which intellectual worth can be measured. Standardized international criteria like citation indexes and peer review by foreign members of the "invisible college" have become the standard ways to confirm the judgment of the local branch.

The fragility of these approaches has been amply documented (Cole et al. 1981), but this has not weakened the imperium of the dogma in academe. Academics continue to reaffirm that these are the only acceptable and reasonable ways to carry out the classification of research projects, programs, and teams.

The invisible college has thus acquired almost a monopoly on the legitimate gauging of the quality of research and knowledge production, and on the right to argue that only certain types of knowledge meeting its standards should be publicly funded. The classification recognized by the academic community is based on virtuosity in puzzle-solving favoured by certain affiliated journals. These standards may bear little relationship to the substantive questions raised in civil society, as there has been a gradual displacement of content by process in the practice of social sciences and humanities. A certain fixation on methodology has generated a "fallacy of misplaced concreteness" and methodological canons have become the common denominator around which the academic community congregates in lieu of former concern over the fundamental problems of the day.

The process of self-selection hidden behind confirmation by peers is not always transparent, but there have been claims that there is a poor match between the *academic* classification and what a *socioeconomic* classification would rank as excellent in competitions for public funding, in the same sense that a scheme using places to explain French wines is irrelevant on the California scene where the kind of grape is the key variable (Douglas 1986).

In the recent past, connoisseurship has developed outside academe, and there have been challenges to the monopoly claimed by academics on granting seals-of-approval to intellectual endeavours (Paquet and von Zur-Muehlen 1989). But academics have continued to use the granting councils as a bulwark in their defense of the perenniality of academic values: the granting councils have been the terrain on which the strategies of dynamic conservatism (selective inattention, containment, least change tactics, etc.) have been most fully deployed (Schon 1971).

Illegitimacy of Delta Knowledge

In classifying, individuals have a certain degree of autonomy, but public classifications derive from communal or social institutions that do the classifying and "the instituted community blocks personal curiosity, organizes public memory, and heroically imposes certainty upon uncertainty. In marking its own boundaries, it affects all lower levels of thinking, so that persons realize their own identities and classify each other through community affiliation" (Douglas 1986). This public production of labels has a significant impact on human beings: it is "making up people," the new labels engender new kinds of people and ensure that they will behave differently (Hacking 1985).

What is left out in academic classification is what academics block out, i.e., what does not fall into the realm of academic disciplines. We have shown elsewhere the extent of the damage done by this reductionism (Paquet 1988e). The tradition originating with René Descartes put the emphasis on a theory-centred style of argument; this has had deleterious effects. There has been a shift from a language of life to general ideas, abstract principles, instrumental reason, and a fixation on methods. This sort of "methodism" has contributed to a reshaping of the notion of interesting knowledge into a new notion of standard output. As a result, work on local, timely, and particular issues has been demoted to the level of uninteresting questions (Toulmin 1988).

The semi-unconscious conspiracy of the academic community against practical knowledge has reached a phase where, in the last half century, an ever narrower range of stylized classes of knowledge has come to be recognized as legitimate by universities. The present social system of production of knowledge has ruled whole categories of useful and usable knowledge — in particular much of what is learned by doing — as mundane, unwholesome, unwanted, illusive, confusing, etc., and discarded it as socially irrelevant (Gilles and Paquet 1989).

We have labeled this "delta knowledge": a broad category of useful and usable knowledge generated by wroughting and wrighting, by practical philosophy and reflection in action (Schon 1983). This delta world has been rejected by academics, rendered illegitimate, and it has consequently been underfunded. There are important costs to these censures: gaping holes in the knowledge base; and distortions in the process of production of delta knowledge (in management or design for example) forced upon it by the mold in good currency in alpha (humanities), beta (physical sciences), and gamma (social sciences) knowledge production. A further cost is attached to this ideological censure: when the occasion arises for the creation of centres to bolster the production of new knowledge, any academic classification scheme likely to be used by public authorities in search of legitimacy is bound to be blind to excellence if it takes a delta form.

GRANTING COUNCIL AS STALLED OMNIBUS**

Some observers have argued that it is the role of granting councils to serve as brokers and innovators in this context. Because these institutions are in principle mixed public/academic agencies, they should be able to strike the right balance between the academic imperatives of quality and other socio-political criteria. The fact that such institutions have to secure budget allocations from their public-sector masters in a politically competitive context has also been seen as making them particularly sensitive to all the relevant socio-politico-cultural dimensions.

Yet most governments have chosen to set up ad hoc institutions to handle the selection of centres of excellence when they have had the opportunity to do so. Implicitly, it may be argued that governments have decided that one cannot count on granting councils as they now stand to perform this brokerage function effectively. This decision stems undoubtedly in part from an evaluation of the composition and the power structure of such councils, but more

---

** I did not feel that I had to modify any of the papers published in this book for the analysis would appear to have sustained well the passage of time. I must make an exception for this particular section of this particular paper. Since the paper was written, some ten years ago, there has been a significant effort made by granting councils to shake off the dominium of disciplinarian academics. Through a new brand of leadership, a membership more broadly representative of the meaningful groups of users of research, and the design of innovative joint ventures with the private, public, and civic sectors, the granting councils have been made much more sensitive to society's demands.

Granting councils have also shown signs of being able to correct the biases of academic evaluation and to allow research demands and social needs to be echoed more fully in the allocation of research resources.

But these changes are not yet part of the ethos of granting councils, as has been clearly revealed by some changes in the leadership in some of the granting councils that have generated important *volte-faces*. Any of the transformations noted above can still be easily reversed. Consequently, one should not underestimate the powers of the Republic of Science and its capacity to re-establish the hegemony of the Republic of Science rules. The idea of the language of needs taking precedence over (or even being considered on a par with) the language of disciplinary worth is still not in good currency.

So my complaints and forebodings may require some sharps and flats, but they are not out of order.

fundamentally from a recognition of the lack of depth of their roots in civil society, of their poor record at gauging the dual constraints of clients' demands and field requirements, and their lack of any mechanism to evaluate priority needs.

Producers' Dominance and Lack of Roots in Civil Society

As they now stand, the granting councils in Canada are institutions that have been all but completely captured by academics. Although academics and nonacademics are appointed by the government, most are chosen from the ranks of professional academics — not so much because of their enlightened view about the place of science in society, but mostly because of some narrow accomplishment in academic disciplines. As for the lay appointees, until recently most were not very knowledgeable in science policy matters, and, consequently, they have been neither vocal nor capable of articulating a coherent philosophy as an alternative to the academic perspective. From time to time, some of the appointees — academic or not — have taken a broader view of the mandate given to granting councils and have been instrumental in triggering some reflection on their social role, but it is fair to say that granting councils have remained largely entrapped by the academic interest groups. This explains why such limited powers and resources have been granted to research councils.

Thus, when governments have felt that they had to address some socio-economic need through an investment in research, they have not found it wise to entrust the decision as to what should be done and by whom to producer-dominated agencies. They felt it wise to set up ad hoc structures. The rationale was that the granting councils did not provide a sufficiently reliable coverage of the diversity of interests in the socioeconomy at large. If granting councils were the classifying institution, major groups of clients and users of research would be disenfranchised and would have little or no opportunity to be heard. The granting councils are neither perceived as capable of acting as surrogates for the forum (Tussman 1977) nor of becoming major players in science policy design.

Client Demands and Field Requirements

Even if better representation on granting councils could be achieved, this would still not make them into sufficiently sensitive instruments to ensure monitoring of the changing constraints imposed by the demands of research clients and by the nature of the field requirements. The academic evaluation process is likely to remain their guiding light, for it is unlikely that any consensus on an alternative will develop. Consequently, the logic of the academic evaluation — which puts little value on the research demands of clients and is more than likely to interpret the field constraints in self-serving ways — is bound to remain dominant.

Indeed, the continuous evolution of fields and the changing priorities of clients have led academics to argue that the best research strategy is to allow the producer to proceed independently on the dual assumptions that (1) whatever the researcher might do will turn out to be most helpful in some way and at some time, and that no useful guidance can be expected from uninformed clients; and (2) whatever the researcher chooses to do has a greater chance of being the right thing to do because he/she is best informed about the texture of the field and the optimal path to new knowledge.

Without the inward biases introduced by the disciplinary framework and self-regulation of the field by professional academics, this approach might be defensible as a viable strategy. It would represent a bet on the free flow of competing ideas in the marketplace, generating, through the workings of the invisible hand, the selection of the best research strategies and the generation of the best complement of usable knowledge. However, this bet on the market as the organizing principle is most problematic. First, knowledge as a commodity has a number of characteristics that make it rather special — a public good component, acute uncertainty, etc. — and as a consequence, much waste is generated by simple competitive systems in the world of knowledge production (see Chapter 4). Second, competition is highly imperfect in this knowledge production market cartelized by the "invisible college." The "invisible foot" marches in, and the rent-seeking activities of academics over distributive shares is likely to generate much waste (Brock and Magee 1984).

No Machinery to Evaluate Needs

Even with additional sensitivity to clients and sounder evaluation of field requirements, granting councils, within their interpretation of their current mandate, are unlikely to develop a list of research needs to be addressed as a matter of priority. This is not part of their ethos.

The members of granting councils perceive themselves as experts asked to define a technically superior method of adjudication between competing applicants. They perceive their role in a *technical* mode, not in a *political* mode. At the core of the problem is a misconception about the political process at work in choosing centres of excellence. Academics do not understand that the issue is not to arrive at a technical optimum, but at a political optimum (Trebilcock et al. 1982). This outcome depends on the interrelated games of politicians, media, bureaucrats, the electorate, and special interest groups — of which academics are but one.

It is unlikely that granting councils as presently constituted can arrive at meaningful answers to national priorities. The cause of this marginalization is that the very idea of a language of needs taking precedence over the language of disciplinary worth is so foreign to granting councils that, were they offered the possibility of managing the whole process of selection of centres of excellence and of identifying national needs, they would probably refuse the job.

USING THE PRINCIPLE OF PRECEDENCE

The decisions made over the last few years about the creation of centres of excellence have reflected a lack of appropriate mechanisms for collective choice. As a result, ad-hocery was instituted as a guiding principle, and the allocation of important sums of money can be defended on the basis of neither academic excellence nor as an echo of socioeconomic priority. We have had the worst of both worlds.

The root cause of this failure has been a false assumption about the whole process: it was assumed that the creation of centres of excellence was a simple technical matter. Expert academics and expert politicians agreed that their standards were different, prepared an ordering and compared their classifications and hierarchies, normalized them over territory and hard disciplines, and tried to arrive at a single ordering. This ordering can in no way be defended as resulting in public expenditures that will ensure the greatest happiness of the greatest number. In most cases, the result is the unintended consequence of three intersecting processes: a self-selection of groups attempting to express their preferences in a manner likely to fit into the announced criteria of the competition, an academic classification according to the professional code, and a superficial political adjudication. There is nothing to establish that the groups that came forward are the ones who are best able to contribute to the welfare of the nation, that the groups selected were evaluated with criteria broad enough to ensure that the most urgent national research priorities would be fostered, and that the political authorities would do more than marginal tinkering over the final determination.

As it is likely that there will be other competitions for centres of excellence, one might usefully speculate about alternative ways to do the job.

Needs and Desires

The point of departure is a distinction between needs and preferences. For if the national collectivity, through its governments, wishes to use resources to promote research, can a general principle help define some national classification of priorities on the basis of needs. David Braybrooke and Harry Frankfurt have developed, independently, what they call a "principle of precedence" (Braybrooke and Schotch 1981; Frankfurt 1984b; Braybrooke 1987). This principle suggests that there is widespread acceptance of the precedence of needs over desires. Even John Crosbie — a key minister in the Mulroney government — was quoted in *The Financial Post* as being in favour of reallocating government resources on the basis of needs rather than wants if cutbacks in government expenditures were necessary (cited in Braybrooke 1987).

Braybrooke and Schotch (1981) have proposed a simple classification that is usable in cost–benefit analysis: first, proposed policies may be subjected to *peremptory considerations* (rights, honour, standing obligation, respect of life, etc.); second, policies may be gauged in terms of their impact on *minimum standards of provision for needs*; third, attention might be given to *preferences*. This set of categories subjects public decisions to the principle of precedence; the optimization process is subjected to the constraint of peremptory considerations and of meeting basic needs first: no harm should be done, and this takes precedence over the fulfilling of volitional wants.

In the allocation of public monies to centres of excellence, one might, therefore, start with *projects one cannot do without*, a norm that gets to the needs level and would require that a language of needs be used by the agency in charge of the adjudication process. To the extent that the number and scope of peremptory considerations is kept in check, the list of needs stays manageably small, and the minimum standards remain manageably low, this is a viable procedure. However, how can one find a way to articulate these needs and to elicit them?

A Language of Needs

A language of needs is necessary to articulate these priorities. Such a language is rooted in what humans need to be human; it is a language that allows us to identify what we are and what we cannot do without if we wish to remain who we are (Ignatieff 1985). In the debate about centres of excellence, it would be useful to start with a classification of what we cannot do without. This might suggest the creation of centres in fields that are strategically important because of the particular circumstances of Canada. For instance, the MacDonald Commission (1985) complained that, even though the Canadian socioeconomy is fundamentally dependent on natural resources and on its relationship with the United States, it had been unable to find the necessary Canadian expertise in those two areas.

To ascertain what we cannot do without, a forum is needed in which individuals and groups can meet and discuss the main threats and challenges to Canadian society today. Such a forum — be it a Council of Social Values or a Committee on the Long Run to be added to the Senate and the House of Commons (Paquet 1968; Braybrooke and Paquet 1987) — would provide the vehicle for arriving at some notion of a list of course-of-life needs, the minimum standards to be maintained, and the elements to be regarded as categorical needs. For the time being, streams of legislation and jurisprudential decisions more or less define the basis for a language of rights. What we need is some thinking about needs to make these categorical need constraints more explicit.

It would be silly to presume that a list of needs and a definition of minimum standards would provide a simple mechanical answer to the question of what research centres should be created; but it would be equally unreasonable to presume that it cannot be done. However, it cannot be done using a top-down procedure. The language of need has to evolve from a multilogue involving all the stakeholders, more or less on the model of any meaningful national consultation carried out to elicit what the priorities of Canadians are. Such a bottom-up approach was used recently in the case of energy (see Chapter 5) but also in numerous forums on entrepreneurship, on employment, etc.

Social Learning

This approach via a broad participative consultation would require a learning organization (Garratt 1987). It may appear to be somewhat roundabout, but it is not. Creating centres of excellence poses a *wicked* problem to policymakers and policy analysts (see Chapter 2): the goals are either not known or very ambiguous *and* the means-ends relationships are highly uncertain and poorly understood (Rittel and Webber 1973). Friedmann and Abonyi's (1976) approach is applicable in this context (see Figure 5 and the discussion in Chapter 2).

One way to effect such learning about needs and national priorities is through search conferences (Emery 1982; Williams 1982). Search conferences are designed with the general purpose of engaging participants "in exploring how wider change is affecting them all, developing shared images of a desirable future, examining present resources and constraints with respect to pursuing desired directions, and planning innovative strategies to enhance mutual prospects" (Williams 1982: 179).

There have been interesting experiments in Canada along these lines: the series of national economic conferences organized by the Economic Council of Canada, where stakeholders from all over the country were grouped in sectoral units to prepare the national overall meeting; the various regional summits and the 1989 *Forum pour l'emploi* in Quebec. But there has been very little instituted continuity and, as a result, very little accumulation of knowledge about priorities. Indeed, much of the evolution of perceptions, attitudes, and values are registered only by private survey firms for their corporate clients without the benefit of feedback to those surveyed so that public learning can be accelerated. Governments use polls for policymaking, but they are not actively engaged in seeking the participation of the citizenry in experimentation, public learning, and priority definition. This is ascribable to the bureaucratic view that reduces citizens to the role of beneficiaries and resists their promotion to the role of clients (Godbout 1987).

To the extent that citizens are invited to become active, they will. They will articulate their needs in the forum in the same manner as they express their preferences in the market, and in so doing will indicate the directions in which investment of public resources should be made. Moreover, the new shared understanding of change acquired through interactive searching and learning should result in joint commitment to active adaptive strategies, such as joint ventures. A good way to ensure that research programs are conducted effectively and the results disseminated widely is to ensure that there is a commitment by other parties to work in concert with the chosen research teams.

CONCLUSION

There is little hope that granting councils will become active in the ways suggested above unless they begin to interpret their mandate much more broadly. This will require not only a dramatic change in the personnel making up these granting councils — to represent all segments of Canadian society — but also attention to the portion of their mandate that requires them to develop policies that reflect the needs and expectations of Canadian society, government and the research community.

In the past, granting councils have been satisfied to cater mainly to the needs and expectations of the research community, and any consultation they have carried out has been focused on that community. This is no longer acceptable. Mechanisms have to be designed to obtain a better view of the needs and expectations of Canadians if granting councils are to perform their job appropriately.

Because they have not set up appropriate mechanisms to articulate these needs, the granting councils have become minor players in the construction of a national network of research centres. Whether there are signs that granting councils are taking sufficient steps toward a refurbishment of their personnel and a redefinition of their role to warrant optimism is a matter of much debate. But before governments can assign them an expanded role and additional financial resources, it will have to be clearly established whether they are still hostages of the academic community and agents of dynamic conservatism or whether they have become agencies of social learning and a locus where Canadian needs and expectations are meaningfully recorded.

Part III

New Directions

CHAPTER 11

THE STRATEGIC STATE*

Government is the most precious of human possessions; and no care
can be too great to be spent in enabling it to do its work in the best way:
a chief condition of which is that it should not be set to work for which
it is not specifically qualified, under conditions of time and place.
– *Alfred Marshall*

Our politics are Greek, but our administration is Roman.
– *Dwight Waldo*

The Canadian state is in crisis — at a point of decision. On the external front,
the ground is in motion. Canada lives in an environment where knowledge-
and time-based competition have become the determining sources of competitive advantage; the mortgage of geography has waned and a dematerialization
of economic activity and a deterritorialization of the economic process have
ensued; a new regionalization of trading blocks has emerged in which cross-
border partnering and new forms of government–business collaboration appear to be required strategies; and growing interdependencies within this
transnational world have made the notions of "domestic firm" and "national
economy" rather fuzzy (Paquet 1990a, 1991).

External pressures from this global knowledge-based economy have translated into greater demands on the state to provide standards, a sense of political
and social identity, and new forms of public–private risk-sharing arrangements. These demands have come at a time when the ligatures pulling society
together have been loosened, old solidarities have been eroded, and Canada's
sociocultural support for the state has weakened in subtle but important ways.
The public realm has come to be governed by warring private interests that
are either paralyzed by conflicting tensions or swayed by decisions appearing
to most citizens as increasingly arbitrary or capricious. And the polity has
imploded after the demise of the Westminster model of "club government"
(based on parliamentary sovereignty and the public service acting as a passive
executant) in the face of internal pressures for accommodation that call for

* Previously published in three parts in *Ciencia Ergo Sum*, 1996, 3(3), 257–261; *Ciencia Ergo Sum*,
1997, 4(1), 28–34; and *Ciencia Ergo Sum*, 1997, 4(2), 148–154. Extracts are from Chrétien, J.
(editor). *Finding Common Ground.* Hull: Voyageur Publishing, 1992, pp. 85–101. Jak Jabes made
most helpful comments on an earlier draft of the paper. The assistance of Anne Burgess and
Chantal Roy is also gratefully acknowledged.

power-sharing and negotiated adjustments within an increasingly heterogeneous and diverse society (Dahrendorf 1988; Marquand 1988; Reich 1991).

The tensions between the new demands for strategic state intervention and the old political apparatus have triggered many reactions. One has been an argument for the deliberate downsizing of the state and a plea in favour of the market as the only mechanism capable of constructing a meaningful order in this maelstrom. This has been articulated by a neoliberal ideology that has brought about a vacuum at the heart of the political economy: the public purpose has come to be seen as the sum of private purposes. Another reaction has been an obstinate defense of the old Keynesian state with all its paraphernalia, even after it has become clear that it is ineffective and that it can be maintained only by saddling the country with unprecedented debt. These are the neoconservative and the neosocialist routes, respectively. There must be a third way.

To discover what this third way might look like, one must go back to first principles: to prospect anew the boundaries of private and public matters and understand the co-evolutionary nature of the public and private realms; to gauge the extent to which the public infrastructure has become inadequate and why; to identify some of the foundational values and the design principles in the construction of the new state and the process of accommodation required from society, polity, and economy; and to examine some of the features of the new state and the sort of leadership it demands.

THE PRIVATE AND PUBLIC SECTORS

The boundaries between the private and the public spheres are neither well-defined conceptually nor well-delineated statistically. This is because they do not correspond to a rigid frontier, but rather to a wavering and evolving fracture zone.

Yet whenever the scope of government activities is debated, there is a frantic search for "technical" characteristics decreeing that an activity should fall in the private or in the public sector. These attempts to propose more or less "objective" criteria of "publicness" or "privateness," to apportion responsibilities between spheres have foundered. The degree of publicness is fundamentally as dependent on values and political choices as it is on technical characteristics of goods and services, and any change in prevailing values or any reorientation of public organizations may redefine the boundaries between the public and the private spheres without much reference to the technical features of the particular activities (Pelletiere 1989).

In the language of Karl Popper (1972), the boundaries between the public and the private spheres are evolving as a result of the interaction between the forces of World 1 (the world of material and geotechnical realities) and the forces of World 2 (the subjective world of values, mind, preferences, plans, and intentions); this constructed boundary zone constitutes a part of World 3 (the world of objective structures — organizations, laws, institutions, rights, etc.) produced wittingly or not by human beings.

The most insightful x-ray of this fuzzy boundary zone has been proposed by François Perroux (and developed independently by Kenneth Boulding a decade later) at a time when humanistic social sciences were still in good currency (Perroux 1960; Boulding 1970). Both identified three generic ensembles of organizations more or less dominated by a different mechanism of integration: *quid pro quo exchange, coercion*, and *gift or solidarity*. These mechanisms were explored by Karl Polanyi (1968) in the 1940s as dominant features of the concrete socioeconomies of the past. To map out this terrain, Boulding used a simple triangle with each of these mechanisms in its purest form at one of the apexes: the inner territory represents organizations and institutions embodying different mixes of these integrative mechanisms (Figure 1, see Introduction).

This approach provides a rough cartography of the organizational terrain into three domains where the rules, arrangements, or mechanisms of coordination are based on different principles: the economic/market domain (B) where supply and demand forces, the price mechanism, and efficient resources allocation are the norms; the state domain (C) where coercion and redistribution are the rules; the civil society domain (A) where cooperation, reciprocity, and solidarity are the integrating principles. This corresponds roughly to the standard partitioning of human organizations into economy, polity, and society (Wolfe 1989).

A careful survey of the Canadian organizational terrain reveals that society, economy, and polity each occupy roughly one-third of the organizational territory, and we sit at about the centre of gravity of the organizational triangle. This does not correspond to the statistical portrait emerging from official agencies, mainly because zone A activities are underreported, and little effort has been made to measure them better. Activities in the home, within not-for-profit associations, and in general beyond the market and the state are poorly recorded and remain largely underground (Paquet 1989a).

A century ago, the state portion of the terrain was quite limited and the Canadian scene was dominated by the other two sets of organizations. From the late 19th century to the 1970s, government grew in importance to the point where probably half of measured activities were state and state-related. More recently, there has been a vigorous countermovement of privatization and deregulation that has reduced the state sector and shifted the boundaries again.

CO-EVOLUTION: RESILIENCE AND SOCIAL LEARNING

Governments are one of the instruments through which collective concerns are addressed in human societies and governments may choose to exert different degrees of coercion: to enforce changes in the behaviour of private agents and in the structure of the economy or society; at least to resist private demands but be unwilling to enforce changes in behaviours of private actors; or simply to be the instrument of pressure groups. Such a choice may have a determining impact on the fate and evolution of the overall socioeconomic organization. In the same manner, the institutions of civil society (family, associations, etc.) may be more or less developed and accordingly more or less of the collective concerns may be addressed through the mobilization of interpersonal and particularistic resources like status, love, and community (Foa 1971; Bruyn and Meehan 1987; Marquand 1988).

One can identify many mixes of political, social, and economic mechanisms (and different modes of interaction among government, business, and society) in different portions of the world. The Anglo-American system tends to emphasize the market mechanism to the point of belittling the scope of state and civil society. But this sort of system represents no more than 25% of the world trade, and a lesser percentage of socioeconomic transactions. Other parts of the world (Western Europe, Japan, etc.) have chosen to assign a much greater role to the state in their national fabric (and to community, culture, citizenship) and unarguably their own brand of mixed organization appears to have generated a much more impressive socioeconomic performance than our own, greater resilience, and faster organizational learning (Choate and Linger 1988).

This resilience has been achieved through a capacity to maintain the right balance between an emphasis on competition and cooperation in the governing appreciative system, on one hand, and on a learned readiness to adjust the governance of the human organization accordingly and, therefore, to change the structures, technologies, and theories in good currency in the economy, society, and polity, on the other. Because these, in turn, echo more or less accurately the basic underlying values of the members and organizations, their information processing and computing capacities, and their ability to learn and adapt quickly, learning echoes value changes and leads to value changes (Mesthene 1970).

The state has an important role in maintaining healthy communication in the forum and workable competition in the market. The state must maintain an important intelligence function if it is to act as catalyst in an innovative learning process (Wilensky 1967). As we saw in Chapter 2, the four subprocesses in social learning are: the construction of appropriate theories of reality, the formation of social values, the design of political strategies, and the carrying out of collective action (Figure 5). Social values define what is *acceptable*; theories of reality depict what is *technically feasible*; political strategies refer to what will ensure a *stable* situation, what is politically feasible; and social action identifies what is *implementable*. Together these subprocesses pose the four questions that are basic to the requisite social learning by the state (Friedmann and Abonyi 1976).

The basic challenge in organizational learning is to develop innovative competence, for the ability to improve and to innovate is a skill that is vital for survival and resilience (Rugman and D'Cruz 1991). But organizational learning requires the discipline of *team learning*, a capacity for the different stakeholders to engage in dialogues, in conversations that begin to have a life of their own, to take all parties in directions that could not have been planned in advance. This sort of conversation enables the stakeholders to discover what is acceptable, technically and politically feasible, and implementable. However, such a conversation requires a facilitator capable of carrying the partners beyond the defensive routines (based on presumptions that are supposedly *undiscussable* and, therefore, preventing learning) toward a willingness to raise the most difficult, subtle, and conflictual issues. This leadership is essential if dialogue is to lead to the collective suspending of assumptions (Senge 1990).

Vertinsky (1987) has analyzed the internal decision processes in Japanese companies, the way intercompany interactions proceed, and the structure of the government decision process and its role in guiding the economy. He has discovered the many ways in which the process of dialogue is being actively promoted at all levels and the manner in which organizational learning appears to proceed effectively. Vertinsky describes in the following terms the situation he has observed in Japan:

> While swift and radical intervention is taken in a crisis to secure the collective survival, it is the market which ultimately prevails. When a crisis dissolves and market forces dominate, government policy retreats to a subsidiary role of keeping options open, disseminating information, and ensuring a smoother transition to the new state dictated by the market.

How is this balance maintained between collective control and cooperation and individual competition? And how is the switching mechanism operated? These are central questions. In animal collectivities (*slugs*) and in sophisticated social organizations (Japan), it would appear that the secret is *not size but flexibility*: adjustment is effected through

> Flexible behavioral mechanisms rather than expensive investment in physiological or morphological adaptations... [in the first case] — and through flexible exercise of controls and influences upon the private sector, rather than the strengthening of a permanent public sector infrastructure and its share in the economy [in the second case]. [Vertinsky 1987]

Co-evolution of polity, society, and economy calls for this sort of flexibility and this depends much on an ongoing multilogue among partners. This, in turn, requires a facilitator, a leader capable of acting as a quarterback in the process of organizational learning, in the balancing of the short-term competitive forces and of the long-term cooperative forces, and in ensuring a smooth transition from one regime to the next. Organizational learning is, therefore, not only *adaptive learning*, i.e., about coping, it is also *generative learning*, i.e., about creating, adjusting goals, norms, and assumptions as required. In this context, the state itself has to become a learning organization and the leader has to develop new skills and abandon moral agnosticism to be effective, for the leader's new work is building learning organizations, and this is not value-free (Senge 1990).

THE PRESENT FLAWED SOCIAL TECHNOLOGY

The present social technology of the Canadian state does not manage resilience and learning well. The state would even appear to have chosen the *wrong strategy*: heavy investment in physiological and morphological modifications, and a bulky, centralized state system geared to producing centralized technical answers to public management problems. This bulky apparatus has had very limited success in designing flexible controls and influences on the private sector: it has generated little resilience and not much learning (Grimond 1991).

The main critiques of the brand of the Keynesian state in good currency in Canada and in many other advanced socioeconomies have been well documented. They may be subsumed under a few headings (Duncan 1985):

- *overgovernment and government overload:* the state is presented as "a kind of arthritic octopus, an inept leviathan" unable, despite massive growth, to do much to meet the demands of the citizenry; as a result, it has triggered weakened citizen compliance, growing civic indifference and much disillusionment (King 1975);

- *a legitimation deficit:* the depoliticized public has by now ceased to believe that the state has any moral authority or technical ability to deal with the issues at hand; this would explain the disaffection and the withdrawal of support by the citizenry (Habermas 1973);

- *a fiscal crisis:* revealing the incapacity of the state to reconcile its dual obligation to attenuate social difficulties and to foster the process of capital accumulation without generating fiscal deficits that are in the long run unbearable (O'Connor 1973);

- *social limits to growth:* the three crucial dimensions of our social organization (liberal capitalism, mass democracy, and a very unequal distribution of both material and symbolic resources) cannot coexist easily: democratic egalitarianism (in society) generates compulsive centralism (in the polity) to redistribute more and more resources with little success in reducing inequality, but growing shackles on the productive capacity of the economic system (Hirsch 1976).

> Modern democratic capitalist states face... a crisis, because they appear incapable of carrying out established and expected tasks, tasks which they have over the years accepted, because of the absence of necessary resources, *both financial and civic*, or because they cannot meet claims and expectations fostered by the economic and social systems themselves. [Duncan 1985: 274]

This overall crisis of the state has been analyzed historically as a two-stage process. First, it evolved as a crisis in the *economic realm*: coordination failures became more and more important in advanced market-type economies, thereby creating a demand for intervention and regulation by the state (the economic crisis was, therefore, shifted to the state). Second, the *state crisis* developed as the legitimation deficit grew: the state was failing to mobilize the requisite commitment of citizens to be able to do the job; out of despair the state made an attempt to effect an "epistemological coup," to obtain a "blank cheque" from the citizenry. The argument was that because management problems were so technically complex, the citizenry should pay its taxes and demand no accountability from the professional experts. This coup has failed, and "cognitive despotism" has not succeeded in suppressing the autonomous power of the community to grant or withhold legitimacy (Habermas 1973; Wiley 1977; Paquet 1977). The polls have recorded this story line.

Why has such a situation developed? The central reason would appear to be that the public institutional framework built after the Second World War was presented to the citizenry as designed for *instrumental purposes*: to combat a depression, raise standards of living, provide public goods not otherwise produced, assist the needy, etc. As a result, citizens have come to define the state in terms of *claims* they could make on it: "claimant politics began to overshadow civic politics." By comparison, "the activities of the private sphere were seen as ends pursued for their own sake." It is hardly surprising that the instrumental goods of the public sphere were regarded as subordinate to the intrinsic goods of private life (Bellah et al. 1991).

Even though governments were major funders, underwriters, and regulators and, therefore, the fundamental bedrock on which the economy and society prospered from the 1940s to the 70s, Canadians have continued to occlude the importance of the state: "the dominant strains in our culture... [remained] a vigorous individualism, a suspicion of interest groups as self-serving and subversive of democracy, and a skepticism about pervasive social and economic planning by the state" (Fournier in Banting 1986). This ideology of Lockean individualism has continued to prevail despite the fact that government activities had grown so much by 1980 that very little remained absolutely private in a meaningful sense.

In a more and more global context, the private sector made ever greater demands on public institutions at a time when the capacity to supply services from the public sphere could not expand further. This was due to the fact that participation, trust, and creative interaction (on which politics and the public sphere are built) had all but disappeared, as had the sense of community that underpinned civil society and the collective/private ways of meeting the needs of strangers.

In this world of rugged individualism where most citizens are strangely unaware that the government has been the prime mover in the postwar period of prosperity, *private enterprise at public expense has become the rule*. The lack of commitment of emotional, intellectual, and financial resources to refurbish the public infrastructure could only lead to demand overload, and the frustration generated by the policy failures of the 1970s set the stage for citizens to suggest that the best way to strengthen democracy and the economy was to weaken government.

Jacques Parizeau saw through this charade:

It is one thing to be convinced that the policies of yesterday have produced a number of unwanted results, that governments have become inefficient, wasteful and slow; it is quite another thing to accept that in a number of areas, government responsibility should be suppressed. [Parizeau 1988]

In a world of ever-growing interdependence on a world scale, *the need for collective decision-making is growing*. The solution, therefore, is not less government or a weaker government, but *a different sort of government*. There is a need for *a new framework*, for a transformation in our democracy (Dahl 1989), but this new framework for social and economic policies, capable of guiding nations in the years ahead, has not yet been articulated in Canada.

FOUNDATIONAL VALUES AND DESIGN PRINCIPLES

Much of what David Marquand (1988) has said about Britain also applies to Canada and to some other advanced socioeconomies: at the core of our difficulties is a *moral vacuum*. The notion of public purpose is alien to us. We need first and foremost a *philosophy of public intervention*, a *philosophy of the public realm*.

First, one must recognize the need to fill that moral vacuum with a "national ethic" (Grimond 1991), then fill it before getting too far into the design of the new state. To proceed otherwise is to presume wrongly that we already know what the public institutions to be constructed are to be in aid of. Second, one must be able to sketch briefly the sort of design principles that are likely to underpin the social architecture of the new strategic and learning state. The leader must be in a position to identify and promote the institutional setting capable of ensuring the requisite amount of social learning in the Canadian system.

Guiding Values

One fundamental element in the definition of the new state is the recognition that, despite statements from social scientists and the fact that it is not fashionable to say so, *the state is a moral agent*, not a morally neutral administrative instrument. Both on the left and on the right, there is a longing for civil society to provide the well-defined codes of moral obligations that underpin the realization of the good society. However, the "built-in restraint derived from morals, religion, custom, and education" that were considered by Adam Smith as a prerequisite before one could safely trust men to "their own self-interest without undue harm to the community" are no longer there (Hirsch 1976).

The disappearance of this sociocultural foundation has been noted and deplored, and much has been written about the need to rebuild it. But it has also become clear that it is futile to hope for some replacement for these values to come about by "immaculate conception" in civil society. So many have called on the state and on political leaders to accept their responsibility as second-best moral agents (Mead 1986; Wolfe 1989). This does not mean that political leaders should impose values on a community; they should provide a *vision*, propose a *sense of direction*, a commitment to ideals, together with the *public philosophy* to realize them.

There are many plausible public philosophies (some based on sheer individual hedonism, others on different degrees of commitment to cater to the needs of others both directly through philanthropy and indirectly through the agency of the state), and they should be confronted and compared in public arenas. The citizenry is entitled to ask that its political leaders declare their public philosophy: what are their ideals, their ethics. Such a public philosophy is both *constraining* (in the sense that it echoes some fundamental choices and, therefore, excludes many possibilities) and *enabling* (in the sense that it provides a foundation on which to build a coherent pattern of institutions and decisions in the public realm).

The choice of a public philosophy must be rooted in the basic values of civil society, and on *enlightened understanding*. This calls not for the least constraining public philosophy, but for one recognizing that the optimal amount of coercion is not zero. Such a position would be the choice of citizens if they had "the fullest attainable understanding of the experience resulting from that choice and its most relevant alternatives" (Dahl 1989). The challenge is to bring about that sort of "fullest understanding" in the population. It means that government can no longer operate in a top-down mode, but has a duty to institute a continuing dialogue with the citizenry.

This will require a language of common citizenship, deeply rooted in civil society: citizens have goals, commitment, and values that the state must take into account. But citizens must also insist that they want an active role in the formation of these values, goals, and commitments, and in the making of policies supposedly generated to respond to their presumed needs (Sen 1987). Only through a rich forum and institutions that enhance citizens' communication competence is an *enlightened understanding* likely to prevail — both as a result of, and as the basis for, a reasonable armistice between the state and the people.

In the past, the state has played housekeeping roles and offsetting functions, but these functions require minimal input from the citizenry. In complex advanced capitalist socioeconomies, the state must now play new central roles that go far beyond these mechanical interventions. It must become involved as a *broker*, as an *animateur*, and as a *partner* in participatory planning if the requisite amount of *organizational learning*, co-evolution, and cooperation with economy and society is to materialize.

To be able to learn, the state must develop a new interactive regime with the citizenry to promote the emergence of a *participation society* (where freedom and efficacy come from the fact that the individual has a recognized voice in the forum on matters of substance and procedures in the public realm and, more important, an *obligation to participate* in the definition of such matters). The citizen should not be confined to living in a rights society where the dignity of individuals resides exclusively in the fact that they have claims. (Taylor 1985).

Design Principles

The design principles for a social architecture in keeping with the guiding values mentioned above are clear. First is the principle of *subsidiarity*, according to which "power should devolve on the lowest, most local level at which decisions can reasonably be made, with the function of the larger unit being to support and assist the local body in carrying out its tasks" (Bellah et al. 1991: 135–136). This applies in the three realms, and the level of empowerment and decentralization may call for the individual or the family or a minute constituency in the market, the society, or the polity to take charge. This empowerment would not translate, for instance, into paralyzing rules that prevent welfare recipients from supplementing their income, but rather into strategies to help them help themselves (Jencks and Edin 1990).

The rationale for this principle is that the institutions closest to the citizen are those most likely to be organic institutions, i.e., institutions that are likely to emerge *"undesigned"* from the sheer pressure of well-articulated needs and to require minimal yearly redesigning. Although subsidiarity reduces the vertical hierarchical power, it increases, in a meaningful way, the potential for participation.

This is not the death of central government, but the demise of big government as the morphological assurance of resilience. When the ground is in motion, the bulkier and the more centralized the government, the more it will flounder. The lean new central strategic state must deal with norms, standards, general directions, and values. The process of ministering to the public and delivering a service well-adapted to its needs must be devolved to the local level. Such a government would provide services within a framework agreed to nationally.

The second design principle is that of *effective citizen-based evaluation feedback* to ensure that the services produced, financed, or regulated by the public realm meet with the required standards of efficiency, economy, and effectiveness and are consonant with the spirit of the agreed standards or norms. This is a central cybernetic loop feature in the refurbished state. It is essential if organizational learning is to proceed as quickly as possible (Crozier 1987).

This sort of evaluation ensures that the process of participation is significantly strengthened. It provides, partially, some content to the *silent relation* or *implicit contract* that prevails between the state and its citizenry. This sort of feedback cannot be presumed to materialize organically. Its objective would be to ensure that state activities, standards, and rules have legitimacy in the beneficiaries' eyes and that they are compatible with everyday morality, rather than incentives to lie or misrepresent their situations. In a way, it would allow the ordinary citizen to be heard better, for "politics is not only the art of representing the needs of strangers; it is also the perilous business of speaking on behalf of needs which strangers have had no chance to articulate on their own" (Ignatieff 1985).

If government is to become *a learning organization*, then ensuring a continuous dialogue with the citizenry and improving the competence of its citizens to communicate will require some organizational development and institution-building: one cannot rely exclusively on organic feedback. If a capacity to learn at the centre (from the citizen and from the agency delivering the service) and a capacity for quick feedback and instantaneous action when government does not appear to do the right thing are to materialize, then new instruments are necessary.

The role of the leader is crucial in this process: producing a language adequate for our times, a language of belonging and common citizenship, a language of problem definition that provides the citizen with translation of his needs, usually expressed in unspecialized language, into categories that are both relevant and inspiring. This would be a language of human good that would serve as an arena "in which citizens can learn from each other and discover an 'enlightened self-interest' in common" (Dionne 1991).

MESO-FORUMS AND THE UNWRITTEN PLAN

These guiding values and design principles, and the language to articulate them, are not cast in stone. Any ideal can be dropped as learning proceeds: our desires and ideals "are not like our limbs: they are not a fixed part of us" (Schick 1984). But the sensible principles developed in the last section entail a somewhat *decoupled organizational form* of social architecture. Because the centre focuses on norms and the periphery on delivery, there is the serious possibility of lack of coordination unless a clear sense of public purpose materializes and new partnerships, new skills (strategic management, consultancy and advice, evaluation, etc.), along with new moral contracts binding the partners are developed to weave this whole enterprise together.

There is no good reason to believe that a central government would be unable to maintain effective control of the direction of the socioeconomy, even if much of the operations were decentralized, as long as it kept some key levers at the norms, standards, and general policy direction levels, and it ensured quick action to modify the current governance regime when special circumstances call for such moves. This has been the logic behind the governance model in vogue in Sweden for the last few centuries. It is also the basic logic behind some of the refurbishment of the state in the United Kingdom in the 1980s (Fudge and Gustafsson 1989).

One might venture a sketch of what is aimed at: a small number of central intelligence units, representing maybe 5% of the civil service (small units concerned with future-oriented and longer-term policy issues, i.e., laws, regulations, appeals, etc.) quarterbacking all sorts of administrative agencies (representing the other 95% of the public service). These agencies would not be given a simplistic role of enforcement of exogenously-generated higher-order government norms, but would be granted the necessary powers to organize activities in a way consonant with the principle of subsidiarity. These agencies must be learning organizations and, therefore, also *interactive*. They must be *negotiating arenas* in which there is significant space for interaction between the agency and the citizens; scope for defining and redefining activities, and for re-orienting them "under conditions of time and place"; and ample provision for dynamic monitoring from above and for continuous feedback from below.

The central challenge posed by this sort of *post-modern state* "with a weak centre acting as a kind of holding company" (Grimond 1991) is obviously the need to maintain the capacity for social learning and for strategic intervention in the underlying network. This, in turn, cannot be effected either through the old hierarchical method of command or through simple sermons. What has to be found is a way to build institutions likely to restore some *bonds of community* in a fragmented society and modularized polity, both permeated by possessive individualism. The required institutions must be neither built on command (like regiments) or on exchange (like bazaars), but on *communication and learning* (like a debating chamber) (Marquand 1988).

Preceptoral Politics, Meso-forums, and the Unwritten Plan

Centrally important in this context is what Charles Lindblom has labeled "preceptoral politics": leaders become educators, animateurs, people called upon to *reframe* our views of the public realm, to design the organization of mutual education, and to "set off the learning process" necessary to elicit, if possible, a latent consensus (Marquand 1988). Such learning is unlikely to occur easily and well in a post-modern society through a forum organized exclusively through national institutions. The requisite institutions will have to be *middle-range* or *meso* institutions, networks designed to promote communication and cooperation on a scale of issues that mobilizes existing communities, and meso-forums (regional and sectional) likely to ensure the commitment of the citizenry to organizations "*à leur mesure.*"

The strategic state must bet on flexible control and on extremely effective organizational learning through such meso-forums. Their triple role — mediating, setting patterns for the provision of services, and educating individuals in their mutual and civil commitments — needs to be revitalized accordingly (Etzioni 1983).

However, this fluid and seemingly scattered system of governance in the post-modern strategic state must be anchored in a clear sense of direction. There must be a *plan*. Most state leaders in advanced socioeconomies outside North America have such a plan, a direction for strategic intervention and a public philosophy that will articulate and rationalize it.

> They do not publish their plan because it would never gain consent. Yet it is not what one ought to call a conspiracy.... The plan is not entirely conscious or systematic, and it cannot be as long as it is not written, published, debated, revised and so on. But it is not what you could call a secret. [Lowi 1975]

The importance of this *unwritten plan* is that it underpins the state's strategic action and serves as a gyroscope in the definition of actions taken by the personnel of agencies and ministries. It serves as the basis for a *double-looped learning* process, as organizational learning must be — not only finding better means of learning to do what we do better, but also, and more important, finding the right goals and learning whether the objectives we pursue are the right ones (Argyris and Schon 1974).

Such learning cannot be accomplished by elected officials alone. Elected officials and bureaucrats must work symbiotically, and elected officials must learn to devolve a greater amount of discretion to bureaucrats, not only in the delivery process, but in terms of feedback from the citizens. Some officials have complained bitterly about the improper devolution of authority from elected officials to bureaucrats (Schaffer 1988; Auditor General of Canada 1991). Such complaints are ill-founded. The bureaucracy's exercise of power is not improper, illegitimate, or inefficient. In fact, cumulative decision-making by bureaucrats, *working within and with a public philosophy appropriately defined*, enables the post-modern state to learn faster through decisions based on the particulars of the case, while maintaining basic standards. Clinging rigidly to the old "parliamentary control framework" of the Westminster model is not necessarily enlightened. What is essential is the development of a *modified* framework, better adapted to the needs of a strategic state.

In that context, the Foreign Investment Review Agency and the voluntary compliance program of the Bureau of Competition Policy represent the new kinds of institutions a strategic state requires. In both cases, the government has been satisfied with providing a problem setting, to frame the context of the situation and the boundaries of public attention, while allowing the bureaucrats to use their tacit knowledge and connoisseurship to deal with specific situations, and to arrive at decisions on the basis of a "reflective conversation with the situation" (Schon 1983; Argyris et al. 1985).

New Partnerships and Moral Contracts

Institutionalizing greater discretion for bureaucrats will mean creating some sort of negotiating tribunal, geared to "*ex ante* harmonization of public and private interests through the guiding conciliation of bureaucrats" (Paquet 1978b). If the governing principles embodied in the unwritten plan become a diffuse but omnipresent public philosophy, the learning process is likely to be accelerated and, therefore, these structures would quickly acquire legitimacy (Paquet 1971).

The meso-networks so generated are the basis on which one may hope to construct new bonds or moral contracts that ensure tighter ethical linkages between the citizenry and public servants and more responsible professional linkages among the many echelons of the public management structure (Paquet 1991–92a).

Because policymakers in the post-modern state face more and more ill-structured or *wicked* problems (where the goals are unclear, and the means–ends relationships are uncertain), elected officials and bureaucrats are ill-equipped to manage in the usual hierarchical, goal-setting, and control mode (Rittel and Webber 1973). The best one can hope for is some *norm-holding*, and a process of policymaking based on intelligence and innovation: a dynamic monitoring by those closer to the issues, which feeds an innovative learning process. But this new form of public management, based on continuous feedback and constant problem reformulation as experiences accumulate, requires, over and beyond a guiding philosophy, new partnerships between the public and the private realms, between elected officials and bureaucrats, etc.

These new partnerships must overcome the important problems of mutual distrust that exist at the moment: *prisoner's dilemma problems*. A prisoner's dilemma is a dilemma of mutual distrust. It is best exemplified by a situation in which two people are arrested for a crime they have committed jointly, but for which the Crown has no definite evidence. Each is urged to "squeal" on the other in return for a light sentence. If neither of them informs, both get intermediate sentences. If both inform, both get harsh sentences; given their mutual distrust, in the absence of a strict moral code about informing, the likelihood of both doing so is high. When such a moral code is adhered to (as in the case of the Mafia code of *omerta* which promises extraordinarily nasty retribution to anyone who squeals) such problems disappear (Leibenstein 1987). The way out of prisoners' dilemmas is the hammering out of conventions or moral contracts.

A prisoner's dilemma exists between employers and employees: unless there is a moral code in the relationship, both will be tempted to shirk, i.e., to work less or to pay less than they should. As a result, a vicious circle is set into motion: the less productive the work, the less pay, and the less pay, the less productive the work. The result is general unproductivity. The same type of problem exists between the citizenry and the state, between government and business, in the federal–provincial arena, and between elected officials and bureaucrats. Mutual distrust leads one partner to shortchange the other, with the result that the other follows suit, and all the benefits of cooperation vanish. All this can be resolved through conventions or negotiated moral contracts among partners. But these contracts must obviously be inspired and molded by the general guiding philosophy contained in the "unwritten plan," and by the modicum of trust injected by the leader.

The new strategic state will be forced to manage, much more than previously, through the values and norms embodied in such moral contracts. These negotiated norms are much less rigid and less likely to foster adversarial relations than if the work is done through formal regulations and rules. "The general idea is that if it is possible to agree on the broad principles that particular sets of regulations strive to achieve, it should be possible to produce a flexible set of arrangements that satisfy the interested parties without hamstringing operations" (Morgan 1988: 163).

LEADERSHIP IN A POST-MODERN STATE

Some may argue that this is not a program for a political party, but, at best, a somewhat different way of thinking about realities and, as such, it is not very useful for a political leader. Others may suggest that such an approach is most unrealistic, inasmuch as it presumes that trust and the bonds of community can be recreated. Finally, some may say that it considerably belittles the stature of political leadership. We disagree on all counts.

Reframing as Lever

In response to the first argument, we believe that there is a fundamental need for a guiding public philosophy as a loose "*projet de société*," and that a *reframing* of Canadians' vision of the world through such a framework is necessary before one proceeds to develop the electoral platform of a future government. Without such a framework, the program likely to be constructed will be fraught with disjointedness, and the related constitutional, institutional, and organizational plumbing found to be unsafe. The leader of a political party must put forward a modest but clear public philosophy as the general "*projet de société*" underpinning the "unwritten plan": this is a *sine qua non* in the politics of the 1990s.

In answer to the second argument, we suggest that this approach may not be as unrealistic as it first appears. Three recent events illustrate the power of this way of thinking, and hint at the feasibility of the proposed strategy. The first is the impact of Prime Minister Brian Mulroney's expression of concern about the state of Canada's educational systems (directly, in the summer of 1989, then indirectly through the Prosperity Forum documents in 1991) and his plea for "a new public consensus on learning goals." This triggered a wave of soul-searching and questioning at all levels, and it is likely that what will come out of it is an agreement on *national educational standards* that should go a long way toward resolving the structural, organizational, and technological problems plaguing our educational systems.

The second example is the impact created by Gérald Tremblay (1991), the Quebec minister of trade, industry, and technology, in his September 1991 diagnosis of Quebec's socioeconomic malaise. Within days, this had heightened Quebeckers' consciousness and made him a catalyst for all sorts of cooperative arrangements, including multiyear, no-strike collective agreements, and a different way of crafting Quebec's industrial strategy as a partnership of government, business, and labour.

A third example of the progress of this way of thinking is the emergence of a new partnership between Canadian environmentalists and polluting chemical and forestry companies to hammer out acceptable environmental standards that they might jointly propose to governments (Geddes 1991).

Leader as Animateur

In answer to the third argument, one must emphasize that far from dwarfing the notion of political leadership, this approach underlines the new realities of leadership in a post-modern state.

Post-modernism is a way of summing up major changes in the socio political and intellectual scene. It connotes four major phenomena: an increasing incredulity toward the broad ideological interpretive schemes of the last century, a new awareness of the dangers of societal rationalization, a concern about the dangers and possibilities of the new information technologies, and a recognition of the new post-materialist values and social movements (feminism, environmentalism, etc.) underpinning local resistance to any broad normalizing force (White 1991). This has led to a fundamental rethinking of public discourse and political theory.

In this fractured and highly uncertain world, nothing seems linear and easily predictable any longer. The leader is no longer able to neatly separate appreciation and policymaking, on one hand, from executive decisions, on the other. All those who are involved must have a *shared appreciative system* to take an active and effective part in this process. The leader cannot exert authority through command in this network, but has to *acquire* this authority through, first, the setting and promotion of certain *governing relations* or norms embodied in the unwritten plan — those "relations" that the state wishes either to maintain or to bring to "some level more acceptable to those concerned than the inherent logic of the situation would otherwise have provided" — and, second, the negotiating of a true *moral contract or pact* between the leader and the led that is likely to inspire the led, to mobilize them to work within this shared appreciative system, to generate enthusiasm, to bring them beyond the limits of sheer executants to become creative and imaginative *intervenants*. All this is to be done in a manner not much different from the creative animation of musicians by the orchestra leader (Vickers 1965; Paquet 1978b).

The heart of the matter is not goal-seeking and control, but intelligence and innovation — the definition of standards and norms and the negotiation of a moral, intellectual, and emotional norm-holding pact built on a multilevel dialogue in which leaders and constituents are in some measure the shaper and the shaped, and the whole institutional process becomes the learning process and the source of the redefinition of norms and standards as a result of experience (Zaleznik 1991).

Leadership is no longer a matter of personal charisma. It has become a complex phenomenon in which the leader as *animateur* is literally a kind of soul of the body politic. Affirming values, motivating, achieving a workable level of unity, explaining, serving as symbol, representing the group externally, and being the continuous source of renewal are only a few of the leader's tasks in this new context. Fundamentally, there is a necessary sharing of these leadership tasks: if the heart of leadership is the taking of responsibility, empowerment of the led by the leader means that leadership tasks are shared and, therefore, responsibility is shared as well (Gardner 1986: 12).

Governing Relations

Whatever the arrangement arrived at, all human systems are subject to deterioration. Consequently, leaders must first and foremost be capable of setting in motion and maintaining the processes of renewal around some guiding public philosophy.

For John W. Gardner (1988: 12), the role of the leader is clearly defined:

(1) To renew and re-interpret values that have been incrusted with hypocrisy, smothered by cynicism or simply abandoned; (2) to liberate energies that have been imprisoned by outmoded procedures and habits of thought; (3) to re-energize forgotten goals or to generate new goals appropriate to new circumstances; (4) to achieve, through science and other modes of exploration, new understandings leading to new solutions; (5) to foster the release of human possibilities through education and lifelong growth.

A former president of the Carnegie Corporation (and secretary of health, education, and welfare in the United States in the mid-1960s), John W. Gardner puts the values component of leadership at the heart of the matter and relegates debates about plumbing to a subsidiary role, unless they have a contribution to make to the greater efficiency of the learning organization.

What is required at this time is a clearer definition of the *governing relations* and a strengthening of the leader-led pact to mobilize this dispersed leadership. From those aspiring to define a third way between neoconservatism and neosocialism, this in turn requires reasserting their conviction that there is an important role for the strategic state and being able to say what it is; and finding a way of renewing the conversation between political parties and citizens of the broad and all-encompassing middle class on the strategic action of the state.

This cannot be accomplished in Canada or in the United States unless and until some limits are imposed on the "moral agnosticism" of political parties. Comments on the fate of the Democrats in the United States have suggested that

Progressives and Democrats have failed to defend the liberal state because Republicans have successfully narrowed the scope for legitimate political action. In that constricted space, from which the middle class feels excluded, and where the government concentrates solely on the fate of the "have-nots" and on the state as safety net for them, the initial support for government initiatives — for acting collectively — quickly dissolves into skepticism and cynicism. [Greenberg 1991]

Politics and the Middle Class

Some forty years ago, the liberal state embarked on an ambitious program of social reform. Beginning in the 1960s, there was some effort to promote the values that the program was trying to defend. Those were the days of the "just society," with which the majority of Canadians could identify. But as time passed, both in Canada and in the United States, the fixation on "have-nots" and the underclass (almost exclusively) and futile attempts to rescue people from poverty have led politics to abandon the working middle class. This explains why they hate politics: politics has abandoned them (Dionne 1991). Families have worked harder, and yet they are losing ground. These people are not against specific broad-based programs, they are against a government that has failed to represent them, that does not seem to address their concerns, that has failed to "articulate a rationale for the government's role in society" (Greenberg 1991).

It is some thirty years ago that political leaders (Lyndon Johnson in the USA and Pierre Elliott Trudeau in Canada) articulated a vision of a "broad-based state." It is hardly surprising that the middle class has lost a sense of its ability to attack problems collectively, as the state has made no effort to communicate a message they can understand or that appears relevant to them. Social programs are in danger because most Canadians are only aware of some of their abuses (although these may turn out to be fiscally trivial); *they are not aware of what the public sector does for them every day*, of the extent to which their standard of living and economic security depend on public policies, of what government is there for. There has been a disconnection between the taxes they pay and the services they are not aware they are getting.

A Language of Common Citizenship

There is a tacit demand for a *language of citizenship* that would echo the concerns and values of the middle class and help it become articulate about politics. In the post-modern context, political leadership no longer consists of charisma and pirouettes — it amounts to providing a philosophy of the public house-hold capable of mobilizing a dispersed citizenry. A case could be made for a *renewed notion of citizenship* (spelling out individual and collective rights and obligations of Canadians, and the exact role of the state in it) as a promising arena where the Canadian identity might be forged, but also where the mandate of the strategic state might be articulated in conversations between the leader and active citizens (Paquet 1989g; Oldfield 1990).

In Canada, these discussions at the federal level (the definition of both the governing relations in the unwritten plan, and the moral pact of the leader with the constituents) call for a gamble on a substantial amount of decentralization. This is a mortgage of the recent past: the echo effect of the federal government's compulsive centralism after the Second World War, and its reluctance to return to the provinces the fiscal and regulatory powers borrowed in a situation of emergency. It is also the result of some unwise "*coups de force*" (especially in the early 1980s) that still linger in provincial memories: the National Energy Program of 1980 for Alberta, and Bill S-31 in 1982 for Quebec.

One cannot proceed as if these circumstances did not exist. Consequently, the degree of political "roundaboutedness" called for is much greater at present than it technically needs to be, or than it would have been one decade ago. But one can accomplish little if one ignores these constraints.

I believe that, despite these circumstances, discussion on a renewed notion of citizenship can serve as a way to jump-start a genuine renewal of politics in Canada. This was envisaged, in a timid way, in the first portion of the Clark proposals for shaping Canada's future, in September 1991. It should be regarded as a good omen that there has been almost no disagreement about this portion of the document. Indeed, some may even suggest that the whole constitutional debate, if reframed as a way to define the rights and obligations of Canadian citizens, might allow the leaders to initiate the sort of creative dialogue that is needed.

CONCLUSION

This overall approach to the scope of government has the merit of re-establishing the centrality of state institutions and exorcizing the various theories of the withering of the state. Economy, society, and polity must share the organizational task of redefining the human political socioeconomy.

The leader of a political party has to jump-start and steer a process of social learning to ensure that the state plays its role as fully as it must, while allowing the other two domains to occupy their own terrains as fully as possible. There are two broad avenues the leader might follow right from the start: one that is modest and one that is more ambitious.

In the modest agenda, the strategic state does not aim at the *optimum optimorum*. Instead, the leader only strives for ways of avoiding excesses, for a loose codifying of a sense of *limits*. This modesty stems from the fact that very few political questions can be handled by simple rules. Therefore, even a wise public philosophy and an efficient process of organizational learning are regarded, at best, as capable of nothing more than establishing agreement on what is *not* moral, what is *not* acceptable. Because we intuitively understand what is unjust more easily than what is just, the challenge is to find the path of minimum regret, for that corresponds to the only hope a leader might reasonably entertain in a post-modern state (Shklar 1989).

In the more ambitious agenda, the challenge is a bit more daunting: the objective is not to seek the utopian just society of yesteryear, but to develop an active leadership role that would promote active citizenship. This agenda is built on the following premises (Buckley 1990):

- the *Tocqueville lament* about the peril of democracy: "not only does democracy induce to make every man forget his ancestors, it hides his descendants and separates his contemporaries from him; it throws him back forever upon himself alone, and threatens in the end to confine him utterly within the solitude of his own heart"; and

- the *John Stuart Mill statement* about social obligations: "every one who receives the protection of society owes a return for the benefit."

From these premises, three sets of actions follow:

- The leader must frame a public philosophy aiming at nothing less than a change in the national ethos.

- The leader must become an "official," i.e., "a person with duties and obligations," not only of foregoing private interests in the name of public duty, but also being capable of "getting the ruled to do what they don't want to do" because what the public wants, or thinks it wants, or thinks is good for it, may not be what the public good requires. This entails a *"devoir d'ingérence."*

- The citizen needs to be persuaded that he has an active burden of office, that a citizen may act unjustly, not only by breaking a law, but also by remaining passive in the face of a public wrong. This means that the citizen has to be *educated* into an active citizenship that entails a *"devoir de solidarité"* (Tussman 1977, 1989).

These agendas are rooted in the development of "a national ethic," but demand different degrees of dynamism on the part of the leader as moral agent. The modest agenda is a backhanded moral approach: a public household that would ensure this sense of limits would already have done much to recreate the civil politics that is so badly needed. The more ambitious agenda would attempt to reframe the national ethos as a way to guide the debate around the size and scope of the state in the year 2000. Such *reframing* is regarded by all political parties as the central challenge they are facing today.

The public philosophy in good currency suggests that the modest agenda is the only viable one. Dwight Waldo (1985), one of the foremost observers of the public administration scene over the last 40 years, reminds us that "we simply do not know how to solve some of the problems government has been asked to solve." For Waldo, the central feature in the discussion of the boundaries between the private and public spheres is the "growth of the 'gray area'... the fading distinction between public and private, caused and accompanied by increasing complexity of organizational arrangements where what is — or was — government meets and interacts with what is — or was — private, usually but by no means exclusively 'business.'" And Waldo adds somewhat sharply that any person who claims to have clear ideas about this "gray area" is "suspect as ideologue, scenario writer, or a con artist."

Yet the times may call for leaders capable of envisaging a real attempt at a somewhat immodest agenda. Enlightened pragmatism, an emphasis on practice guided by a modest public philosophy, an ongoing and somewhat directed conversation with the situation, "under conditions of time and place," are the bedrock of the new modern and modest strategic state. But this enlightened pragmatism need not be amnesic and myopic; it must forge new concepts and new symbols, new options and, as "options are thus changed or expanded, it is to be expected that choice behavior will change too, and changed choice behavior can in turn be expected, given appropriate time lags, to be conceptualized or 'habitualized' into a changed set of values" (Mesthene 1970).

This hemi/semi/quasi immodest agenda is not echoed in the triumphant politics of principle developed by supposedly great political leaders, and likely to convulse society, but in the solution of particular cases in an innovative way. Already, there is agreement on the profile of the new type of leader that the times call for. The key features are a capacity to listen, to learn and to entice others to learn, to change and adapt to change, and to inform the public clearly and serenely about the general orientation of the guiding public philosophy;

the courage to change one's mind when circumstances and problems demand it; but centrally, an "ethical attitude" acting as a gyroscope and permitting no concession to opportunism (King and Schneider 1991).

It is not clear whether what is needed to kick-start this transformation is a fully worked out *"projet de société,"* an *avventura comune*, or nothing more than what Aristotle identified as "concord" (*"homonoia,"* "a relationship between people who... are not strangers, between whom goodwill is possible, but not friendship... a relationship based on respect for... differences" [Oldfield 1990]). What is clear is that the leader of the strategic state needs to find a way to energize the nervous system of the economy, society, and polity, for, as Joseph Tussman (1989: 11) would put it, a modern democracy is committed to "governance not by the best *among* all of us but by the best *within* each of us."

CHAPTER 12

BETTING ON MORAL CONTRACTS*

We need a new "declaration of interdependence."...
                                              – *Warren Bennis*

We already know much about the most important challenges that public management in Canada is likely to face over the next decade. Further, we have good reason to believe that administrative restructuring, technological fixes or gadgets, and soft-headed sloganeering about total quality or client-orientation will not provide an adequate answer, but, at the same time, we appear to be unwilling to engage in the difficult task of engineering the "mores revolution" that might hold the key to our difficulties. I believe that we should and can effect that revolution.

Mores are defined either as "the established, traditional customs or folkways regarded by a social group as essential to its preservation and welfare" or as "the accepted conventions of a group or community" (*Funk & Wagnall's Standard College Dictionary* [Canadian ed.]. 1976, p. 981).

Although the diagnosis is unlikely to prove controversial, the proposed cure may be discarded offhandedly because it entails nothing less than a cultural revolution. Yet, the proposal should at least be debated in the public forum. This is especially important because two major Canadian public institutions — the Office of the Auditor General and the Public Service Commission — could effectively kick-start the whole process of change if they were swayed by the argument.

THE CHALLENGES

There are two major families of challenges facing public management in the 1990s. First, modern societies like Canada are becoming more plural, open, and liberal. Most people now strongly assert their right to be in the know. It is no longer easy to ensure that only the centrally interested stakeholders are informed; public managers live in a goldfish bowl. As a result, it is all but

* This chapter first appeared in *Optimum* 1991–92; 22(3): 45–53. The critical comments of Jak Jabes have been very helpful, and the challenging questions and probing of many participants in the October 1991 meeting of the Ottawa Chapter of the Planning Forum helped sharpen the argument.

impossible to avoid procedural complications in almost every area of public management, as the most powerful resource is *public attention* and any well-organized minority can more or less define the public agenda.

This development has been perceived as a tragedy by old-style public servants for whom "a duty of complete disclosure would render impossible the effective operation of government" (Bennis 1976). But this is only the second part of the well-known pronouncement of Edward Levi (former dean of the Chicago Law School and former attorney general of the United States): the first and complementary part of the statement is that "a right of complete confidentiality in government could not only produce a dangerous ignorance but also destroy the basic representative function of government" (Bennis 1976). Obviously, one has to strike a balance between these two evils of excessive disclosure and excessive confidentiality.

Governments still operate with undue confidentiality. This has undermined their legitimacy and authority and, as a result, they are almost paralyzed. The state cannot command; nobody feels that they have to obey; it cannot persuade or organize; preaching does not work; and even sophisticated structures cannot maintain order for the uninformed citizens put all their energy into trying to circumvent what they regard as unwarranted constraints placed on them. As a result, at a time when there is a need for more collective decisions in our information society (for markets do not always handle information very effectively [Paquet 1987a]), it has become more and more difficult to effect them.

One important consequence is the omnipresent temptation of bureaucrats to use shortcuts: the public servant condemned to be a frustrated public educator and *animateur* is often unwittingly led to become a son of *homo manipulator*. As a result, ethical issues become the new daily bread of the public manager in Canada and almost everywhere else in democratic societies.

Second, in Canada, but also in many other countries, this new liberal pluralism has become a greater challenge, because of a particular malaise that may be ascribed to what one might call the collapse of the social consensus.

From the 1950s to the 1970s, one cannot but notice an extraordinary decay of the degree of solidarity in Britain and in Canada, to mention only two well-documented cases (Marquand 1988; Paquet 1991). In Canada, for example, the 1950s were the era when equalization payments policy (an echo of interregional solidarity) and many welfare programs (an echo of intersocial group solidarity) were created. In the 1970s, this sense of interregional solidarity had all but disappeared: this was the era of the Alberta bumper sticker that read, "Let those eastern bastards freeze in the dark." There have also been signs of a weakening of intergroup, intergenerational, and even interethnic solidarity that have translated into an erosion of welfare programs and heightened intergroup tensions.

This collapse of social consensus since the Great Depression and the Second World War has had an impact on the governance of the country. The public service, as an institution, can only reflect and echo the malaise of the broader society in which it is embedded and which it serves. A quantum leap in anomie has been noted in Canada (Bibby 1990). As a result, it has become even more difficult to manage the public household in this country (and a number of others), and the tension and frustrations of public servants have been heightened accordingly.

THE IMPACT

The result of this sociopolitical degradation has been a particularly debilitating disease for the public service in Canada. Using the language of Robert Pirsig in *Zen and the Art of Motorcycle Maintenance*, I would call it *loss of gumption*. Gumption is defined by Funk and Wagnall as "bold energetic initiative, courage to act, shrewd common sense" — from the Middle English "gome" meaning "care." This illness originated as a result of the forces described in the last section, but these have been catalyzed by two additional major factors that have hit the Canadian scene particularly hard.

The first one is *demographic* in nature. Canada had a most extraordinary population explosion between 1951 and 1966: some seven million Canadians were born during this period. This cohort generated a phenomenal growth in the demand for governmental services (health, education, etc.), but it also produced what John Kettle (1980) has called "a new kind of people." On one hand, this cohort was overprotected and "cajoled with promises of a bright future," but, on the other hand, it has been provoked and made more and more frustrated as overcrowding generated alienation and violence, and as their naive "me-generation" expectations have been put to a terrible test.

By now, this generation has come to be well represented, mostly in the lower and middle echelons of the Canadian public service. These "Baby Boomers" are a new kind of people with new attitudes to work: more questioning; less confidence in authority figures; more valorization of family and community than their elders; frustration, as their probability of promotion is much lower than the previous cohort; and so forth.

The oldest members of this cohort are now in their 40s, the 35 to 49 age group will continue to grow dramatically during much of the 1990s. This is the very age group most likely to be hit by an identity crisis and a midlife crisis, with its characteristic vulnerability and equivocation. This is the time when gumption traps like anxiety, boredom, and impatience are most damaging (Scrosone 1990).

The second factor is *organizational* in nature. The massive demands for government services from this me-generation have brought a lot of pressure to bear on the public service. The old-style senior public servants, mostly born before the Second World War, were forced by such external circumstances to deal with the new pluralist reality in a very direct way. Moreover, given the new values of the day, they had to attend to these demands in a sensitive way. Consequently, they developed an explicit *language* of care — the vision statements and the slogans they have hammered out to expound their commitment are all about client-orientation and quality of service to client publics.

But, internally, the old Taylorian logic of the feudal hierarchical system was still in place. Both at the federal and provincial levels (but also in many large private bureaucracies administering companies that have been in place for quite a while), there is ample evidence that the bunker mentality is not dead. Dissent is still not in good currency, and scapegoating is still a way of conducting business. Indeed, given the increased external vulnerability of the public service bureaucracy in this fish-bowl world, scapegoating (from its radical version, *firing*, to its softer version, *shelving*) is increasingly a tool of management.

In this somewhat schizophrenic world, junior civil servants try their sanity as they are squeezed between the explicit rhetoric of client service uttered by their superiors for external consumption and the Taylorian language and practices experienced internally. Without the benefit of an inclusive public philosophy or guiding professional culture to help these junior civil servants interpret and reconcile both types of utterances and guide them in adapting creatively to ever-changing circumstances, this situation generates extraordinary existential strains.

Kets de Vries and Miller (1985) have psychoanalyzed the sort of neurotic organization that results. It appears that the current scene in Canada corresponds closely to what they identify as one type of dysfunctional organization — *the paranoid organization*. The paranoid organization is marred by suspicion and mistrust of others. The result is a "desire for perpetual vigilance and preparedness for emergencies" through a centralization of power in the hands of the top executives. The strategies of such organizations are essentially reactive, with a sizable element of conservatism, and a "loss of capacity for spontaneous action because of defensive attitudes."

DEFENSE MECHANISMS

This world of contradictory signals is a great source of double binds. In town hall-type meetings, senior bureaucrats use language that encourages subordinates to feel empowered, but then do not hesitate to accuse them of incompetence, disloyalty, and disobedience when they take initiatives and the outcome is not entirely "politically correct." This is a typical Catch-22 situation in which conflicts are suppressed and an atmosphere of false consensus is encouraged. Such confused interpersonal and superior–subordinate interactions generate all sorts of tensions, insecurity, disenchantment, and resentment among second-tier managers and their subordinates. And the situation is yet more serious when the lower and middle echelons are "the new kind of people" generated by the Big Generation.

The situation is so tense that public servants in the middle echelons are led either to internalize these tensions — "some conscious pretense, emotional suppression, or cognitive unawareness concerning the factors that induce fear... in a crisis situation" (Kets de Vries and Miller 1985: 136) — or to design escape routes — "cooperation with all its half-measures and half-satisfactions is no longer enough. I want it all. I want out" (Scorsone 1990).

The *internalization route* may take one of the many forms well-known to psychoanalysts and management specialists like Kets de Vries and Miller (1985) — *repression* of desires, emotions, and thoughts, *regression* to passive, child-like behaviour, *projection* (creating distortions of representations designed to attribute to persons and circumstances all responsibility for the uneasy situation), or identification (leading one to adopt values and patterns of behaviour of those in power. And, finally, a way out of this uncomfortable pew is reaction formation (internalizing one's deeply felt sentiments and externalizing exactly the reverse).

Through this internalization process, personnel acquire a capacity to cope and muddle through one day at a time, but, in the long run, it is rather debilitating and counterproductive. The neurosis that has hit a portion of the middle-rank public service has translated into disenchantment, and public servants have been shown to lack commitment to their superiors (Zussman and Jabes 1990).

As for the *escape route*, it can also take many forms. Some have simply *migrated within* and withdrawn into a mercenary role, belittling, by example if not always by formal utterances, the importance of both ethics in relations with the clientele and a professional culture of solidarity within the organization. Others have effectively *opted out*, sometimes by leaving the public service altogether, which is an unfortunate but easy-to-defend action under the circumstances. But others have *opted out while staying in*, either by submerging themselves in some form of nirvana (which is another way to suppress emotions) or by arguing openly in favour of massive privatization of the public service, as a way out of their quandary and misery.

The adoption of a *mercenary* role is a betrayal of public trust. Public servants are not meant to be robots, but rather important elements within government as a learning organization. Their multiple roles vis-à-vis their client publics and their colleagues in the rest of the organization are pregnant with positive freedoms, that is, obligations and duties that go much beyond the mechanical despatch of orders received from above. Public servants have ruling work to do.

Withdrawing into a passive role amounts to not meeting these obligations and failing to provide clients and colleagues with what they are in a position to demand as a matter of right. At best, it reveals weakness of will; at worst, it generates what Warren Bennis (1976) has labeled "*petit* Eichmannism."

This *opting out* by middle-echelon public servants, and even, at times, by younger or relatively senior bureaucrats into a blind espousal of deregulation/privatization (as a way to cleanse the system by making public management more like private management) is also a dereliction of duty. Many activities may effectively be shifted from the public to the private sector, with some efficiency gains and no meaningful loss on other fronts. And, indeed, these should be so shifted. In the same way, activities currently under the authority of the federal public management system might be allocated to provincial or local authorities as a matter of economy, efficiency, and effectiveness. However, the nature of the activities that can be shifted this way can only be ascertained on the basis of a reasoned discussion of what the market can and cannot handle appropriately and of what different levels of government can deliver. It is the responsibility of public servants to understand and explain to the citizenry and the politicians the porous, but fundamental, border between public and private matters and between federal, provincial, and local matters.

Allowing ideological sloganeering to sway a debate, or to carry a decision without the key decision-makers being fully briefed on all its implications, represent failure by public servants to live up to the *"obligation de diligence"* and the *"devoir de diligence"* that are part and parcel of their positive freedoms. The famous *"obligation de réserve"* should never translate into an *"obligation de mutisme."* Bureaucrats who do not accept these obligations are less an aid to enlightened public decision-making than a hindrance to governments as learning organizations. The inescapable and changing responsibilities of active citizens and public servants, even when these are unpleasant, are to make full use of their positive freedoms, that is, of their obligation to participate (Tussman 1989; see also Chapter 5). This is the sense in which it is said that public servants, like citizens, have ruling work to do.

THE WAY OUT

Senior bureaucrats have a central responsibility in the design of a solution: ethical standards begin at the top. Given their important brokerage function between the public service and its clientele, and their complementary tutelage function vis-à-vis public servants within the organization, one has to recognize first and foremost that they face a *prisoner's dilemma* on both fronts.

A prisoner's dilemma is one of mutual distrust (see *New partnerships and moral contracts* in Chapter 11). Although there is an incentive to betray one's partner in crime, if both partners inform on each other, the penalty is the maximum. The same type of problem exists between the citizenry and the state or in the federal–provincial arena: mutual distrust leads one partner to short-change the other, with the result that the other follows suit and all the benefits of cooperation vanish.

All this can be resolved by negotiating moral contracts. Ideally, our senior bureaucrats would be the key designers in the development of new conventions/moral contracts, both *within* (in their dealings with the different layers of the bureaucracy) and *without* (that is, in their dealings with client publics) as a way out of their dilemmas. For all kinds of reasons, they have not performed this task to the necessary degree. However, it is quite possible to remind them of this central responsibility and to provide incentives for them to engage in moral contract activities.

What conventions might constitute a way out in the circumstances we have described? Our labels for the internal moral contracts that need to be hammered out between high and low *fonctionnaires*, and for the *external* moral contracts between public servants and the general public are rather simple: professionalism and ethics. And, they are closely interrelated.

Professionalism

A moral contract between senior and junior civil servants must be based not only on a sense of respected identity, but also on rules of mutual obligation and a sense of *quid pro quo*. Professionalism refers to both "practical knowledge and social skills that are conducive to savvy functioning within the social and political context of an organization or field" (Messick 1988). It also refers to a culture — "a set of intellectual glasses to interpret reality with," as R.M. Pirsig (1991) puts it — the ensemble of values underpinning this culture and the unwritten agreement in which the mutual obligations these entail are recorded.

As it stands these days, no one is a civil servant first, not in Canada nor in most of the countries Canada usually associates with (Crozier 1987). People are accountants, economists, plumbers, *animateurs*, engineers, or oenologists first: they identify with their craft rather than with their *métier* (from the Latin *ministerium*), which is to serve the public. This primary identification refers to a bond, an esprit de corps that binds as much as it empowers. It often carries with it not only a sense of pride, but also a code of ethics.

People can be public servants first; indeed, there are important models of people who have celebrated that profession as their primary self-label (Bloch-Lainé 1976). However, for such self-identification to prevail, the *métier* of public servants must be refurbished and repromoted to the rank of "honorable profession." This, in turn, calls for a milieu in which openness, candour, and deliberation (i.e., a true, open, internal forum) exist and there is respect for responsibility.

Such professionalism could be the basis of a new *strategic state* — one that would do things better with fewer resources because of the new possibilities opened by networks of mutual trust within the organization. This is a funda-mental requirement if one is to experiment with institutional design along the lines suggested by the *strategy of special operating agencies* or by the more ambitious Swedish model, in which 5% of public servants deal with policy and legislation and 95% deal with management in relatively autonomous agencies. In such contexts, the existence of a common philosophy of public service is essential; the organizational culture ensures some cohesion in decision-mak-ing, along with much cooperation and networking, with the result that the principle of subsidiarity can be fully applied without the usual ailments that flow from decentralization in a paranoid organization.

Ethics

A new moral contract with the citizenry must be based not only on great respect for citizens' right to know, but also on client publics' right to be involved in the evaluation of the public service. This is much more than client-orientation rhetoric: it is a sort of *quid pro quo* involving the protection of public servants from abuse and harassment by clients, and the protection of citizens from the arbitrariness and negligence of public servants.

For the time being, there is a fixation on *quality of service* in the rhetoric of client-orientation. There is a danger that such a phrase can mislead more than it enlightens, for in matters of quality of service in the public sector (at least in the absence of any user fees), the optimum is not, in all likelihood, the maximum. Indeed the notion of "total quality" may be quite misleading. Quality of service in the absence of any price rationing is a bottomless pit. Why should the citizen not demand more if it is free? There develops a logic of entitlements in the clientele to which the public servant responds with a liturgy of service: both parties pretend to be acting in good faith while knowing full well they are not (Paquet 1985d).

By establishing more clearly, via a moral contract, both the entitlements of citizens (within limits) and the obligations of public servants (but also the limitations that might reasonably apply), *and* having a transparent evaluation process for public service based on the participation of citizens, one might expect the establishment of a different rapport between public servants and clients and an enforcement mechanism limiting encroachment on both sides.

For the time being, the two sets of moral contracts linking headquarters to the field and both of them to the citizenry have not been developed into a proud and integrated culture of professional public service. As a result, "*la fonction publique manque de patrons*" (Crozier 1987) in the two senses of the term: leaders and models. Senior headquarters managers, whatever their zeal or good intentions, cannot avoid sending dual messages: the words (that is, the rhetoric of client-service, openness, etc.) do not always jibe with the music (the old arrogant logic of the internal administration of yesteryear), and the rapport between civil servants and the citizenry is based on misunderstanding, because of the indeterminate nature of the moral contract binding the parties.

GUIDING PRINCIPLES

The content of these moral contracts must be explicitly and openly negotiated. But, because the sort of moral agreements that are likely to ensue are to be designed as a way of avoiding excesses and of codifying, somewhat, a sense of *limits*, it may be helpful to go back to the four cardinal virtues (sometimes called natural virtues) proposed by Plato as primary guiding values. They are *temperentia* (the sense of limits, of not going too far), *justitia* (a sense of what is good), *fortitudo* (a capacity to take into account context and the longer time horizon) and *prudentia* (the sense of pursuing reasonable and practical objectives). Schumacher (1973) could not find any better set of principles when he was searching for values likely to guide modern choices at the end of *Small Is Beautiful*.

These principles may not hold the key to the question of what is moral, but they are most helpful in establishing by negotiation what is not moral. Indeed, this is exactly the plausible framework suggested for "locating and developing post-modern insights in relation to justice," according to Stephen White (1991). We often intuitively know better what is unjust than what is just.

Judith Shklar (1991) goes even further and revives an old distinction of Cicero between passive and active injustice to remind her readers that a citizen may act unjustly not only by breaking a law, but also by remaining passive in the face of a public wrong.

This is a backhanded approach, but one that is likely to define the bounds within which the moral contracts might be kept by *convention* of all stakeholders, that is, the tolerable and intolerable bounds of active and passive immorality within which the parties will agree to stay.

WHO SHOULD KICK-START THE NEGOTIATION PROCESS?

For the process of negotiation of moral contracts to proceed quickly, at least two agencies should be involved, thereby triggering the sound emulation and the requisite competition likely to produce results in short order. Two federal agencies stand above all others, in terms of independence and mandate and, therefore, might be considered as extraordinarily well-suited to kick-start the process: the Office of the Auditor General (OAG) and the Public Service Commission (PSC).

The PSC might be charged with the primary responsibility of negotiating the professionalism contract. A redefinition of the role of the PSC is already in progress, not only as a result of internal restructuring, but also as a result of a process of critical thinking in the whole Commonwealth about the roles of PSCs (see Chapter 9). In addition, the Auditor General's (1990) annual report for the fiscal year ending 31 March 1990 began a critical examination of the underlying issues at stake in the definition of such a contract. This might provide many insights into how to do the job.

The OAG might take primary responsibility for negotiating the ethics contract. It has already gone quite a distance toward comprehensive auditing, i.e., asking not only if public service is provided economically and efficiently, but also asking if it is done effectively. However, it has done this work timidly, without much explicit government support and almost entirely without direct, explicit, or powerful involvement of citizens. Professional experts are acting on behalf of the public: this is not good enough. Even in the private sector, where one has the benefit of a market discipline, the lags involved in waiting for the market test are too long, and potential mistakes too costly for one to rely entirely on this feedback mechanism. Private firms now use real customers as focus groups, to evaluate how well they are doing and to determine in what way their product should be improved. An extension of the auditing function to cover effectiveness, and a direct involvement of client publics in the evaluation of effectiveness, would extend the role of the OAG considerably and provide a basis for negotiation of the moral contract between the public service and the citizenry.

CONCLUSION

A strategy based on the definition of moral contracts would contribute much to solving the prisoner's dilemma that plagues public management in Canada and elsewhere. It would define, as clearly as possible, the mutual expectations of both parties, the legitimate entitlements and obligations they might have, and the corridor or boundary limits within which it is imperative or less imperative to effect these entitlements and to honour these obligations.

First, it would rebuild the trust of client publics in the public service community and redefine the centrality of the positive freedoms of public servants in dealing with the public. A greater possibility of cooperation between the citizenry and the state would ensue, and the resulting empowerment of the intellectual resources of the bureaucracy would allow public servants not only to serve the public better, but also to be an integral part of the co-evolution of government, society, and business that is the key to international competitiveness (Archibald et al. 1990).

Second, it would provide the basis for refurbishing the collective decision-making capability within government at a time when it is badly needed and for rebuilding a proud culture of public service within governmental circles with loyalties and commitments attached to it. Further, it would contribute, in no minor way, to eliminating the schizophrenia that plagues public management and prevents it from delivering public services economically, efficiently, and effectively.

In a sense, these new instruments within the public administration apparatus are nothing more than a concretization and an extension of what has already begun to evolve in the relationships between the state and civil society on the broader political scene.

Over the last half century, the role of the state has changed considerably in advanced, modern capitalist economics. From simple housekeeping functions, the state has graduated to Keynesian, off-setting functions as a result of the great instability that used to plague advanced industrial economies and paralyze their effectiveness. Lately, it has become clear that off-setting will no longer suffice. We are now entering an era where cooperation between government, business, and civil society is becoming a basic ingredient of national competitiveness and prosperity. As a result, all advanced industrial countries have reworked, more or less explicitly, their participatory/planning functions, and it may be said that they all have a "plan." As Theodore Lowi (1975) put it, "they do not publish their plan because it would never gain consent. Yet, it is not what one would call a conspiracy.... The plan is not entirely conscious or systematic, and it cannot be as long as it is not written, published, debated, revised and so on. But, it is not what you could call a secret." Lowi has called on political science "to discover what the plan is and, in discovering it, stopping it or improving it as the case may be."

The same sort of agenda is now facing specialists in public administration when it comes to the moral contracts we have referred to earlier. There are important new instrumentalities in the realization of the "plan." Public managers will not only have to continue to deliver their usual services, but they will also have to take part in some social architecture to design the moral contracts likely to create the best structure of public management. The challenge for senior public servants can be likened to the one facing an orchestra leader trying to restructure the orchestra while conducting the concert — shrieks and other ungodly noises can be expected!

Yet, only through joint pressures generated by an informational age requiring a much larger and very different public sector output and by an era of legitimate fiscal restraint where public-sector deficits command that resources be rationed to the public household can a public strategy of *working smarter and cooperatively* be given a real chance to come into being.

No simple rules will do: nothing is black or white — all is grey. This is the area where evolving negotiated moral contracts are going to work best, and this is why they will be the new tool of public management in the 1990s.

CHAPTER 13

DISTRIBUTED GOVERNANCE AND TRANSVERSAL LEADERSHIP*

The obverse of hope is trust.

– James O'Toole

Québec–Canada constitutional carpentering has become a national cottage industry. For years now, aficionados have met in different forums in different weeks of the year to debate slightly different versions of the same basic scenarios. After a while, these ballet-like exchanges have ceased to generate excitement because they are the re-enactment of the same constitutional charades. Yet failure at this game is exacting a heavy toll on the country, and there is a danger of fatigue syndrome among the citizenry.

For the sovereignist camp, the way out of this stalemate is through *hope*. The separatist movement, however flimsy the basis on which it is constructing such hope, is providing permission to dream. For a large number of Quebeckers living in regions where the unemployment rate is oscillating around 30%, the dream of a future where things might not be as bad, of a future that will materialize magically the day Quebec is free from the bondage of Canada, is an attractive proposition. This is not unlike a modern version of the "cult of the cargo" or "some day my prince will come." Passively and effortlessly, the present dreadful state of affairs will be cured by separation.

So far, the federalist camp has either fantasized about instant constitutional reform or been satisfied to try to puncture separatists' hope. It should be clear by now that no magic constitutional refurbishment will materialize and that one cannot expect to win over the hearts and souls of Quebeckers by dashing their hopes. Nor can one expect to win them with promotional brochures about how good Quebeckers have had it within Canada over the last 130 years.

The only way out for the federalist camp is to find ways to rebuild *trust*. This calls for refocusing the debates on the best use of the nonconstitutional route and for new, principled but pragmatic leadership along that road. This, in turn, requires a refurbished notion of governance and a renewed notion of

* This chapter also appeared in Trent, J.E., Young, R., Lachapelle, G. (editors). *Québec–Canada: What Is the Path Ahead?/Nouveaux sentiers vers l'avenir.* Ottawa: University of Ottawa Press, 1996, pp. 317–332.

leadership rooted in earned confidence based on the accomplishments of the leader as servant. This sort of governance and leadership is feared not so much by the have-nots (who are often uninvolved and passively hopeful), but by the haves who have invested so much in the status quo (status, beliefs, values, power) that they are unlikely to allow change to perturb their comfort and security.

Challenging this collective myopia of the haves and their "somnambulistic certainty" about the rectitude of the existing governance process and the sort of leadership in good currency is the task facing those who want to earn trust (Mannheim 1936; O'Toole 1995).

FROM CENTRALIZED TO DISTRIBUTED GOVERNANCE

Governance is about guiding: it is the process through which an organization is steered. Fifty years ago, in Canada, governance was debated in the language of management science. It was presumed that public, private, and social organizations were strongly directed by leaders who had a good understanding of their environment, of the future trends in the environment if nothing were done to modify it, of the inexorable rules of the game they had to put up with, and of the goals pursued by their own organization. Those were the days when social sciences were still Newtonian: a world of deterministic, well-behaved mechanical processes where causality was simple because the whole was the sum of the parts. The challenge was relatively simple: building on the well-defined goals of the organization to design the control mechanisms likely to get the organization where it wanted to be.

Many issues were clearly amenable to this approach, but as the pace of change accelerated and the issues grew more complex, private, public, and social organizations became confronted more and more with "wicked problems" (Rittel and Webber 1973; see Chapter 2) requiring a new way of thinking. The governance system evolved accordingly, and rather smoothly over the last decades. However, what is not always understood is that it has been transformed as a result of a number of rounds of adaptation to provide the requisite flexibility and suppleness of action. The ultimate result of these changes is a composite governance system built on unreliable control mechanisms in pursuit of ill-defined goals in a universe that is chronically in a state of flux. This composite governance process has emerged in four stages of increasing complexity (Boisot 1987; Paquet 1994b).

At first, when organizations were relatively small and under the direction of autocratic leaders, governance had a fiefdom quality: information flows were very informal, and they were strongly focused on a small group around the leader. But as problems grew more complex, this pattern of governance faltered. More elaborate structures and more formal rules had to evolve to meet the organization's changing needs, but these formal rules remained the preserve of those at the top of the hierarchies. From these emerged the more-or-less standard bureaucratic forms of organization that played an important role during "*les trentes glorieuses années*" between the 1940s and the 1970s.

As the pace of change accelerated, problems became ever more complex, less easily structured and ever-changing, and the bureaucratic system, with its inability to transform quickly enough, began to show signs of dysfunction. This led to efforts to partition private, public, and social bureaucracies into smaller self-contained and more flexible units that were likely to be more responsive to clients. This market-type governance, built on the price system, had the benefit of being more inclusive, for price information is widely shared. In the private sector, large companies began a process of segmentation, creating a multiplicity of relatively independent profit-centred organizations likely to be more attentive to the changing needs of the clients and to be more adaptable to evolving circumstances. After a lag time, public bureaucracies went the same route with, for instance, the creation of executive agencies in the United Kingdom and special operating agencies in Canada. Organizations came to be governed — to a much greater extent than before — by the "invisible hand" of the market.

But information flows in market-type organizations are anonymous and highly stylized; thus, the price-driven steering mechanism often proved to be less than perfect. For instance, it was insensitive to third-party effects and external economies and incapable of appreciating either synergies within the organization or the various forces at work in the external environment. More important, the myopia of the market led to short-term opportunistic competitive behaviour that proved disastrous for organizations. As a result, an effort was made to establish or re-establish, within the decentralized units, the informal cooperative links — *les liens moraux* — that might give an organization a sense of shared values and commitments. Corporate culture acquired a new importance as the sort of social glue that enabled organizations to steer themselves better through better use of informal moral contracts based on shared values.

Although private-sector organizations were quick to develop these new informal channels of communication, public organizations were much slower to recognize the central importance of these clan-type relations. In Canada, the Public Service 2000 exercise was perhaps one of the first occasions when these issues gained prominence.

This shift in the centre of gravity of the governance system is captured well in Max Boisot's (1987) information space in which he identifies the different types of governance schemes that correspond to more or less codified and more or less diffused information flows (Figure 4 in Chapter 1). Although earlier forms of governance continue to persist and endure, the whole organizational architecture has come to be dominated less and less by the sort of centralized formal decision-making and hierarchical control that characterize the governance of fiefdoms and bureaucracies, and more and more by informal and distributed governance systems like those of markets and clans. Within a complex and multifaceted governance process, the center of gravity of Boisot's information space has been shifting broadly from a bureaucratic focus to a market-cum-clan focus over the last decades.

When the ground is in motion, organizations can only govern themselves by becoming capable of learning both their goals and the means to reach them *as they proceed*, by tapping the knowledge and information in the possession of active citizens and getting them to invent ways out of the predicaments they are in. This more decentralized governance intervenes strategically as an animateur and a catalyst. Such a governance system deprives the leader of his or her monopoly on the governing of the organization. For the organization to learn quickly, everyone must take part in the *conversation* and bring forward each bit of knowledge and wisdom he or she has that has a bearing on the issue (Webber 1993; Piore 1995; see also Chapter 11).

The new governance structures (more modular, network-like, and integrated either by the invisible hand of the market or by informal moral contracts) are only one half of the learning process. The other half is the work of the leader as animateur. Instead of building on the assumption that the leader is omniscient and guiding autocratically, a distributed governance process builds on social learning and on the capacity of the leader to listen and to lead through a critical dialogue with the stakeholders to ensure that everyone learns about the nature of the problem and about the consequences of various possible alternatives.

In this manner, the citizenry and clienteles learn to limit unreasonable demands, managers and administrators learn to listen and consult, and other stakeholders learn enough about one another's views and interests to gauge the range of compromise solutions that are likely to prove acceptable. As a result, the distributed governance process predicated on social learning builds on the answers to four questions posed to all stakeholders in this variety of meso-forum: Is it feasible? Is it socially acceptable? Is it too destabilizing? Can it be implemented? (Friedmann and Abonyi 1976).

A THREE-PRONGED STRATEGY

In a context of rapid change, the best learning experience can be effected through decentralized and flexible teams woven by moral contracts and reciprocal obligations negotiated in the context of evolving partnerships (Nohria and Eccles 1992; de la Mothe and Paquet 1994). According to this gauge, the Canadian governance system would appear to suffer from learning disabilities. There seems to be a strong institutional residue from the fiefdom and bureaucratic eras. Indeed, some might suggest that those elements still dominate much of the Canadian governance landscape.

For the federal government, the challenge of distributed governance is important. It calls for the definition of a new role for the central government, one that depends to a great extent on its capacity to earn the trust of Canadians and to explain the manner in which it can play its role of animateur and leader within the new governance system.

To effect a transition in our governance system likely to rekindle the commitment of the citizenry and to regenerate trust in the federal government by the population of all regions, three major and difficult tasks must be undertaken: a reframing exercise, a retooling exercise, and a mobilization exercise.

Reframing: The reframing effort entails a shift from debates on government to debates on governance. This will refocus discussions away from the fight between coalitions trying to seize power and establish their hegemony *toward* an examination of the best way to design the system so that it learns faster and more effectively. Our socio-politico-economic system is like our immune system: it is bombarded with new bacteria and viruses continually and it has to learn, develop, and transform to cope effectively with them. Focusing on governance requires that we reflect on the required changes in our governance system. This raises a meta-problem: the question of the rules that are to be used when changing rules.

Some of this reframing has already been initiated at the federal cabinet level. It has been suggested that *a meta-rule could be provided by the principle of subsidiarity* (Burelle 1995; Janigan and Fulton 1996). Such a principle or philosophy of governance leaves completely open the precise allocation of responsibilities; it simply suggests a set of principles to help decide who should do what.

It is difficult to imagine any party refusing *ex ante* to enter a debate on governance based on this principle. Indeed we have reason to believe from statements of endorsement from such staunch sovereignists as J.F. Lizée (on the back cover of André Burelle's [1995] book) that such an approach would even be acceptable to Quebec. This approach also has the merit of putting the responsible citizen at centre stage; underpinning a division of labour not only between Quebec and the rest of Canada but among the private, not-for-profit, and public sectors based on efficiency and proximity; and undergirding a distributed notion of governance and a transverse notion of leadership.

Retooling: The retooling effort needed to support the reframing strategy sketched above entails the development of political and administrative instruments to ensure that the transformation of the governance system is effected in an orderly manner. First, at the symbolic level, one requires a sketch of an inspiring *political vision* of where the governance system might be heading if a subsidiarity strategy were adopted. A plausible beacon might be Switzerland, but there might be other models. Although such a broad fuzzy objective is vague and most certainly not meant to be binding in any way, it would have the advantage of providing the citizenry with a reference point. It is very difficult to understand how trust could be regained by the federalist camp without such a vision. Yet, there seems to be quite a bit of diffidence on the part of federal public officials in providing any vision of where their strategy might lead.

Second, at the realities level, one requires a sketch of the *administrative means* through which the reallocation of responsibilities will proceed. The obvious administrative routes might well be Program Review (in a refurbished format) and the Efficiency of the Federation Initiative (in a rekindled form) as leading instruments to establish beyond reasonable doubt the degree of seriousness of the federal government in proceeding with a streamlining of its own operations in keeping with the philosophy of subsidiarity. This would entail massive devolution with compensation.

Mobilizing: The mobilization exercise calls for a proactive strategy to neutralize the dynamic conservatism of those in power and to expose the various stratagems to derail the process of change. But one must also find ways to elicit a strong commitment to the new philosophy of governance. Education, information, and communication must play an important role in this effort. Central to this process is the recognition of the power of the ideology of comfort and the importance of a new form of values-based leadership mobilizing the positive freedom of the citizenry.

SOCIAL LEARNING AND TRANSVERSAL LEADERSHIP

At the core of this mobilization process, one finds social learning and transverse leadership. To cope with a turbulent environment, organizations must use the environment strategically, the way a surfer uses a wave, to learn faster, to adapt more quickly. This calls for expropriation of the steering power from the top managers. There must be constant negotiation and bargaining with partners. Managers must exploit all favourable environmental circumstances and the full complement of imagination and resourcefulness in the heart and mind of each player. They must become team leaders in task force-type projects, quasi-entrepreneurs capable of cautious suboptimizing in the face of a turbulent environment (Leblond and Paquet 1988).

This sort of strategy calls for lighter, more horizontal and modular structures, networks and informal clan-like rapports (Bressand et al. 1990) in units that are freer from procedural morass, empowered to define their mission and clienteles more precisely, and to invent different performance indicators. Not only in the public sector, but also in the private sector, the "virtual corporation" and the "modular corporation" are the new models (Business Week 1993; Tully 1993).

These new modularized private and public organizations cannot impose their views on clients or citizens. Like the state, the firm must consult. Deliberation and negotiation are everywhere: away from goals and controls, deep into intelligence and innovation. A society based on participation, negotiation, and bargaining is replacing one based on universal rights. The strategic organization has to become a broker, a negotiator, an animateur: in this network socioeconomy, the firm and the state are always in a consultative and participative mode (Paquet 1992a).

In these forums that cut across bureaucratic hierarchies and vertical lines of power, fraught with overlapping memberships, personal ties, temporary coalitions, special-task organizations, "the organizational structure of the future is already being created by the most as well as the least powerful" within the new paradigm (Hine 1977). Indeed, to the extent that middle-range regional and transnational networks and forums are cutting across usual structures, the interactions distill in an evolutionary way an always imperfectly bounded network.

The new competencies that are going to be essential in this world have not been fully documented yet, and there would be much disagreement in any discussion about what should be on any priority list. But one may draw a provisional list from the work of Donald Michael (1980, 1988a,b) and Gareth Morgan (1988). These new competencies fall into four general groups: contextual competencies, interpersonal and enactment skills, creating an effective corporate climate, and systems values. This last group is particularly important as it draws attention to the new ethic driven by interconnectedness and interdependence: "our values still emphasize rights and autonomy while the actual circumstances of life make imperative the acceptance of obligations and interdependence" (Michael 1988a). This ethic is one that forces a redefinition of leadership: away from leaders as generals to leaders as leaders of leaders — those removing obstacles that prevent followers from making creative and effective decisions themselves (O'Toole and Bennis 1992).

For the social system to adapt (i.e., to learn) as much and as fast as possible, some basic conditions must be realized: the conversation between leaders and followers must be conducted with *tact and civility*; and within a context where the ethos is sufficiently rich and supportive to make possible the *avventura comune*. These are conditions for transversal leadership.

Tact would appear to be a very limited requirement for the conversation to yield social learning. Indeed, many have felt that it cannot be a sufficient condition. Yet, Gadamer (Kingwell 1995) defines *tact* as "a particular sensitivity to situations, and how to behave in them, for which we cannot find any knowledge from general principles." This is a screening not at the level of the types of problems or issues to tackle, but at the level of permissible arguments. It embodies the basic condition for the conversation to continue — a dual requirement of not saying just anything that comes to mind and of keeping a certain openness vis-à-vis the arguments of others.

With regard to the sort of "communautarian" fabric likely to support a fruitful conversation, it is also difficult to establish precise conditions for its emergence. It may originate in various ways and be woven according to quite different logics. It is clear, however, that the conversation is much more fruitful in a "contextualist" world of multiplexed relations of mutual interdependence and caretaking, of group-oriented social relations. In a network society like Japan, the contextualist culture has been shown to facilitate greatly conversation and social learning on a large scale (Kumon 1992).

Leadership is the leavening force that is required to ensure effective social learning. Effective leaders lead change by reflecting the values of their followers after having done much listening. For effective leaders are principled but also pragmatic. They tend to bring their followers beyond their limits, but not unreasonably fast and not unreasonably beyond such limits.

To be followers, team members must first respect their leader and be persuaded that *their* welfare is the leader's objective. The burden of office for a leader is, therefore, first a requirement to listen and to "refine the public views in a way that transcends the surface noise of pettiness, contradiction and self-interest" (O'Toole 1995:10–12). The leader must earn the trust of the followers by persuading them that he or she has their needs and aspirations at heart. The leader's ability to lead is a by-product of the trust he or she has earned by serving the followers (O'Toole 1995: 28).

Transversal leadership cannot function unless the leader and the followers develop a capacity to appreciate the limits imposed by their mutual obligations. This form of leadership does not depend on a matrix where vertical-functional and horizontal-process rapports are supposedly keeping one another in check. Rather, processes are dominating and the reaction to external challenges is for the different stakeholders to coalesce laterally to create informal links and multifunctional teams capable of promoting faster and more effective learning (Tarondeau and Wright 1995).

Transversality is built on a multifunctional *esprit de corps* that provides fertile ground for social learning. It is based on the existence of a social capital of trust, reasonableness, and mutual understanding that facilitates debate and generates a sort of basic pragmatic ethic likely to promote interaction and synergies among the many partners in the organization. Transversal leadership is based on the ligatures among functions effected by individuals or groups that have accepted the distributed nature of governance and are building on new modes of cross-functional coordination. Although much of this new coordination is fuzzy and built on moral contracts, it must be clear that it represents the only effective way to guide the organization and nudge it in different directions (Putnam 1995).

What is at stake in leadership is "the ability to stay the course while 'rocking the boat' to enhance organizational readiness and competitiveness in an unpredictable environment" (Vicere 1992). This ability cannot be imparted effectively except through experiential and action learning.

RESISTANCE TO CHANGE

Leadership is first and foremost a moral issue. It is based fundamentally on a conversation between leader and followers in which the burden of office of the leader entails listening carefully and taking responsibility. In that sense, the leader is a servant. The official is

> A person with duties and obligations, not merely an insatiable center of gigantic appetites, a person with things to do that may be the death of his

private self, that may make the office seem less an opportunity than a burden. And sometimes, even without the aid of flaws, a tragic burden. In fact, if we do not understand the office and its burdens we may not understand about tragedy. [Tussman 1989: 15]

The nature of the burden of office of the transversal leader is best illustrated by Jan Carlzon (1987), the CEO of Scandinavian Airlines and author of *Moments of Truth*. When he had occasion to explain how he had chosen to empower his employees and to make them totally responsible for the 50 million "moments of truth" that occur annually when an employee of the company has a direct one-on-one contact with a customer, he was often asked how many of these moments of truth had gone sour. Carlson always readily confessed that there had been half a dozen serious instances of costly errors in approximately six years. When asked how the employees responsible for costly errors had been punished, he would answer,

> Punish them? Why should we have punished them when it was *our* fault? We believe the task of leaders... is to articulate the values of the organization, to create a system in which people can be productive, and to explain the goals that the system was established to achieve.... If we in top management had done those jobs properly... those few errors would not have occurred. That is why we went back to evaluate our own communication skills. [O'Toole 1995: 59]

When a group is demoralized, when junior officials have lost their trust in their leaders, as is the case in Canada now, we are faced with a form of *vertical solitude*. In the case of the Canadian public service, this phenomenon has been gauged very precisely through surveys (Zussman and Jabes 1990), but the phenomenon goes much beyond this group. In most cases, surveys reveal the lack of trust of citizens and junior officials in their leaders, but the leaders are quite satisfied to ascribe such results to extraneous circumstances, to the flaws of their subordinates, or to the ignorance of the citizenry.

Our experience suggests that there are systemic reasons for the lack of trust and for the political stalemate in Canada. These reasons fall into three general categories: the existence of a centralized mindset, the development of the adversarial syndrome, and the burden of envy and resentment inherited from our egalitarian tradition of the last 50 years.

A Centralized Mindset

Over the last 125 years, circumstances have often endangered Canadian prosperity. Canada has had to learn ways and means to cope with these challenges in a manner that reconciled the geotechnical and sociopolitical constraints it operated under with the values, plans, and idiosyncrasies its diverse population had given priority to at the time. A *habitus* has evolved: a system of habitualized dispositions and inclinations to use certain institutional devices or stratagems that appear to do the job of reconciling all those constraints most effectively.

The *economic culture* that has evolved in this fashion has underpinned the governance of the Canadian economy over the last century and has been based *decentralized Canada*

on two fundamental elements: the extensive use of *public enterprise* and *interregional redistribution* of the economic surpluses (Hardin 1974). These two root stratagems have been used repeatedly from the very early days of the federation and at most stages in the country's first century of evolution.

Recently, both these tenets of the Canadian economic culture have come under attack. There has been a massive disengagement by the federal government from its public enterprises, and large-scale interregional redistribution of resources has been questioned. This has come about for many reasons. Disenchantment with guidance from the centre has led to decentralization. Many public enterprises have been privatized or have ceased to play a central policy role, and the weakening of the central government's financial capacity has eroded its ability to make massive interregional transfers.

But this has in no way diminished the extraordinary propensity to centralize that has come to characterize Canada. This is not only a Canadian trait; it is a widely shared bias. Mitchel Resnick (1994) has analyzed the bizarre *travers* that explains that, in an era of decentralization in every domain, centralized thinking is remaining prevalent in our theories of knowledge, in our ways of analyzing problems, and in our search for policy responses. "Politicians, managers and scientists are working with blinders on, focusing on centralized solutions even when decentralized approaches might be more appropriate, robust, or reliable" (Resnick 1994: 36).

This centralized mindset appears to be stronger in Canada than elsewhere, and the strategies to immunize the traditional centralized mindset from challenges and erosion have been very sophisticated. These have gone through many phases. First, there was the *denial posture*. Using public spending patterns as benchmarks, many have argued that Canada is one of the most decentralized countries in the world. The fact that spending at the subnational level was commanded by conditional transfers appears to have been ignored.

A second line of defense suggests that further devolution might well balkanize the country, which would be disastrous (McCallum in McKenna 1995). But Migué (1994) has shown rather persuasively that centralization — and not decentralization — is the source of balkanization in Canada.

A third defense is that the glue that binds this country together is the egalitarian economic culture of redistribution. National standards are the fabric of this country, so central control cannot be reduced. Moreover, the central government must retain the role of enforcer because of international agreements that Canada is party to (Banting 1996; Leslie in McKenna 1995). This would appear to be the Queen's defense, and we have shown elsewhere that it is not very potent (Paquet 1996c).

A fourth argument is that decentralization is necessary, but it must be postponed until we have uncovered "Canadian core values" that might be used in determining the nature, extent, and character of "acceptable" decentralization (Maxwell 1995).

These arguments are often mere sophistry when they are not explicit devices to slow down the process of change, but they constitute *in toto* a most effective strategy for resisting change, and this sort of strategy is explicitly propagated by those officials who have most to fear from massive decentralization.

The Adversarial Syndrome

The conflict between the centralized mindset of Canadian leaders and the forces underpinning the dispersive revolution has directly generated some resistance to change, but it has also catalyzed the coalescence of a national adversarial system in Canada (Valaskakis 1990). This regime has developed less as a matter of design than as a result of (1) adversarial relations becoming the modus operandi and the new underlying philosophy and (2) conflictive equilibria (situations where nothing can be resolved except by cooperation, but collaboration appears extremely difficult if not impossible) in government–business–society relations, in the labour–management world, but also within each sector (private, public, and social) as between large and small firms, between the federal and provincial levels, or between various environmental groups.

One should not unduly malign competition nor excessively lionize decision-making by consensus, but it seems that Canada is fractured by those re-enforcing adversarial systems to the point where the public policy forum has not hesitated to blame them for much of the erosion of Canada's competitiveness. The adversarial syndrome has undoubtedly been the source of some paralysis in Canada's wealth-creation process as a result of the multiple stalemates it has engendered, but it has also contributed significantly to the reduction of the surplus potentially available for redistribution.

This adversarial syndrome corresponds to the strong taste for competition in the Anglo-American space (Choate and Linger 1988), but it also echoes a profound social decapitalization in North America (Putnam 1995, 1996). It has thrived on the loss of civic engagement based on networks, norms, and social trust that facilitate coordination and cooperation for mutual benefit, but it has also accelerated the process of social decapitalization.

According to Hollingsworth (1993), this civic disengagement has triggered a weakening of the sociocultural underground on which cooperation is built for firms and public and social organizations. It has also contaminated the core of the basic values on which our sociopolitical system has been built. This explains the difficulties in generating the requisite processes to solve the challenging problems of coordination created by the new world of distributed governance.

Egalitarianism, Envy, and Resentment

A third general set of forces has contributed to a "climate of unreasonableness" and a sociocultural underground that has proved more likely to generate division than cohesion. It has its roots in the promotion of egalitarianism as a basic value and a democratic dogma in a world more and more segmented along ethnocultural lines. This has generated a heightened degree of tension and envy at the intercultural interface (Laurent and Paquet 1991).

The nature of these jealousies and the deep resentment created by the propaganda about egalitarianism in a world where differences are omnipresent have been suppressed, but the profound public sentiment that one cannot be "equal and different" has prevailed and remains prevalent in all recent inter-provincial deliberations and all constitutional forums throughout the country.

It may well be that nothing less than a new social contract built on the principle "different but united" can accommodate the requisite separateness, complementarities, and hierarchies and reduce envy and contain violence. But we are still far from willing to confront the demons of egalitarianism and the social capital of envy and resentment that has been accumulated by top-down efforts to force acceptance of terms that seem to attempt to square the circle of "equal and different." They have not only generated much social anomie, but they are also responsible for the failure of the Meech Lake and Charlotte-town accords. Moreover, they still represent fundamental mental blocks to much-needed discussion about the possibility of any viable asymmetric regime.

This has fueled much social decapitalization and reinforced the intransi-gence of egalitarians demanding a new drive for centralization capable of guaranteeing the necessary renewed powers of redistribution to ensure stand-ardization. Although the likelihood of a "different but united" social contract may appear utopian, the proposed alternatives for managing this intercultural interface (separateness and encapsulation) appear unpalatable (Laurent and Paquet 1991: 177–178).

THE LONG ADMINISTRATIVE ROUTE AS A SHORTCUT

The bells and whistles of constitutional conferencing usually overshadow the more pedestrian way of addressing difficult issues using the administrative state, i.e., the decisions of public officials. A most divisive and explosive issue like *universality* has been handled in this manner in Canada. Canadians knew very well that addressing this issue head-on would be too politically destabiliz-ing, so it was adroitly handled by the administrative state. Universality has now all but disappeared, and new arrangements have come to take its place without a major national confrontation.

Many of the real concerns (as opposed to the symbolic ones) over which the various parties agonize could be handled in this manner. Indeed, no less than 70% of what Charlottetown and Meech were trying to achieve could be accomplished through administrative rearrangements. The Efficiency of the Federation Initiative, introduced late in 1993, and Program Review in 1994 were promising instruments to effect much of that work. Their minimal success so far should not be interpreted as an indication of a congenital flaw in these processes. Their failures are ascribable much more to the centralized mindset of the government in power than to any other force (Paquet 1996b, Paquet and Shepherd 1996).

Social Learning

Most of the high-level constitutional debates get bogged down in posturing, in negotiation through the media, in extraordinarily intricate and unfortunate wording that proves to be cast in stone as soon as it hits the street. This generates important learning disabilities. It is much less difficult to proceed through a major reframing of issues or to negotiate important compromises when one is not in Macy's window. This is the reason why we have had such a long tradition of successes using the administrative route.

One can point to the social learning by all parties that has marked decades of negotiations of the Tax Structure Committee or generations of anonymous committees of public officials who have been particularly effective at reframing issues and have allowed the federation to evolve quickly and fruitfully over the last century.

Social learning may materialize in the constitutional debate, although there are reasons to feel pessimistic, as any group of malcontents may cause the whole process to crash. In dealing with high-profile, symbolic issues, no other channel can provide an easy resolution of disputes at this level. The "distinct society" conundrum is a good example of such issues. But, for most substantive issues, the administrative route is much more promising because of its capacity to generate faster learning and its greater probability of being successful in reframing issues. This road holds the promise of rapid progress, whereas the constitutional route appears to be paved with bad intentions.

Social Learning Through Panic

There has been a slow, but irreversible, awakening to the new realities as a result of the October 30th (1995) referendum. This has triggered new thinking at the federal cabinet level, if one is to believe the revelations about the famous "master plan" calling for devolution of 25% or more of federal program activities in the very near future (Janigan and Fulton 1996). But, given the schizophrenic mind of the federal cabinet on this front, time is of the essence. The panic effect might easily fade away and the original good intentions may be squashed and derailed by the not inconsiderable group of federal public officials who still adhere to the view that nothing would be more disastrous for Canada than the erosion of Ottawa's power.**

Not all social learning is a feed forward process. One might suspect that those most opposed to a transformation of the Canadian governance system also feel a sense of urgency. Their rear-guard action will not take the form of

---

** As of early 1999, as we are going to press, the federal–provincial social union discussions are embroiled in controversies, and it would appear clear that the federal government is intent on reconditionalizing federal–provincial transfers for medicare. The panic effect has faded away, the centralized mindset looms large, and social learning has gone awry.

counterproductive inflammatory denunciations of the devolution process. In all likelihood, it will consist of a broad focus on alternative program delivery and a quality service-centred federalism. Such a strategy might be a genuine way out of the constitutional conundrum, but it can equally well be a decoy and a thwarting maneuver designed to give the appearance of transformation of federal governance without any substantial reduction of the federal hegemony. In this dark scenario, a multitude of federal special operating agencies and a focus on quality of service might even succeed in getting Ottawa's central agencies to increase their power base.

On the other hand, a more optimistic scenario of a rekindled administrative route to change in the governance system might help the parallel work along the constitutional highway. Such a scenario would call for a reframing of perspectives along the lines suggested by Burelle (1995) and others: a vision of Canada that would proceed comfortably toward decentralization à la Switzerland, a general philosophy of governance based on subsidiarity (i.e., a strong push toward the responsibilization of the citizen and a recognition that one can best attend to citizens' needs at the level closest to the citizens), a renewal of the notion of citizenship replacing the entitlement mentality with a sense of mutual obligation, and a move away from the state's heavy top-down omnipresence toward a light-handed strategic state ensuring bottom-up and more distributed governance (Paquet 1994b; Burelle 1995).

Toward a New Deal

If the federal "master plan" is to be carried out at all, it must be implemented quickly. It would call for a rejuvenation of the Efficiency of the Federation Initiative and for a refurbishment of the Program Review. The explicit objective should be to achieve, through administrative negotiation over the next six months, so much progress toward the reallocation of responsibilities among the federal government, the provinces, the not-for-profit sector, and the private sector, that it would be impossible for the crusaders on the high stage of constitutional talks not to acknowledge that there has been a reframing of the central issues.

Then one might be able to focus on some fundamentals that are, for the moment, drowned by ideologic harangues. These fundamentals are (1) the extraordinary interregional economic interdependence that still exists in Canada and that one would not wish to destroy lightly (Helliwell and McCallum 1995), but also (2) the recognition that Canada is, fundamentally, a "community of communities" much like Switzerland and that attempts to homogenize it unduly and to thrust national standards on these diverse communities can, at best, balkanize the country and, at worst, fracture it (Migué 1994).

Decentralization does not entail breaking the economic union or balkanizing the social union: it simply means forcing local and provincial governments to provide the level of services they can afford. If anything, by foisting onto provinces standards they could not afford, past efforts at decentralization have, in fact, distorted prices, diminished provincial responsibility, and prevented interregional adjustments of human and financial resources. Indeed with the dead weight impact of equalization payments, the provinces are put in an ignominious position: "the more inefficient the provinces are, the more they are compensated by the central authority" (Migué 1994: 117).

CONCLUSION

There is no hope of our getting out of our present stalemate by focusing all our efforts on the constitution. We must be ready to recognize that, to cut through this mess, our political scissors need two blades: a constitutional one to deal with symbolic issues and an administrative one to deal with substantive issues. Moreover, it is only when the second blade is sharp that the first can really come into play.

There has been much skepticism about the effectiveness of the administrative route. Public officials in Ottawa have feared that route from the very beginning; so much so, that they have successfully derailed many genuine efforts to make good use of it (Paquet and Roy 1995; Paquet and Shepherd 1996).

The panic social learning triggered by the referendum results provides a unique window of opportunity to revive the administrative strategy before it becomes re-encapsulated by the forces of dynamic conservatism.***

*** The ethnographic evidence available would appear to show that while much pessimism is in order at the level of political negotiations, much optimism is permissible when one focuses on the federal–provincial discussions at the bureaucratic level.

THE BURDEN OF OFFICE, ETHICS, AND CONNOISSEURSHIP*

> Civilization is an achievement in the face of difficulties,
> a precarious achievement. It is the state of mind of the magician
> who tremblingly invokes the powers he would use, knowing that
> if he gets the ceremony wrong what he invokes will destroy him.
>
> – *Joseph Tussman (1989)*

The notions of *accountability* and *ethics* are poorly understood, and the adequacy of existing frameworks for analyzing them may be responsible for much of our inability to contribute to more effective institutions of public policy (Uhr 1992; Dubnick 1996). Although both terms are used freely by public administrators, academics, and ordinary citizens, they are often used inappropriately.

At a time when there is so much public outcry over our society having lost its moral anchor and its sense of responsibility, carelessness in the use of these words has become even more costly. In fact, the misuse of these concepts by legal, political, and managerial authorities has been denounced as deceit that is no less damaging than if the Bank of Canada were to issue counterfeit currency. This explains the quest for precise rules, standards, and norms to serve as guidelines and benchmarks for what constitutes responsible, accountable, and ethical behaviour under various circumstances. This is a futile quest.

This does not mean that one cannot ground these concepts somewhat better in a reality capable of illuminating them. But, the degree of precision one can hope for in this venture is quite limited: accountability and ethics are fundamentally contentious because of the fact that the notion of the burden of office, on which they are built, is an essentially contested concept.

THE BURDEN OF OFFICE AS A CONTESTED CONCEPT

In a democracy, each citizen is an official, a person with duties and obligations. He or she has ruling work to do and is not simply a consumer of governance but also a producer. Indeed, it is only because citizens as citizens have duties

---

* This chapter first appeared in *Canadian Public Administration* 1997, 40(1), 55–71.

and obligations that they are entitled to civil rights that ensure they are fully equipped with the power to meet their obligations. But there is not much meaningful debate about the nature of this burden of office; when there is, agreement does not necessarily ensue (Tussman 1989).

The same fuzziness holds for more "important" officials, i.e., those holding higher office, be they prime minister, chief of defense staff, etc. They are persons with higher obligations and duties that are often rather ill-defined in our complex world. This vagueness is unfortunately unavoidable. It is a consequence of the fact that the concept of burden of office is socially based; it is based on "a shared set of expectations and a common currency of justifications" (Day and Klein 1987) that are quite difficult to define consensually. We underline this state of affairs when we say that the burden of office is an essentially contested concept.

Gallie (1964: 158) identified a whole range of concepts as essentially contested, i.e., concepts "the proper use of which inevitably involves endless disputes about their proper uses on the part of the users." He has identified five conditions for a concept to be essentially contested: it must be (1) appraisive, in the sense that it accredits some kind of valued achievement; (2) this achievement must be complex in character and its worth attributed to the achievement as a whole; but (3) variously describable in its parts, with the possibility of various components being assigned more or less importance, and (4) open in character to the extent that it admits considerable modification in the light of changing circumstances. Moreover, to qualify as an essentially contested concept, (5) each party must recognize that its own use of the concept is contested by other parties (Gallie 1964: 161). A good example of such a concept may be "championship" in a sport like figure skating, which can be judged in a number of different ways, with differential attention being paid to method, strategy, style, etc.

My argument is that the notion of burden of office (like the concepts of democracy and social justice [Gallie 1964: 178–182]) is an essentially contested concept, and it is quite impossible to find a general principle to determine which party is using the concept best.

It came to my attention after this paper was written that there is another way of stating the problem. Michael Harmon (1995: 5) has sharply criticized the rationalist discourse on government by arguing that the notion of responsibility with "ethical correctness and the conformity of action with authoritative ends [is]... necessarily flawed in a fundamental way." Paradox is everywhere in public administration.

BURDEN OF OFFICE, ACCOUNTABILITY, AND ETHICS

If the burden of office is an essentially contested concept, the notions of accountability and ethics are in some way infected. The fuzziness of the former concept projects some haziness into the definition of the latter two.

Accountability refers to the requirement to "answer for the discharge of a duty or for conduct." This presupposed an agreement on what constitutes acceptable performance and what constitutes an acceptable language of justification for actors defending their conduct (Day and Klein 1987). But, in the complex world in which we now live, officials are confronted with many interfaces with different stakeholders with different claims to authority (hierarchical superior, professional colleagues, clients, etc.); demands for many types of accounts (political, managerial, legal, professional, etc.); and much complexity, heterogeneity, and uncertainty in the circumstances surrounding the activities for which they are accountable. Thus, the very complexity of the burden of office results in much fuzziness in the definition of accountability.

Ethics is a form of goodness-of-fit that evolves in and from reflection in action, deliberation, or "argumentation — among particular people, in specific situations, dealing with concrete things, with different things at stake" (Toulmin 1988). Judgement is embodied in action. *A reflective conversation with the situation* resolves moral issues in the same manner that it resolves the problem faced by an industrial designer: in both cases, the challenge is to find a form that fits the circumstance, given the constraints. When a designer interacts with a situation, the interactive triggers the generation of a goodness-of-fit between two intangibles: a form that has not yet been designed and a context that cannot be properly and fully described, because it is still evolving (Alexander 1964; Cloutier and Paquet 1988; Paquet 1991–92b, 1997f). This is the way of the "reflective practitioner" (Schon 1983). The notion of ethical fitness calls for the same fit between the standard defined by the burden of office and those that take into account the circumstance. And again, the essentially contested nature of the notion of burden of office makes it impossible for ethical conduct to escape a degree of fuzziness.

The fact that the notion of burden of office is essentially contested will not prevent contestants from claiming that their use of the concept is "the only one that can command honest and informed approval" (Gallie 1964: 189). Consequently, there will be different views about accountability and ethical behaviour. This is not without danger, for, as the essential contestedness of the concept transpires, there is always a *real danger* that those in authority may grow impatient with trying to persuade and be led to "a ruthless decision to cut the cackle, to damn the heretics and to exterminate the unwanted"(Gallie 1964). The conversation and the deliberation are interrupted, and democracy is in danger.

DEALING WITH INCOMMENSURABLES

But even when the conversation does not stop, there is a tendency to deny the essential contestedness of the concept and to search for ways to simplify the notion of burden of office to ensure well-behaved trade-offs among the various interfaces with stakeholders. In fact, what many refuse to accept is that the burden of an official in a multidimensional world of hierarchical superiors,

professional colleagues, clients, etc., amounts to choices among incommensurables. The search for simple rules can only result in formulas that claim to
reduce incommensurables to commensurability. For that reason, it is hardly
surprising that this approach fails.

Defining accountability in a single direction, with reference to only one
stakeholder, or without taking account of the context is extremely dangerous.
It would amount to assuming that only one dimension is important and
presuming that all other forms of accountabilities can be regarded as irrelevant or secondary in some sense. The famous 1919 case between the Dodge
brothers and Ford is a case in point. At the time, the court chastised Ford's
corporate board for not paying exclusive attention to the interests of the
shareholders in their decisions. This considerably limited their burden of
office. This situation has evolved over the last 80 years, and the burden of
office of corporate directors has now changed and become much more
complex. Currently, a few dozen U.S. states have legislation that clearly
establishes that corporate boards may take into account other stakeholders'
interests (de la Mothe and Paquet 1996).

Even though the burden of office of corporate directors has been prudently
extended, the notion of accountability is still not widely regarded as a 360-de-
gree process, that is, as pertaining to all the stakeholders surrounding the
official. And yet, focus on a single dimension is likely to be fundamentally
contested. So, the only way to get agreement about what constitutes *acceptable
performance* and *acceptable justification* is through deliberation, not through the
unilateral imposition of one set of views.

The same may be said about ethics. Ethics is by definition "agonistic"—
from the Greek *agon*, meaning competition, rivalry, conflict of characters in
tragic dramas (Gray 1995: 1). One must make moral sense in the presence of
conflicting and incommensurable alternatives. Consequently, moral reasoning
cannot proceed on the basis of the comfort of universal ethical rules or codes.
Indeed, it cannot rely on any simplistic theory that purports to provide answers
to ethical dilemmas by pretending to gauge incommensurable situations with
a single measuring stick. Nontrivial ethical issues involve rival goods and evils
and dilemmas that cannot be solved or decided by rational reflection. The
rationalistic normative theories (utilitarianism, contractarianism, right-based
principles, etc.) are futile, because they are swayed by simplistic universalism
(i.e., the belief that there are universal rules that will arbitrate all moral
dilemmas) (Clarke and Simpson 1989).

In the name of utilitarianism, one falls into total disrespect for the
individual; right-based approaches condone the most awesome inequities. As
for the Rawlsian (1971) contractarian approach, it is silent on the nature of the
redistribution required to ensure satisfactory allocation of the so-called "primary" goods. Consequently, no clearly acceptable criteria for action can be
derived from these general principles, because they are all too completely
disconnected from a full appreciation of context and, therefore, are of no
practical use (Paquet 1994c, 1997f).

Insistence on only one dimension of the burden of office or of the accountability framework (legal, organizational, professional, or political) or a lack of prudence in balancing the moral push (to live up to one's values) with the moral pull (the need to respect the values of the other various stakeholders) can only lead to abusive, dangerous, and truncated notions of burden of office, accountability, and ethics (Dubnick 1996). There is no easy way out: there must be discussion, dialogue, and deliberation leading to social learning and to an always imperfect and incomplete reconciliation of these different dimensions.

Value relativism is often presented as the only alternative to universal principle: it is the world of "anything goes." To most people, this appears rather abhorrent, which is why *pluralism that is regarded* as *a sort of halfway house* has acquired such a good press (Keyes 1993). Pluralism is first and foremost against monism. Pluralists reject the view that there is only one system of values leading to the good life. However, they must agree to find some grounds to impose reasonable limits on what is acceptable and some justification for imposing these limits on the possibilities that individuals may pursue. Although relativists do not believe that any such limits can have an objective basis, pluralists do. But how can this be done?

It can only materialize through social learning, through the erratic process of bouncing off the limits of tacit convention and making the highest and best use of scandals, because scandals are events pointing to unacceptable situations or behaviours (Paquet 1994c). This is not likely to result in a high degree of marksmanship. But it is only through an oblique process of this sort that the limits of the unacceptable are defined and jurisprudence slowly redefines the boundaries beyond which current convention does not hold. In the same way, scandals act as *révélateurs* to signal that certain limits have been crossed, but there is some randomness in the scandal-generating process. Learning is recognizing the difference between what is expected and what happens, and embracing this error as a way of evaluating and adjusting action (Michael 1993).

But this learning can only occur under some conditions: (1) if the conversation with the situation is conducted within a context where the ethos is sufficiently rich and supportive (i.e., the sum of characteristic usages, ideas, and codes by which a group is differentiated is strong enough to allow a meaningful conversation to be carried out); and (2) if the conversation, deliberation, and accumulation of judgements is conducted with tact and civility, with a capacity to span boundaries and to synthesize multiple logics. Without a supportive "communautarian" fabric and a fruitful and open conversation, it is difficult to see how learning can occur effectively and how a somewhat objective basis that might define the reasonable limits on which pluralists need to agree can be determined (Schon 1983; Kingwell 1995; Paquet and Pigeon 1995).

Even though Michael Harmon's (1995) work focuses on a general cartography of the paradoxical world of responsibility rather than on ways to navigate in this world of paradoxes, there is a certain family resemblance between my insistence on the essentially contested nature of the burden of office and his insistence on the essentially paradoxical nature of responsibility. For Harmon, responsibility is at best a paradox-ridden locus of creative tension among freedom of will (agency), answerability to some institutional authority (account-ability), and obligation to meet externally generated norms. This leads him to search for a way out — not in unassailable criteria (together with their retinue of obedience and "blameability"), but in a celebration of "practice" and "dialogue." Thus, his philosophical analysis, conducted at a much more abstract level than mine, converges with my celebration of the "reflective practitioner" (Schon 1983).

MORAL REASONING AND INTERMEDIATE CASES

We are then confronted with two very different accounts of ethics and morality: one that seeks "eternal, invariable principles, the practical applications of which can be free of exceptions and qualifications, and the other, which pays closest attention to the specific details of particular moral cases and circum-stances" (Jonsen and Toulmin 1988: 2). The first is an *absolutist version* that oversimplifies the discussion of moral issues; the dogmatism of codes and rules does not allow any middle road between absolutism and relativism. But the second, *pluralist version* also generates major challenges: it relies on human perceptiveness, appreciation, and discernment; it does not prohibit rules, but it condemns them to a limited and conditional role in moral reasoning.

This pluralist stand has been under attack by those who, from Pascal on, have labeled it casuistry or case ethics and have denounced any moral reason-ing based on "cases"or "circumstances" as "an invitation to excuse the inexcus-able" (Jonsen and Toulmin 1988: 11).

Indeed, the pluralist position tries to avoid both absolutism and total value relativism by a rehabilitation of casuistry as the practical resolution of particular moral perplexities. It cannot ensure, however, that the conversation with the situation carried out by the citizens and other officials in the forum and the bearing of the burden of office working itself through in the context of habits, patterns, and institutions (making up the appreciative system and the ethos) will necessarily lead to effective social learning. But double-looped learning (i.e., not only learning better ways to achieve given objectives, but also learning new goals, values, and objectives as circumstances change) is possible.

Ensuring that conversation is conducted in a manner likely to foster social learning requires a process of adaptation of values and an improvement of the "goodness-of-fit" between values and context. For the social system to adapt (i.e., to learn) as much and as fast as possible, some basic conditions must be realized. Some pertain to process, some to new competences, and others have to do with the robustness of the supportive moral contracts in the ethos.

In terms of process, Wittgenstein's (1953) *Philosophical Investigations* may provide some cues. For Wittgenstein, understanding emerges from dialogue: it is mutual understanding. It materializes by looking at a multiplicity of cases, describing examples, drawing analogies, and "drawing attention to the inter-mediate cases so that one can pass easily from familiar cases to the unfamiliar and see the relation between them" (Tully 1995: 108).

Tully notes that this practical form of reasoning is akin to the reasoning in individual cases in common law. This common-law view is typical of the Renaissance humanist culture. It is a commitment to conversation, to listening to the other side, to accepting that the only way to develop reason as a practical skill is to compare and contrast, to exchange and negotiate alternative descriptions.

The sort of learning generated by dialogue does not necessarily congeal in formalized conclusions. It remains very much tacit knowledge, a capacity to deal effectively with matters of practice and to deal with such matters in a timely manner and with a full appreciation of the local and particular context. Such accumulated *tacit knowledge* is predicated on the fact that, through experience, we learn much and that, at any time, we know more than we can tell (Polanyi 1996). This is the way knowledge evolves in common law: case by case and often in a tacit way.

Through the assimilation of evidence, the individual's diagnostic capabil-ity grows. The specific experience is the essence of connoisseurship; it is developed by relating and comparing within a field of knowledge (Freedberg 1989). Connoisseurship, like skill, is communicated by experience and exam-ples, not by precepts. One cannot develop an appreciation of human physiog-nomies except through a long course of experience. The skill of a wine taster or the capacity to swim or ride a bicycle is acquired this way (Polanyi 1958: 54). There is no spontaneous emergence of connoisseurship. It arises out of a combination of some basic capability and extensive exposure to a large number of intermediate cases.

Connoisseurship can never be the application of simple explicit rules. It is a tacit "*savoir-faire*" and "*savoir-être*" and becomes part of the fabric of the trainee. It generates instinctively a responsible decision in the face of complex and uncertain circumstances, a response that appropriately balances agency, accountability, and obligation *hic et nunc*.

Learning values is like learning how to swim: it is done by eliminating misfits, by correcting errors, by continuous realignment to ensure goodness-of-fit between elusive standards and circumstances. But there can be no learning unless one recognizes and embraces error as a fundamental building block in social learning, as a crucial way of fuelling fruitful deliberations. This is true as much for the citizen or the simple soldier as it is for military leaders.

However, the new competences in such learning systems will develop only under certain conditions. There must be an acknowledgment that the high level of uncertainty is irreducible; an explicit will to embrace error as the difference between what is expected and what happens; and a willingness to span boundaries across perspectives (Michael 1993).

Harmon (1995) does not focus on connoisseurship. He spells out the practical implications of viewing responsibility paradoxically, but he proffers no advice. Our focus on the "practitioner" rather that on "practice" forces us to be bolder and to insist on the need, not only to recognize the practical implication of viewing the notion of burden of office as essentially contested in nature, but also to develop practical strategies and to reflect on the sort of competencies likely to lead to workable notions of accountability and ethics.

A robust underlying ethos is also very important for effective social learning. It is embodied in a number of more or less explicit moral contracts linking the various stakeholders; for example, the moral contracts between the citizenry and the bureaucracy, and between the bureaucrats and their leaders (Paquet 1991–92b and Chapter 12). What we mean by a robust ethos is a "contextualist" one in which there are vibrant multiplexed relations of mutual interdependence and caretaking, a contextual fabric rich in networking and in social capital (Putnam 1995). The more trust and esprit de corps, the more effective the social learning.

We know from experience that sometimes faster learning is a matter of survival. Our immune system is bombarded constantly by new viruses, and it must learn and adapt quickly if we are to survive. At times, there is even the possibility that our immune system may not learn fast enough, so it becomes necessary to use a vaccine, a lever to help it learn faster about the best way to fight a disease. The same can be said about any social system. And leadership is the lever in this case.

If the conversation is to be carried on truthfully, the leader must earn the trust of his followers by persuading them that he has their needs and aspirations at heart. The leader's ability to lead and to foster effective social learning is a by-product of the trust he has earned by serving his followers, as well as the capacity of the existing ethos to generate such trust (O'Toole 1995; Paquet 1997f).

For political leaders, the dual moral responsibility to both the citizenry and their followers is quite daunting. For military leaders, because of the fact that there is always a potential life-and-death dimension to their decisions, the stakes are even higher. They must manage high-stakes moral contracts: the citizenry must grant some latitude in the use of violence by armed personnel against a guarantee of higher moral standards among them than what is expected from the ordinary citizen; armed personnel must make a commitment to selflessness in the face of difficult circumstances in exchange for a guarantee of the appropriate level of financial, material, and symbolic resources necessary to ensure minimal casualties.

If these moral contracts between citizens and armed forces, and between leaders and followers within the military, are explained, they may prove less difficult to implement than is generally perceived. For, as Akerlof (1984) suggests, there may be advantages for a well-identified group like the armed forces to instill in its members certain moral values and certain virtues that limit the pursuit of individual personal interests but that significantly improve the probability of promotion within the ranks. To the extent that this is the case, one may see how the two moral contracts (between the military and the citizenry, and between leaders and followers within the military) are interconnected: the military offers the citizenry a commitment to virtuous behaviour as a quid pro quo for civilian support of the military, and military leaders offer their followers progress through the ranks on the basis of those very virtues that are important to the citizens (Ricks 1996).

CONNOISSEURSHIP, SOCIAL LEARNING, AND "BLAMEABILITY"

To foster stronger accountability and ethical fabric, a three-pronged strategy that can be built on the highest and best use of education, deliberation, and social capitalization is necessary. Anything that provides greater moral connoisseurship and responsible behaviour or that fosters a wider use of moral reasoning, facilitates a more open deliberation process in the forum, or strengthens the ethos by endowing it with denser relations and a higher degree of trust promotes more effective social learning and, therefore, the likelihood of a more robust accountability and ethical fabric. Anything that generates blockages in these three directions can only slow down social and moral learning.

There are important impediments and stumbling blocks on these three roads. They may vary in form and intensity, from time to time and place to place. However, one major distortion deserves special attention. It is the sort of "judicial usurpation of politics" that has distorted the whole social learning process and the fluid common-law-type emergence of an effective evolving accountability and ethical framework. This distortion is caused by the myopic search for "blameability" that has become the trademark of the judiciary.

Politics consists of free people deliberating the question of how we ought to order our life together. When questions that are properly political are unduly narrowed, legalized, or "speciously constitutionalized," the conversation is truncated and distorted and social learning falters (First Things 1996). It is an even more dramatic distortion when morality is declared legally suspect and a threat to the public order and when political deliberative institutions are undermined by the arrogance of those who insist on redefining judicially the political questions.

The main reason why judicial commissions of inquiry headed or fuelled by the legal perspective have proved quite unsatisfactory has to do with the tendency of such bodies to be mesmerized by experts in the business of interrogating and punishing. Those people are neither trained to analyze nor really prepared to handle issues of malfunctioning institutions or flawed administrative systems. As a result of their narrow legalistic perspective, the notions of burden of office, accountability, and ethics are redefined in a flawed and reductive way.

For them, error is not a source of learning but rather a source of blame, and it demands punishment. Consequently, years after some of these commissions have been appointed, it is still unclear what was flawed in the system they were investigating. So, the citizen cannot be sure that this flaw has been corrected. These commissions are in hot pursuit of culprits and people to blame instead of trying to repair defective institutional architectures.

It is not clear whether one can easily eliminate such a massive source of distortion in our political and administrative systems. Indeed, there are instances abroad where the judicial usurpation of politics has progressed beyond anything we have experienced in Canada. But it would be unwise to develop a fixation on this sole blockage.

There are other impediments to moral and social learning: a diminished role of moral connoisseurship in our education system, the presence of too many taboo topics that cannot be openly discussed, the social decapitalization denounced by Putnam (1995) and others. However, this should not lead one to conclude that action to improve the moral fabric is not possible or is condemned to be fruitless.

On the education front, the central concern is the explicit recognition that connoisseurship is not necessarily an innate quality. It must be learned by example as much as by training. It must also be reconciled with the rest of the value system defined by the ethos.

It is as unfair to demand moral connoisseurship from public servants or military personnel, without the appropriate moral apprenticeship, as it would be to ask one to fly an F-18 without training. Consequently, unless the public sector begins to spend as much money as Toyota in selecting suitable recruits and in allocating throughout their training period as much time to developing accountability and ethical skills as it does to technical skills, connoisseurship will not materialize.

On the deliberation front, the process of democratic participation in the production of governance has to be understood as a daunting task. When a problem of some magnitude is revealed by scandal, it often cannot be understood easily and repaired quickly. In the case of a malaise in the armed forces, it may demand an overhauling of the corporate culture, a fundamental rethinking of recruitment practices and nothing less than a sanitization of the "traditional" way of life of the organization. Moreover, it may require no less than a full generation (some 15 years) to "cleanse" the present ethos from its bacteria.

It is only too understandable that in the face of such a mammoth task, the tendency has been to turn one's attention to more tractable problems: for instance, blameability. This is especially the case when acknowledging the problem may lead to one's having to admit that one does not know what to do. This explains why it becomes a taboo problem (Michael 1988b).

On the social recapitalization front, even if it is not clear what the contours of the new institutional fabric will be, moral connoisseurship cannot simply be transplanted to the existing ethos. It can be fitted within it only by making major repairs to the ethos.

An ethos is a permanent construction site. It is evolving constantly and represents a complex set of social armistices between geotechnical constraints and values and plans. A refurbished ethos may have to start with a few reiterated points, as was done in the *Magna Carta*: *primum non nocere* as one of the few absolutes; higher moral standards required from the public servant than from the citizen; a greater awareness of the basic moral contracts making up the ethos; the essentially contested nature of the burden of office and the great limits it imposes on accountability and ethics consensus; the fundamental importance of error-embracing and social learning; the connoisseurship nature of moral reasoning; the recognition that social and moral learning is bound to be a trial-and-error process.

All this is both extremely simple and extremely profound. It recognizes that any social recapitalization is bound to take much time and to require long and difficult deliberations. Although it is quite easy to destroy institutions, it is difficult to construct an institutional order and it often requires both a major reframing of perspective and much effort to reconfigure the ethos and even to neutralize or displace the present politics of denial that prevent any coordinated effort to mount a new construction site (Paquet 1995).

However, this major task of reframing cannot be undertaken unless it is first recognized that the usual rationalist representation of accountability and ethics is an "irresponsible masquerade"; it cannot escape the paradoxes it attempts to abolish (Harmon 1995: 65). Only when the ground is clear, can one hope to build a more practical and useful representation.

Even though Harmon (1995) refuses to be programmatic, he has identified four major challenges that need to be met head on in the process of social learning: the need to keep in mind and maintain balance (1) between personal responsibility and commitment to others; (2) between freedom and responsibility; (3) between individual and collective "answerability" and entitlement; and (4) between political and professional responsibility.

The temptation in each case is to postulate a split between these different poles and to assert the dominance of one over the other. This can only produce pathologies through the atrophy of one of the constituent principles and an undue simplification of the "fundamental, unresolved, and perhaps unresolvable tensions" that characterize human behaviour (Hirschman 1985).

But avoiding such pathologies cannot suffice. Reframing entails a transformation of these treacherous dyads into creative dialectical relationships that need tone worked out through deliberation at the practical level in a manner that ensures that all the relevant stakeholders and all the constituent principles are fully engaged in the creative dialogue and the creative practice from which viable compromises emerge. This entails a 360-degree accountability and ethics: a complicated conversation that is both inevitable and unlikely to yield anything but an ongoing and unending multilogue.

Hirschman (1985) and Harmon (1995) might be rightly accused of having contributed significantly to a complication of the social–science discourse. Theirs have been pleas to recognize complexity where it exists instead of denying it. These complications may be troublesome, but they are not posing unresolvable problems. They only force a reframing of our approach to social phenomena that takes into account the basic tensions with which humanity must live.

CONCLUSION

One of the fundamental reasons why the problem of inappropriate connois-seurship has not been resolved is that leaders have been unwilling to acknow-ledge it as a problem. The denial syndrome emerged from the fact that the leaders have been regarding this issue as one with which they did not know how to cope; so there was denial, and the real problem remained a taboo topic. Consequently, scandals have been dealt with as anomalies, and bad apples have been removed (or regiments disbanded), as if such actions resolved the issue. This has been both futile and dangerous: futile, because the problem was simply occluded; dangerous, because the suppressed problem was ever-present like a denied generalized cancer.

For example, it is very difficult for civilians, who are not especially well-informed, except through the popular press, to understand how the violence-based apprenticeship of the Canadian Airborne Regiment could not but lead to violence in a context requiring saintly tolerance, humanitar-ian patience, and quiet diplomacy. Making scapegoats of the regiment or some of its officers without raising questions about the ethos of their training and the system of command that led the military to assign a group so specialized in violence to such a delicate task, can only leave civilians puzzled. Disbanding the regiment did not deal with the central issues; it allowed everyone to avoid dealing with it.

Conferences and papers about ethics may be necessary and useful, but they are hardly sufficient to deal with the systemic problem at hand. They are at best a useful first step toward admitting that there is problem. In that sense, they may foster courage, because it requires much courage to stop denying the problem when one has no solution. This is the sort of courage that has been witnessed recently in the military, but also in numerous other areas of the private, public, and social domains. Now that it has become possible to talk about these questions without being accused of treason, it is essential that the conversation not be derailed into trivial pursuits. The central questions are not the preparation of a compulsory three-hour course on ethics or the concoction of a code of ethics engraved on a plasticized card. The central concerns have to do with the burden of office of the various officials and with the account-ability and ethical frameworks that are required if officials are to perform their tasks in a manner that meets the expectations of the citizenry.

It may take 15 years of deliberation and clarification (of the moral contracts between the citizenry and the military, and between the military leaders and their followers, for instance) before the problem receives, not a solution, but a workable response. As Nowlan (1968) remarked some 30 years ago, "puzzles have solutions, problems don't; problems have responses and one man's response will inevitably give rise to another man's objection." This is the world of paradoxes and essentially contested concepts. No anodyne instrumental logic will do.

But 15 years is only a shade more than 5000 days. This is the realistic time-frame that the United States has accepted for transforming the ethos of their military establishment, and there are reasons to believe that this approach has proved effective (Ricks 1996).

Whether such a farsighted approach can be adopted by Canadian officials in the military and elsewhere remains to be seen. However, there is growing awareness that the problem is unlikely to go away and that an effective response is unlikely to be of the Band-Aid variety. That is why one may feel that there are reasons to hope — not to be optimistic but to hope (Michael 1988b).

References

Acs, Z., De la Mothe, J., Paquet, G. 1996. Local Systems of Innovation. In Howitt, P. (Editor). *The Implications of Knowledge-based Growth for Micro-economic Policies*. Calgary: University of Calgary Press. 339–359.

Adams, R.J. 1980. *Training in Canadian Industry: Research, Theory and Policy Implications*. Hamilton: McMaster University, Faculty of Business. Research and Working Papers Series 168.

Adie, R.F., Thomas, P.G. 1982. *Canadian Public Administration*. Scarborough: Prentice-Hall.

Aharoni, Y. 1981. *The No-Risk Society*. Chatham, NJ: Chatham House Publishers, Inc.

Akerlof, G. 1984. *An Economic Theorist's Book of Tales*. London: Cambridge University Press.

Akerlof, G.A., Dickens, W.T. 1982. The Economic Consequences of Cognitive Dissonance. *American Economic Review*, 72(3):307–319.

Alexander, C. 1964. *Notes on the Synthesis of Form*. Cambridge, MA: Harvard University Press.

—. 1971. *De la synthèse de la forme, essai*. Paris: Dunod.

Allison, G.T. 1971. *Essence of Decision*. Boston: Little Brown.

Alt, J.E., Shepsle, K.A. 1990. *Perspectives on Positive Political Economy*. Cambridge: Cambridge University Press.

Amin, A., Thrift, N. 1995. Institutional Issues for the European Regions: From Markets and Plans to Socioeconomics and Powers of Association. *Economy and Society*, 24(1):43–66.

Anderson, R.J., Hughes, J.A., Sharrock, W.W. 1986. *Philosophy and the Human Sciences*. London: Croom Helm.

Andreski, S. 1974. *Social Sciences as Sorcery*. Harmondsworth: Penguin Books.

Ansoff, H.I. 1960. A Quasi-analytic Method for Long Range Planning. In Churchman, C.W., Verhulst, M. (editors). *Management Sciences — Models and Techniques*. London: Pergamon Press.

Archibald, K.A. 1970. Three Views of the Expert's Role in Policy Making. *Policy Sciences*, 1, 73–86.

Archibald, C., Galipeau, C., Paquet, G. 1990. Entreprises, gouvernements et société civile : une perspective co-évolutive. *Gestion*, 15(4):56–61.

Argyris, C., Schon, D.A. 1974. *Theory in Practice*. San Francisco: Jossey-Bass.

—. 1978. *Organizational Learning: A Theory of Action Perspective*. Reading, MA: Addison-Wesley.

Argyris, C., Putnam, R., McLain, D. 1985. *Action Science*. San Francisco: Jossey-Bass.

Arnal, M. 1986. Canadian Values and Canadian Citizenship: Challenges for the Future. In Gadacz, R.R. (editor). *Challenging the Concept of Citizenship*. Edmonton: CSC Consulting Services.

Auditor General of Canada. 1990. *Report to the House of Commons for Fiscal Year Ended 31 March 1990*. Chapter 7. Values, Service and Performance. Ottawa: Government of Canada.

—. 1991. *Report to the House of Commons for Fiscal Year Ended 31 March 1991*. Ottawa: Government of Canada.

Authier, M., Levy, P. 1992. *Les arbres de connaissances*, Paris: Éditions La Découverte.

Badot, O., Paquet, G. 1991. Quasi-firme et secteur public : un pari sur le franchisage. *Gestion 200 – Management et Prospective*, 7(4):15–31.

Baldwin, B. 1986. Free Trade, Deregulation and Privatization. *Canadian Labour*, April.

Banfield, E.C. 1958. *The Moral Basis of A Backward Society*. New York: Free Press.

Banting, K. 1986. *The State and Economic Interests*. Toronto: University of Toronto Press.

—. 1996. Notes for comments to the deputy ministers' luncheon. 5 January 1996. 14 pp.

Barney, G.O., Freeman, P.H., Ulinski, C.A. 1981. *Global 2000: Implications for Canada*. Toronto: Pergamon Press.

Barzelay, M. 1992. *Breaking Through Bureaucracy*. Berkeley: University of California Press.

Basken, R., Task Force on Harnessing Change. 1988. *Focus 2000 — Report of the Task Force on Harnessing Change*. Ottawa: Canadian Chamber of Commerce.

Beam, R.D. 1983. Fragmentation of Knowledge: An Obstacle to its Full Utilization. In Boulding, K.E., Senesh, L. (editors). *The Optimum Utilization of Knowledge*. Boulder, CO: Westview Press. 160–174.

Becker, T.L. 1991. *Quantum Politics*. New York: Praeger.

Bell, D. (editor). 1984. New Directions in Modern Thought. *Partisan Review*, 51(2):215–320.

Bell, J.D., Vickery, G. 1988. *International Perspectives on Technology and Free Trade*. Paris: Organisation for Economic Co-operation and Development. Mimeo, 29 pp.

Bellah, R.N., Madsen, R., Sullivan, W.M., Swidler, A., Tipton, S.M. 1991. *The Good Society*. New York: Alfred A. Knopf.

Bennis, W. 1976. *The Unconscious Conspiracy*. New York: AMACOM.

Bennis, W.G., Benne, K.D., Chin, R. 1961. *The Planning of Change*. New York: Holt, Rinehart, Winston.

Berry, J. 1977. Multiculturalism and Intergroup Attitudes. In Dubois, S.V.C. (editor). *Conference on multiculturalism in education*. Toronto: Ontario Association for Curriculum Development.

Bettinger, C. 1978. *La concession de service public et de travaux publics*. Paris: Berger-Levrault.

Bibby, R.W. 1990. *Mosaic Madness*. Toronto: Stoddart.

Bissonnette, L. 1987. The Midforum Briefing. In *Proceedings of the National Forum on Post-Secondary Education*. Halifax, NS: Institute for Research on Public Policy. 81–82.

—. 1989. La formation fondamentale : au delà des clichés. In Andrew, C., Esbensen, S.B. (editors). *Who's Afraid of Liberal Education?* Ottawa: University of Ottawa Press. 21–31.

Bloch-Lainé, F. 1976. *Profession : fonctionnaire*. Paris: Seuil.

Block, W. 1990. *Economics and the Environment: A Reconciliation*. Vancouver: Fraser Institute.

Bloom, A. 1987. *The Closing of the American Mind*. New York: Simon & Schuster.

Blouin, J. 1986. *Le libre-échange vraiment libre ?*, Québec: Institut Québécois de recherche sur la culture.

Boisot, M. 1987. *Information and Organizations — The Manager as Anthropologist*. London: Fontana.

—. 1995. *Information Space — A Framework for Learning in Organizations, Institutions and Culture*. London: Routledge.

Bonin, B., Desranleau, C. 1988. *Innovation industrielle et analyse économique*. Montréal: Gaëtan Morin.

Bouchard, L. 1989. Statement before the Standing Committee on Environment of the House of Commons of Canada, 2nd session of the 34th Parliament, October 26, 1989.

Bouchard, L. 1990. *A Framework for Discussion on the Environment*. Ottawa: Supply and Services Canada.

Boulding, K.E. 1970. *A Primer on Social Dynamics*. New York: The Free Press.

Bourdieu, P. 1972. *Esquisse d'une théorie de la pratique*. Geneva: Droz.

Braybrooke, D. 1974. *Traffic Congestion Goes Through the Issue-machine*. London: Routledge & Kegan Paul.

—. 1987. *Meeting Needs*. Princeton: Princeton University Press.

Braybrooke, D., Paquet, G. 1987. Human Dimensions of Global Change: The Challenge to the Humanities and the Social Sciences. *Transactions of the Royal Society of Canada*, Series V, Vol. II. 271–291.

Braybrooke, D., Schotch, P.K. 1981. Cost-benefit Analysis Under the Constraint of Meeting Needs. In Bowie, N.E. (editor). *Ethical Issues in Government*. Philadelphia: Temple University Press. 176–197.

Bressand, A., Distler, C., Nicolaidis, K. 1989. Vers une économie des réseaux. *Politique Industrielle*, 507, 155–168.

Breton, R. 1984. The Production and Allocation of Symbolic Resources: An Analysis of the Linguistic and Ethnocultural Fields in Canada. *Canadian Review of Sociology and Anthropology*, 21(2):123–144.

—. 1986. Multiculturalism and Canadian Nation-building. In Cairns, A., Williams, C. (editors). *The Politics of Gender, Ethnicity and Language in Canada*. Toronto: University of Toronto Press. 27–66.

Brock, W.A., Magee, S.P. 1984. The Invisible Foot and the Waste of Nations. In Colander, D.C. (editor). *Neoclassical Political Economy*. Cambridge: Ballinger.

Brotz, H. 1980. Multiculturalism in Canada: A Muddle. *Canadian Public Policy*, Winter. 6(1):41–46.

Brundtland, G. 1987. Our Common Future: Report of the World Commission on Environment and Development. New York: Oxford University Press.

Bruyn, S.T., Meehan, J. 1987. *Beyond the Market and the State*. Philadelphia: Temple University Press.

Buchanan, J.M., Tollison, R.D., Tullock, G. 1980. *Toward a Theory of the Rent-seeking Society*. College Station: Texas A&M University Press.

Buchholz, R.A. 1985. *Essentials of Public Policy for Management*. Toronto: Prentice-Hall.

Buckley, W.F. 1990. *Gratitude*. New York: Random House.

Burelle, A. 1995. *Le mal canadien*. Montréal: Fides.

Burnet, J. 1976. Ethnicity: Canadian Experience and Policy. *Sociological Focus*, April.

Business Week. 1984. Small Is Beautiful Now in Manufacturing. 22 October.

—. 1993. The Virtual Corporation. 8 February.

Cairncross, A. 1972. Government and Innovation. In Worswick, G.D.N. (editor). *Uses of Economics*. Oxford: Basil Blackwell. 1–20.

Caldwell, L.K. 1988. Environmental Impact Analysis: Origins, Evolution, and Future Directions. *Policy Studies Review*, 8(1):75–83.

Cameron, D. (editor). 1986. *The Free Trade Papers*. Toronto: Lorimer.

Canada, Government of. 1986. *Strengthening the Private Sector/University Research Partnership — the Matching Policy Rules*. Ottawa: Ministry of Supply and Services.

Cardozo, L.A. 1988. In Defence of the Federal Government's Multiculturalism Policy. *The Ottawa Citizen*, 19 January.

Carlzon, J. 1987. *Moments of Truth*. New York: Harper & Row.

Carmichael, C.L. 1986. Improving the Organization and Management of Civil Service Training in Zambia. *Public Administration and Development*, 6(2):187–201.

Castells, M. 1996. *The Rise of the Network Society*. Oxford: Blackwell.

—. 1997. *The Power of Identity*. Oxford: Blackwell.

Caves, R.E. 1982. *Multinational Enterprise and Economic Analysis*. Cambridge: Cambridge University Press.

CEPII (Centre d'études prospectives et d'informations internationales). 1985. *Économie mondiale 1980–1990 : la fracture ?* Paris: Economica.

Charreaux, G., Couret, A., Joffre, P., Koenig, G., de MontMorillon, B. 1987. *De nouvelles théories pour gérer l'entreprise.* Paris: Economica.

Cheng, L. 1984. International Trade and Technology: A Brief Survey of the Recent Literature. *Weltwirtschaftliches Archiv*, 120, 165–189.

Chichilnisky, G., Heal, G. 1986. *The Evolving International Economy.* Cambridge: Cambridge University Press.

Choate, P., Linger, J. 1988. Tailored Trade: Dealing with the World as It Is. *Harvard Business Review*, 66(1):86–93.

Clark, H. 1989. Strengths and Weaknesses of Liberal Education: A Comment. In Andrew, C., Esbensen, S.B. (editors). *Who's Afraid of Liberal Education?* Ottawa: University of Ottawa Press. 39–45.

Clark, W.C., Munn, R.E. (editors). 1986. *Sustainable Development of the Biosphere.* Cambridge: Cambridge University Press.

Clarke, S.G., Simpson, E. (editors). 1989. *Anti-theory in Ethics and Moral Conservatism.* Albany: State University of New York Press.

Cloutier, M., Paquet, G. 1988. L'éthique dans la formation en administration. *Cahiers de recherche éthique*, 12:69–90.

Coddington, A. 1968. *Theories of the Bargaining Process.* Chicago: Aldine.

Cohen, M.D., March, J.G., Olsen, J.P. 1972. A Garbage Can Model of Organizational Choice. *Administrative Science Quarterly*, 17(1), 1–25.

Cohen-Tanugi, L. 1985. *Le droit sans l'État.* Paris: Presses universitaires de France.

Cole, S., Cole, J.R., Simon, G.A. 1981. *Peer Review At the National Science Foundation: The Results of an Experiment.* New York: Center for the Social Sciences, Columbia University (mimeo 34 pp.)

Coleman, J.S. 1987. Norms as Social Capital. In Radnitzky, G., Bernholz, P. (editors). *Economic Imperialism — The Economic Approach Applied Outside the Field of Economics.* New York: Paragon. 133–155.

Collingridge, D. 1982. *Critical Decision Making.* London: Frances Pinter.

Cooke, P., Morgan, K. 1993. The Network Paradigm: New Departures in Corporate and Regional Development. *Environment and Planning D: Society and Space*, 11, 543–564.

Courchene, T.J. 1980. Towards a Protected Society. *Canadian Journal of Economics*, 13(4):556–577.

—. 1995. Glocalization: the Regional/International Interface. *Canadian Journal of Regional Science*, 18(1):1–20.

Cova, B., Cova, P. 1991. Procédure de passation des marchés publics européens : les limites du paradigme concurrentiel. *Gestion 2000 – Management et Prospective*, 7(5):13–42.

Crookell, H. 1973. The Transmission of Technology Across National Boundaries. *Business Quarterly*, 38(3):52–60.

Cross, J.G. 1969. *The Economics of Bargaining.* New York: Basic Books.

Crozier, M. 1987. *État modeste, État moderne*. Paris: Fayard.

Crozier, M., Thoenig, J.C. 1976. The Regulation of Complex Organized Systems. *Administrative Science Quarterly*, 21.

Culbertson, J.M. 1986. The Folly of Free Trade. *Harvard Business Review*, 64(5):122–128.

Dahl, R.A. 1989. *Democracy and Its Critics*. New Haven: Yale University Press.

Dahmen, E. 1988. Development Blocks in Industrial Economics. *Scandinavian Economic History Review*, 36(1):3–14.

Dahrendorf, R. 1988. *The Modern Social Conflict*. New York: Weidenfeld and Nicolson.

—. 1995. A Precarious Balance: Economic Opportunity, Civil Society and Political Liberty. *The Responsive Community*, 5(3):13–39.

Dales, J.H. 1968. *Pollution, Property and Prices*. Toronto: University of Toronto Press.

Daly, H.E., Cobb Jr, J.B. 1989. *For the Common Good*. Boston: Beacon Press.

Dasgupta, P., David, P. 1987. Information Disclosure and the Economics of Science and Technology. In Feiwel, G. (editor). *Arrow and the Ascent of Modern Economic Theory*. London: McMillan. 519–534.

Dasgupta, P., Stiglitz, J. 1980. Industrial Structure and the Nature of Innovative Activity. *Economic Journal*, 90, 266–293.

Dasgupta, P., Stoneman, P. (editors). 1987. *Economic Policy and Technological Performance*. Cambridge: Cambridge University Press.

Davidow, W.H., Malone, M.S. 1992. *The Virtual Corporation*. New York: Harper Collins.

Davidson, M. 1983. *Uncommon Sense*. Los Angeles: J.P. Tarcher Inc.

Day, P., Klein, R. 1987. *Accountabilities: Five Public Services*. London: Tavistock.

D'Cruz, J.D., Rugman, A.M. 1992. *New Compacts for Canadian Competitiveness*. Toronto: Kodak Canada Inc.

De Bono, E. 1969. *The Mechanism of Mind*. Harmondsworth: Penguin.

De Bresson, C. 1987. The Evolutionary Paradigm and the Economics of Technological Change. *Journal of Economic Issues*, 21(2):751–762.

Defaveri, I. 1986. *Jaenen on Multiculturalism in Multiculturalism: Perspectives and Reactions*. Edmonton: Department of Educational Foundations, University of Alberta. Occasional paper 86-1.

de la Mothe, J., Paquet, G. 1994. The Dispersive Revolution. *Optimum*, 25(1):42–48.

—. (editors). 1996. *Corporate Governance and the New Competition*. Ottawa: Program of Research in International Management and Economy (PRIME).

—. 1997. Coordination Failures in the Learning Economy. In de la Mothe, J., Paquet, G. (editors). *Challenges Unmet in the New Production of Knowledge*. Ottawa: Program of Research in International Management and Economy (PRIME). 3–26.

Détienne, M., Vernant, J.P. 1974. *Les ruses de l'intelligence*. Paris: Flammarion.

Dewey, J. 1935. *Liberalism and Social Action*. New York: Putnam.

de Wilde, J. 1985. Global Competitor or Farmteam Economy: Canada's Real Trade Debate. *Business Quarterly*, Winter, 50(4):37–40.

Diamond, P. 1965. The Evaluation of Infinite Utility Streams. *Econometrica*, 33, 170–177.

Dionne, E.J. 1991. *Why Americans Hate Politics*. New York: Simon & Schuster.

Dlugos, G., Weiermair, K. (editors). 1981. *Management Under Differing Value Systems*. New York: Walter de Gruyter.   .

Doern, G.B. 1986. The Tories, Free Trade and Industrial Adjustment Policy: Expanding the State Now to Reduce the State Later. In Prince, M. (editor). *How Ottawa Spends, 1986–87*, Toronto: Methuen. 61–94.

—. 1989. *The Limits of Energy Deregulation: the Interplay Between Economic and Social Regulatory Dynamics*. Ottawa: School of Public Administration, Carleton University. 26 pp. (mimeo).

—. 1990. *The Economic Imperative: Market Approaches to the Greening of Canada*. Toronto: C.D. Howe Research Institute.

Doern, G.B., Phidd, R.W. 1983. *Canadian Public Policy*. Toronto: Methuen.

Doern, G.B., Toner, G. 1985. *The Politics of Energy*. Toronto: Methuen.

Dosi, G., Freeman, C., Nelson, R., Silverberg, G., Soete, L. (editors). 1988. *Technical Change and Economic Theory*. London: Pinter Publishers.

Douglas, M. 1986. *How Institutions Think*. Syracuse: Syracuse University Press.

Douglas, M., Wildavsky, A. 1982. *Risk and Culture*. Berkeley: University of California Press.

Drucker, P.F. 1988. The Coming New Organization. *Harvard Business Review*, 66(1):45–53.

Drummond, I.M. 1986. On Disbelieving the Commissioners' Free Trade Case. *Canadian Public Policy*, 12(suppl):59–67.

Dubnick, M.J. 1996. Clarifying Accountability: An Ethical Theory Framework. Presented at the 5th International Conference of Ethics in the Public Service, Brisbane, Australia, 5–9 August.

Dumezil, G. 1987. L'excellence introuvable. *Autrement*, 86:14–21.

Dumont, L. 1983. *Essais sur l'individualisme*. Paris: Esprit/Seuil.

Dumouchel, P., Dupuy, J.P. 1979. *L'enfer des choses*. Paris: Seuil.

Duncan, G. 1985. A Crisis of Social Democracy? *Parliamentary Affairs*, 38(3):267–281.

Dwivedi, O.P. 1987. Moral Dimensions of Statecraft: A Plea for Administrative Theology. *Canadian Journal of Political Science*, 20(4):699–709.

Dwivedi, O.P., Engelbert, E.A. 1981. Education and Training for Values and Ethics in the Public Service: An International Perspective. *Public Personnel Management Journal*, 10(1):140–145.

Dyer, G. 1990. Green Report Card on Five World Leaders. *New Environment*, premier issue.

Economist, The. 1990. The State of the Nation-state. *The Economist*, December 22, 43–46.

Ellul, J. 1954. *La technique ou l'enjeu du siècle*. Paris: Armand Colin.

Emery, F. 1980. *Educational Paradigms — An Epistemological Revolution*. December. (Mimeo)

Emery, F.E., Trist, E.L. 1965. The Causal Texture of Organizational Environments. *Human Relations*, 18, 21–32.

Emery, M. 1982. *Searching — for New Directions/in New Ways/for New Times*. Canberra: Centre for Continuing Education, Australian National University.

Errens, W., Paquet, G. 1990. L'entreprenariat de l'entreprenariat. *Revue de gestion des petites et moyennes organisations*, 5(2):55–61.

Etzioni, A. 1983. *An Immodest Agenda*. New York: McGraw Hill.

Fayol, H. 1949. *General and Industrial Management*. London: Pitman.

Feibleman, J.K. 1961. Pure Science, Applied Science, Technology, Engineering: An Attempt at Definitions. *Technology and Culture*, 2(4):305–317.

First Things. 1996. Symposium: the End of Democracy? The Judicial Usurpation of Politics. *First Things*, 67(November):18–42.

Fitzgerald, F.S. 1945. *The Crack-up*. New York: New Directions.

Florida, R., Kenney, M. 1993. Innovation-mediated Production. *Futures*, 25(5):637–651.

Foa, U.G. 1971. Interpersonal and Economic Resources. *Science*, 3969:345–351.

Fogel, R.W. 1964. *Railroads and American Economic Growth: Essays in Econometric History*. Baltimore: Johns Hopkins University Press.

—. 1979. Notes on the Social Saving Controversy. *Journal of Economic History*, 39, 1–54.

Foray, D., Lundvall, B.A. 1996. The Knowledge-based Economy: From the Economics of Knowledge to the Learning Economy. In *Employment and Growth in the Knowledge-based Economy*. Paris: OECD. 11–32.

—. 1997. Une introduction à l'économie fondée sur la connaissance. In Guilhon, B., Huard, P., Orillard, M., Zimmerman, J.B. (editors). *Économie de la connaissance et organisations*. Paris: Harmattan. 16–38.

Foster, G.M. 1972. The Anatomy of Envy: A Study in Symbolic Behavior. *Current Anthropology*, 13(2).

Fraas, A.G., Munley, V.G. 1989. Economic Objectives Within a Bureaucratic Decision Process. *Journal of Environmental Economics and Management*, 17(1):35–53.

Frankfurt, H.G. 1984a. *The Importance of What We Are About. (Necessity and Desire)*. Cambridge: Cambridge University Press.

—. 1984b. Necessity and desire. *Philosophy and Phenomenological Research*, 45(1).

Freedberg, S.J. 1989. Berenson, Connoisseurship and the History of Art. *The New Criterion*, 7(6):7–16.

French, R.D. 1980. *How Ottawa Decides*. Toronto: Lorimer.

Friedenberg, E.Z. 1975. *The Disposal of Liberty and Other Industrial Wastes*. New York; Doubleday.

Friedmann, J. 1973. *Retracking American Theory of Transactive Planning*. New York: Doubleday.

—. 1978. The Epistemology of Social Practice: A Critique of Objective Knowledge. *Theory and Society*, 6(1):75–92.

—. 1979. *The Good Society*. Cambridge, MA: MIT Press.

Friedmann, J. 1987. *Planning in the Public Domain: From Knowledge to Action*. Princeton: Princeton University Press.

Friedmann, J., Abonyi, G. 1976. Social Learning: A Model for Policy Research. *Environment and Planning A*, 8, 927–940.

Fry, R.E., Pasmore, W.A. 1983. Strengthening Management Education. In Srivastva, S. & Associates. *The Executive Mind*. San Francisco: Jossey-Bass. 269–296.

Fudge, C., Gustafsson, L. 1989. Administrative Reform and Public Management in Sweden and the United Kingdom. *Public Money and Management*, Summer, 29–34.

Gabel, J. 1962. *La fausse conscience*. Paris: Minuit.

Gallagher, J., Robinson, R. 1953. The Imperialism of Free Trade. *Economic History Review*, 6(1):1–15.

Gallie, W.P. 1964. *Philosophy and the Historical Understanding*. London: Chatto & Windus.

Galston, W.A. 1998. A Public Philosophy for the 21st Century. *Responsive Community*, 8(3):18–36.

Gans, H. 1979. Symbolic Ethnicity. *Ethnic and Racial Studies*, 2(1):1–20.

Gardner, J.W. 1986–1988. *Leadership Papers* 1–12. Washington: Leadership Studies Program, Independent Sector.

Garratt, B. 1987. *The Learning Organization*. London: Fontana.

Gastil, R.D. 1972. A general framework for social science. *Policy Sciences*, 3(4):385–403.

Gauthier, D.F. 1963. *Practical Reasoning*. Oxford: Clarendon Press.

Geddes, J. 1991. How Business Can Affect Politics. *The Financial Post*, 18 November.

Geertz, C. 1965. The Impact of the Concept of Culture on the Concept of Man. In Platt, J.R. (editor). *New Views of Man*. Chicago: University of Chicago Press.

—. 1983. *Local Knowledge*. New York: Basic Books.

—. 1986. The Uses of Diversity. *Michigan Quarterly Review*, 25(1):105–123.

Georgescu-Roegen, N. 1975. Bio-economic Aspects of Entropy. In Kubat, L., Zeman, J. (editors). *Entropy and Information in Science and Philosophy*. New York: Elsevier. 125–142.

Gibbons, M., Limoges, C., Nowotny, H., Schwartzman, S., Scott, P., Trow, M. 1994. *The New Production of Knowledge*. London: Sage Publications.

Gibson, J.J. 1979. *The Ecological Approach to Visual Perception*. Boston: Houghton Mifflin.

Giersch, H. 1984. *New Opportunities for Entrepreneurship*. Tübingen: Mohr.

Gilles, W., Paquet, G. 1989. On Delta Knowledge. In Paquet, G., von Zur-Muehlen, M. (editors). *Edging Toward the Year 2000*. Ottawa: Canadian Federation of Deans of Management and Administrative Studies. 15–30.

—. 1991. La connaissance de type Delta. In Paquet, G., Gélinier, O. (editors). *Le management en crise : pour une formation proche de l'action*. Paris: Economica. 19–36.

Glaser, T. (editor). 1988. Dossier : administration. *The Courier*, 109, May-June.

Godbout, J.T. 1987. *La démocratie des usagers*. Montréal: Boréal.

Goffman, E. 1969. Strategic Interaction. Philadelphia: University of Pennsylvania Press.

Goldstaub, J. 1981. Social Value Change and Economic Development: Idiosyncrasies and Non-linearities. In Dlugos, G., Weiermair, K. (editors). 1981. *Management Under Differing Value Systems*. New York: Walter de Gruyter. 157–174.

Gordon, H.S. 1970. *Social Science and Modern Man*. Toronto: University of Toronto Press.

—. 1975. The Political Economy of Big Questions and Small Ones. *Canadian Public Policy*, I(1):97–106.

Gordon, R.L. 1981. *An Economic Analysis of World Energy Problems*. Cambridge, MA: MIT Press.

Granovetter, M. 1973. The Strength of Weak Ties. *American Journal of Sociology*, 78(6):1360–1380.

Grant, J.K. 1989. Thoughts on the Three Solitudes — Business, Government and the Universities. In Andrew, C., Esbensen, S.B. (editors). *Who's Afraid of Liberal Education?* Ottawa: University of Ottawa Press. 33–37.

Gray, J. 1995. *Berlin*. London: Fontana Press.

Greenberg, S.B. 1991. From Crisis to Working Majority. *The American Prospect*, 7 (Fall):104–117.

Greve, M.S. 1989. Environmentalism and Bounty Hunting. *The Public Interest*, 97, Fall, 15–29.

Grimond, J. 1991. For Want of Glue: A Survey of Canada. *The Economist*, June 29, 18.

Guéhenno, J.M. 1993. *La fin de la démocratie*. Paris: Flammarion.

Gunderson, M. 1978. Training in Canada: Progress and Problems. In Pettman, B.O. (editor). *Government Involvement in Training*. Bradford: MCB Publications. 109–131.

Habermas, J. 1971. *Knowledge and Human Interests*. Boston: Beacon Press. Part II.

—. 1973. *Legitimation Crisis*. Boston: Beacon.

Hacking, I. 1985. Making Up People. In *Reconstructing Individualism*. Stanford: Stanford University Press. 222–236.

Halpern, D., Osofsky, S., Peskin, M.I. 1988. Taylorism as Applied to the Public Sector. *Journal of Business Issues*, 17(1).

Handy, C. 1990. *The Age of Unreason*. London: Arrow Books.

—. 1992. Balancing Corporate Power: A New Federalist Paper. *Harvard Business Review*, 70(6):59–72.

—. 1998. *The Hungry Spirit*. New York: Broadway Books.

Hardin, H. 1974. *A Nation Unaware — the Canadian Economic Culture*. Vancouver: J.J. Douglas Ltd.

Harmon, M.M. 1995. *Responsibility as Paradox*. London: Sage Publications.

Harris, R.G. 1985. *Trade, Industrial Policy and International Competition*. Toronto: University of Toronto Press.

Harris, R.G., Cox, D. 1985. *Trade, Industrial Policy, and Canadian Manufacturing*. Toronto: Ontario Economic Council.

Hartle, D.G. 1978. The Expenditure Budget Process in the Government of Canada. Toronto: Canadian Tax Foundation.

Harvey, D. 1988. Urban Places in the Global Village: Reflections on the Urban Condition in Late 20th Century. In Mazza, L. (editor). *World Cities and the Future of the Metropolis*. Milan: Electra.

Haworth, L. 1977. *Decadence and Objectivity*. Toronto: University of Toronto Press.

Held, D. 1995. *Democracy and the Global Order*. Stanford: Stanford University Press.

Helliwell, J.F., McCallum, J. 1995. National Borders Still Matter for Trade. *Policy Options*, 16(5):44–48.

Herendeen, J.B. 1975. *The Economics of the Corporate Economy*. New York: Dunellen.

Hine, V.H. 1977. The Basic Paradigm of a Future Socio-cultural System. *World Issues*, April/May, 19–22.

Hirsch, E.D. Jr. 1987. *Cultural Literacy*. Boston: Houghton-Mifflin.

Hirsch, F. 1976. *Social Limits to Growth*. Cambridge, MA: Harvard University Press.

Hirschman, A.O. 1945. *National Power and the Structure of Foreign Trade*. California: University of California Press.

—. 1985. Against Parsimony: Three Easy Ways of Complicating Some Categories of Economic Discourse. *Economics and Philosophy*, 1(1):7–21.

Hirst, E. 1990. Electricity: Getting More with Less. *Technology Review*, July.

Hodgkinson, C. 1983. *The Philosophy of Leadership*. Oxford: Basil Blackwell.

Hollingsworth, R. 1993. Variation Among Nations in the Logic of Manufacturing Sectors and International Competitiveness. In Foray, D., Freeman, C. (editors). *Technology and the wealth of nations*. London: Pinter. 301–321.

Horsman, M., Marshall, A. 1994. *After the Nation-state — Citizens, Tribalism and the New World Disorder*. London: HarperCollins.

Howard, R. 1989. Call to Link Arms Replaces Battle of Words at Environment Meeting. *The Globe and Mail*, 28 December,

Hurtig, M. 1985. Giving Away the Store. *Canadian Business*, June, 265–271.

Hutchison, T.W. 1977. *Knowledge and Ignorance in Economics*. Oxford: Blackwell.

Iglesias, E. 1987. *Energy 2000 — A Global Strategy for Sustainable Development*. London: Zed Books Ltd.

Ignatief, M. 1985. *The Needs of Strangers*. New York: Viking.

Islam, N., Henault, G.M. 1979. From GNP to Basic Needs. *International Review of Administrative Sciences*, 14(2).

Jacobs, J. 1992. *Systems of Survival*, New York: Random House.

Jacquemin, A. 1995. Capitalism, Competition, Cooperation. *De Economist*, 143(1):1–14.

Jaenen, C.J. 1986. *Multiculturalism: An Historian's Perspectives in Multiculturalism: Perspectives and Reactions*. Edmonton: Department of Educational Foundations, University of Alberta. Occasional paper 86-1.

Janigan, M., Fulton, E.K. 1996. The Master Plan: A Draft for a New Canada Goes Before the Cabinet. *Maclean's*, 109(6):18–19.

Jencks, C., Edin, K. 1990. The Real Welfare Problem. *The American Prospect*, Spring, 31–50.

Jenks, L.H. 1944. Railroads as an Economic Force in American Development. *Journal of Economic History*, 4, 1–20.

Johansen, L. 1979. The Bargaining Society and the Inefficiency of Bargaining. *Kyklos*, 32(3):497–522.

Johnson, H.G. 1960. The Cost of Protection and the Scientific Tariff. *Journal of Political Economy*, 68(4):327–345.

—. 1963. *The Canadian Quandary*. Toronto: McGraw Hill. Chapter 11.

—. 1971. *Spectator*, 13 October.

Jones, R.S. 1983. *Physics as Metaphor*. New York: Meridian.

Jonsen, A.R., Toulmin, S. 1988. *The Abuse of Casuistry*. Berkeley: University of California Press.

Jussawalla, M., Cheah, C.W. 1984. International Trade and Information: Some Welfare Implications. In Jussawalla, M., Ebenfield, H. (editors). *Communication and Information Economics: New Perspectives*. Amsterdam: North Holland. 51–71.

Kahn, A.E. 1966. The Tyranny of Small Decisions: Market Failures, Imperfections and the Limits of Economics. *Kyklos*, 19, 23–47.

Kallen, E. 1982a. Multiculturalism: Ideology, Policy and Reality. *Journal of Canadian Studies*, 17(1):51–63.

—. 1982b. *Ethnicity and Human Rights in Canada*. Toronto: Gage Publishing Ltd.

Kapp, R.O. 1960. *Toward a Unified Cosmology*. New York: Basic Books.

Karelis, C. 1989. General Education Curriculum Trends in the United States. In Andrew, C., Esbensen, S.B. (editors). *Who's Afraid of Liberal Education?* Ottawa: University of Ottawa Press. 47–58.

Kash, D.E., Rycroft, R.W. 1984. *U.S. Energy Policy — Crisis and Complacency*. Norman: University of Oklahoma Press.

Katouzian, H. 1980. *Ideology and Method in Economics*. New York: New York University Press.

Kelly, K. 1994. *Out of Control*. Reading, MA: Addison-Wesley.

Kemball, P. 1984. A Scalpel for Government. *Policy Options*, 5(6):15–18.

Kets de Vries, M.F.R., Miller, D. 1985. *The Neurotic Organization*. San Francisco, Jossey-Bass.

Kettle, J. 1980. *The Big Generation*. Toronto: McClelland & Stewart.

Keyes, J. 1993. *The Morality of Pluralism*. Princeton: Princeton University Press.

Kierans, T. et al. 1988. *Energy and Canadians into the 21st Century*. Ottawa: Energy, Mines and Resources.

Kindleberger, C.P. 1978. *The Aging Economy*. Kiel: Institut für Weltwirtschaft.

King, A. 1975. Overload: Problems of Governing in the Seventies. *Political Studies*, June-September, 284–296.

King, A., Scheider, B. 1991. *Questions de survie*. Paris: Calmann-Lévy.

King, M.L. 1968. The Role of the Behavioral Scientist in the Civil Rights Movement. *Journal of Social Issues*, 4(1):1–12.

Kingwell, M. 1995. *A Civil Tongue: Justice, Dialogue and the Politics of Pluralism*. University Park, PA: Pennsylvania State University Press.

Kirby, M.J. 1980. *Reflections on the Management of Government in the 1980s*. Alan B. Plaunt Memorial Lecture. Ottawa: Carleton University.

Kolb, D.A. 1984. *Experiential Learning*. Englewood Cliffs, NJ: Prentice Hall.

Kolm, S.C. 1984. *La bonne économie*. Paris: Presses Universitaires de France.

Kooiman, J. (editor). 1993. *Modern Governance*. London: Sage Publications.

Kumon, S. 1992. Japan as a Network Society. In Kumon, S., Rosovsky, H. (editors). *The Political Economy of Japan* (Vol. 3). Stanford: Stanford University Press. 109–141.

Lachmann, L.M. 1971. *The Legacy of Max Weber*. Berkeley: Glendessary Press.

Lancaster, K. 1973. The Dynamic Inefficiency of Capitalism. *Journal of Political Economy*, 81(5):1092–1109.

Laplante, L. 1988. *L'université — questions et défis*. Québec: Institut québécois de recherche sur la culture.

Larkin, J., McDermott, J., Simon, D.P., Simon, H.A. 1980. Expert and Novice Performance in Solving Physics Problems. *Science*, 208, 1335–1342.

Lasswell, H.D. 1971. A Preview of Policy Sciences. New York: Elsevier.

Latouche, S. 1984. *Le procès de la science sociale*. Paris: Anthropos.

Laumann, E.O., Knoke, D. 1988. The increasingly organizational state. *Society*, 25(2):21–28.

Laurent, P., Paquet, G. 1991. Intercultural relations: a Myrdal-Tocqueville-Girard scheme. *International Political Science Review*, 12(3):171–183.

—. 1998. *Épistémologie et économie de la relation: coordination et gouvernance distribuée*. Lyon/Paris: Vrin.

Laxer, J. 1986. *Leap of Faith — Free Trade and the Future of Canada*. Edmonton: Hurtig.

Le Bas, C. 1993. La firme et la nature de l'apprentissage. *Économies et Sociétés* (Série dynamique technologique et organisation), 1(5):7–24.

Leblanc, F.E. 1987. *Federal Policy on Post-secondary Education*. Report of the Standing Senate Committee on National Finance. Ottawa: Supply and Services.

Leblond, A. and Paquet G. 1988. Stratégie et structure de l'entreprise de l'an 2000. In Jabes, J. (editor). *Gestion stratégique internationale*. Paris/Reims: Economica/Groupe ESC. 19–37.

Lefebvre, H. 1961. Utopie expérimentale : pour un nouvel urbanisme. *Revue française de sociologie*, 2(3):191–198.

Leibenstein, H. 1976. *Beyond Economic Man*. Cambridge: Harvard University Press.

—. 1987. *Inside the Firm*. Cambridge: Harvard University Press.

Leontief, W. 1982. Academic Economics. *Science*, 217, 104–105.

Leroy, R. 1990. L'économiste du travail en quête du social. In Michon, F., Segrestin, D. (editors). *L'emploi, l'entreprise et la société*. Paris: Economica. 27–40.

Light, I.H. 1972. *Ethnic Enterprise in America*. Berkeley: University of California.

Lindblom, C.E. 1959. The Science of Muddling-through. *Public Administration Review*, 19, 79–88.

Lipnack, J., Stamps, J. 1994. *The Age of the Network*. Essex Junction, VT: Omneo.

Lipsey, R.G. 1986. Will There Be a Canadian-American Free Trade Association? *The World Economy*, 9(3):217–238.

Llerena, D. 1997. Coopérations cognitives et modèles mentaux collectifs: outils de création et de diffusion des connaissances. In B. Guilhon et al. (editors). *Économie de la connaissance et organisations*. Paris: Harmattan. 356–382.

Lowi, T.J. 1975. Toward a Politics of Economics: The State of Permanent Receivership. In Lindberg, L.N., Alford, R., Crouch, C., Offe, C. (editors). *Stress and Contradiction in Modern Capitalism*. Lexington: D.C. Heath. 115–124.

Luke, D.F. 1986. Trends in Development Administration: The Continuing Challenge to the Efficacy of the Post-colonial State in the Third World. *Public Administration and Development*, 6(1):73–85.

Lundvall, B.A. 1992. *National Systems of Innovation — Towards a Theory of Innovation and Interactive Learning*. London: Pinter.

Lundvall, B.A., Johnson, B. 1994. The Learning Economy. *Journal of Industry Studies*, 1(2):23–42.

Lupul, M.R. 1982. The Political Implementation of Multiculturalism. *Journal of Canadian Studies*, 17(1):93–102.

Macdonald Commission (Royal Commission on the Economic Union and Development Prospects for Canada). 1985. Final report (vol. 2). Ottawa: Ministry of Supply and Services.

Macpherson, C.B. 1985. *The Rise and Fall of Economic Justice and Other Essays.* Oxford: Oxford University Press.

Macrae, N. 1982. Intrapreneurial Now. *The Economist,* April 17.

Magee, S.P., Brock, W.A., Young, L. 1989. *Black Hole Tariffs and Endogenous Policy Theory.* Cambridge: Cambridge University Press.

Majone, G. 1980. Policies as Theories. *Omega,* 8(2):151–162.

Mannheim, K. 1936. *Ideology and Utopia.* New York: Harcourt Brace.

Manzer, R. 1984. Public Policy Making as Practical Reasoning. *Canadian Journal of Political Science,* 17(3):577–594.

March, J.G. 1976. The Technology of Foolishness. In March, J.G., Olsen, J.P. (editors). *Ambiguity and Choice in Organizations.* Oslo: Universitetsforlaget. 69–81.

—. 1978. Bounded Rationality, Ambiguity and the Engineering of Choice. *The Bell Journal of Economics,* 9:587–608.

—. 1991. Exploration and Exploitation in Organizational Learning. *Organization Science,* 2(1):71–87.

Marquand, D. 1988. *The Unprincipled Society.* London: Fontana.

Marshall, A. 1907. The Social Possibilities of Chivalry. *The Economic Journal,* 17(3):7–29.

Masuda, Y. 1982. Information Epochs and Human Society. *World Future Society Bulletin,* Nov–Dec, 17–23.

Maxwell, J. 1995. Build on Core Values. *The Ottawa Citizen,* 15 November, A17.

McAllister, I. 1987. Canadian Aid for the Training of Public Servants in Ghana and Zimbabwe. *Public Administration and Development,* 7(3):289–307.

McCloskey, D.N. 1985. *The Rhetoric of Economics.* Madison: University of Wisconsin Press.

McCurdy, H.D. 1988. Free Trade to Hurt Canadian Research. *The Montreal Gazette,* 16 August, B-3.

McCurdy, H.D., Lenihan, D.G. 1988. *Research and Development and the Free-trade Agreement.* Ottawa: University of Ottawa. Mimeo, 8 pp.

McKenna, B. 1995. Ottawa's Grip on Economy at Issue in Debate Over Powers. *Globe and Mail,* 13 November, B1-2.

McLean, R.I.G. 1986. Three Men in a Boat: A Discussion of Tree Trade. *The Idler,* 9, 17–27.

Mead, L. 1986. *Beyond Entitlement: The Social Obligations of Citizenship.* New York: The Free Press.

Meade, J.E. 1955. *Trade and Welfare.* London: Oxford University Press.

Mégrelis, C. 1980. *Keys for the Future.* Toronto: Lexington.

Messick, S. 1988. Testing for Success: Implications of New Developments in Measurement and Cognitive Science. *Selections*, Autumn, 1–12.

Mesthene, E.G. 1970. *Technological Change*. New York: Mentor Books.

Michael, D.N. 1980. *The New Competence: The Organization as a Learning System*. San Francisco: Values and Lifestyles Program.

—. 1983. Competence and Compassion in an Age of Uncertainty. *World Future Society Bulletin*, Jan.–Feb.

—. 1988a. The Search for Values in the Information Age. *Western City*, 64(9):10–18.

—. 1988b. *Can Leaders Tell the Truth and Still Remain Leaders?* Paris: 20th Anniversary Conference of the Club of Rome. 20 pp. (mimeo).

—. 1993. Governing by Learning: Boundaries, Myths and Metaphors. *Futures*, 25(1):47–55.

Migué, J.L. 1994. The Balkanization of the Canadian Economy: A Legacy of Federal Policy. In Palda, F. (editor). *Provincial Trade Wars: Why the Blockade Must End*. Vancouver: Fraser Institute. 107–130.

Milgrom, P., Roberts, J. 1992. *Economics, Organization and Management*. Englewood Cliffs, NJ: Prentice Hall.

Millon-Delsol, C. 1992. *L'état subsidiaire*. Paris: Presses Universitaires de France.

Mills, D.Q. 1993. *Rebirth of the Corporation*. New York: Wiley.

Mintzberg, H. 1985. Emergent Stategy for Public Policy. Ottawa: Faculty of Administration, University of Ottawa. J.J. Carson Lecture.

—. 1987. Crafting Strategy. *Harvard Business Review*, 65(4):66–75.

Mitges, G. 1987. *Multiculturalism — Building the Canadian Mosaic* (Report of the Standing Committee on Multiculturalism). Ottawa: Government of Canada.

Mitnick, B.M. 1980. *The Political Economy of Regulation — Creating, Designing and Removing Regulatory Forms*. New York: Columbia University.

Mitroff, I.I. 1983. *Stakeholders of the Organizational Mind*. San Francisco: Jossey-Bass.

Monnerot, J. 1946. *Les faits sociaux ne sont pas des choses*. Paris: Gallimard.

Montgomery, J.D. 1986. Life at the Apex: The Functions of Permanent Secretaries in Nine Southern African Countries. *Public Administration and Development*, 6(3).

Morales, R. 1994. *Flexible Production*. Cambridge: Polity Press.

Morgan, G. 1986. *Images of Organization*. Newbury Park, CA: Sage Publications.

—. 1988. *Riding the Waves of Change*. San Francisco: Jossey-Bass.

Morgan, N.S. 1981. *Nowhere to Go?* Montréal: Institute for Research on Public Policy.

—. 1985. *Implosion*. Montréal: Institute for Research on Public Policy.

Morin, E. 1990. *Introduction à la pensée complexe*, Paris: ESF éditeur.

Mukherjee, B. 1985. *Darkness*. Harmondsworth: Penguin Books.

Murnane, R.J., Nelson, R.R. 1984. Production and Innovation When Techniques Are Tacit. *Journal of Economic Behavior and Organization*, 5, 353–373.

Naisbitt, J. 1994. *Global Paradox*. New York: Morrow.

Nanus, B. 1982. Developing Strategies for the Information Society. *The Information Society*, 1(4):339–356.

National Task Force on Environment and Economy. 1987. *Report*. Ottawa: Canadian Council of Resource and Environment Ministers.

Navarre, C. 1986. L'état-stratège. *L'Analyste*, 13:48–51.

NFPE (National Forum on Post-secondary Education). 1987a. *The Forum Papers*. Halifax, NS: Institute for Research on Public Policy.

—. 1987b. *Proceedings of the National Forum on Post-secondary Education*. Halifax, NS: Institute for Research on Public Policy.

Neilson, W.A.W., Gaffield, C. 1986. *Universities in Crisis: A Mediaeval Institution in the Twenty-first Century*. Montréal: Institute for Research on Public Policy.

Nohria, N., Eccles, R.G. (editors). 1992. *Networks and Organizations*. Boston: Harvard Business School Press.

Norgaard, R.B. 1984. Coevolutionary Development Potential. *Land Economics*, 60(2):160–173.

—. 1994. *Development Betrayed: the End of Progress and a Coevolutionary Revisioning of the Future*. London: Routledge.

Norgaard, R.B., Dixon, J.A. 1986. Pluralistic Project Design: An Argument for Combining Economic and Coevolutionary Methodologies. *Policy Sciences*, 19(3):297–317.

Nowlan, D.M. 1968. Centrifugally Speaking: Some Economics of Canadian Federalism. In Lloyd, T., McLeod, J. (editors). *Agenda 1970: Proposals for a Creative Politics*. Toronto: University of Toronto Press. 177–196.

O'Connor, J. 1973. *The Fiscal Crisis of the State*. New York: St Martin's Press.

OECD (Organisation for Economic Co-operation and Development).1979. *Face au futur : pour une maîtrise du vraisemblable et une gestion de l'imprévisible*. Paris: OECD.

Ogilvy, J.A. 1986–87. Scenarios for the Future of Governance. *The Bureaucrat*, 15(4):13–16.

Oldfield, A. 1990. *Citizenship and Community*. London: Routledge.

Orgogozo, I., and Sérieyx, H. 1989. *Changer Le Changement*, Paris: Seuil.

O'Toole, J. 1995. *Leading Change*. San Francisco: Jossey-Bass.

O'Toole, J., Bennis, W. 1992. Our Federalist Future. *California Management Review*, 34(4):73–90.

Ouchi, W.G. 1980. Markets, Bureaucracies and Clans. *Administrative Science Quarterly*, 25:120–142.

Paquet, G. 1968. The Economic Council as Phoenix. In Lloyd, T., McLeod, J. (editors). *Agenda 1970: Proposals for Creative Politics*. Toronto: University of Toronto Press. 135–158.

—. 1971. Social Science Research as an Evaluative Instrument for Social Policy. In Nettler, G.E., and Krotki, K. (editors). *Social Science and Social Policy*. Edmonton: Human Resources Research Council, 49–66.

—. 1977. Federalism as Social Technology. In Evans, J. (editor). *Options*. Toronto: University of Toronto Press. 281–302.

—. 1978a. Un appel à l'indiscipline théorique. In Lebel, M., Marchand, C. (editors). *Présentations à la Société Royale*. Québec: Société Royale. 109–118.

—. 1978b. The Regulatory Process and Economic Performance. In Doern, G.B. (editor). *The Regulatory Process in Canada*. Toronto: Macmillan of Canada. 34–67.

—. 1980. A Political Economy Perspective of the Early 1980s. In Barrett, C.A. (editor). *Key Economic and Social Issues of the Early 1980s*. Ottawa: The Conference Board of Canada. 71–81.

—. 1982. Econocrats Versus Situationologists: A Question of Rationalities. 17 pp. (mimeo).

—. 1985a. The Optimal Amount of Coercion Is Not Zero. In Souque, J.P., Trent, J. (editors). *Social Science Research in Canada: Stagnation or Regeneration?* Ottawa: Science Council of Canada. 98–115.

—. 1985b. Entrepreneurship et université: le combat de Carnaval et Carême. *Revue de gestion des petites et moyennes organisations*, 1(5):4–7.

—. 1985c. An Agenda for Change in the Federal Public Service. *Canadian Public Administration*, 28(3):455–461.

—. 1985d. La qualité des services en l'absence de marchés. *L'Analyste*, 9:48–51.

—. 1986. Entrepreneurship canadien-français: mythes et réalités. *Transactions of the Royal Society of Canada*, Series IV, Vol. 24, 151–178.

—. 1987a. The New Telecommunications: A Socio-cultural Perspective. In Estabrooks, M.F., Lamarche, R.H. (editors). *Telecommunications: A Strategic Perspective on Regional, Economic and Business Development*. Moncton: The Canadian Institute for Research on Regional Development. 45–68.

—. 1987b. Le goût de l'improbable : à propos d'une stratégie de sortie de crise pour les sciences humaines. In Paquet, G., von Zur-Muehlen, M. (editors). *Education Canada? Higher Education on the Brink*. Ottawa: Canadian Higher Education Research Network. 61–92.

—. 1987c. Toward a Canadian Network of Social Science Laboratories: An Exercise in Epistemo-economics and Social Architecture. In Artibise, A.F.J. (editor). *University Research Centres in the Social Sciences and Humanities*. Ottawa: Social Science Federation of Canada. 190–205.

—. 1988a. Two Tramps in Mud Time or the Social Sciences and Humanities in Modern Society. In Abu-Laban, B., Rule, B.G. (editors). *The Human Sciences*. Edmonton: University of Alberta Press. 165–198.

—. 1988b. La solution Catoblépas : le pari sur l'innovation à Montréal. *Revue de gestion des petites et moyennes organisations*, 3, 48–56.

—. 1988c. Training and Development: The Shadow Higher Education System in Canada. In Watts, R.A. (editor). *Canada–United Kingdom Colloquium on Postsecondary Education*. London: Gower Press. 189–202.

—. 1988d. Le salut du secteur public par la concurrence ? In Séguin, F., Lemelin, M. Parenteau, R. (editors). *La concurrence dans le secteur public.* Montréal: Les Éditions Agence d'Arc. 5–22.

—. 1988e. Le goût de l'improbable. In Paquet, G., von Zur-Muehlen, M. (editors). *Education Canada? Higher Education on the Brink* (2nd ed.). Ottawa: Canadian Higher Education Research Network. 61–92.

—. 1989a. The Underground Economy. *Policy Options,* 10(1):3–6.

—. 1989b. *The Promotion of Entrepreneurship and the Development of an Entrepreneurial Culture.* Quebec: National Forum on Entrepreneurship. 12–19.

—. 1989c. Virtuous Scheming. *Policy Options,* 10(6):8–12.

—. 1989d. Vers une nouvelle dynamique de localisation des entreprises. In *Proceedings of the Colloque sur les conditions du développement technologique de l'entreprise en région.* Québec: Conseil de la Science et de la Technologie du Québec. 73–94.

—. 1989e. La grande offre publique d'achat (OPA) des années 1960 dans l'électricité au Québec: petit essai d'ethnographie interprétative. In Comeau, R. (editor). *Jean Lesage et l'éveil d'une nation.* Sillery: Presses de l'Université du Québec. 282–297.

—. 1989f. Pour une socio-économie franco-ontarienne. In *Les voies de l'avenir franco-ontarien : Actes du Colloque de l'Association canadienne française de l'Ontario.* Ottawa: ACFO. 53–68.

—. 1989g. Pour une notion renouvelée de citoyenneté. *Mémoires de la Société Royale du Canada,* 5(4):83–100.

—. 1990a. Internationalization of Domestic Firms and Governments: Anamorphosis of a Palaver. *Science and Public Policy,* 17(5):327–332.

—. 1990b. L'adaptation du processus de travail : pour une stratégie à deux vitesses. *Gestion,* 15(2):33–44.

—. 1990c. The Canadian Economy of the Year 2000: A Case of Managed Trade. In Newton, K., Schweitzer, T., Voyer, J.P. (editors). Perspective 2000. Ottawa: Economic Council of Canada. 80–90.

—. 1990d. Pour une approche co-évolutionnaire au développement viable. In Beaumont, J.P. (editor). *Environnement et économie : pour un développement viable.* Montréal: ACFAS. 11–31.

—. 1991. The Canadian Malaise and its External Impact. In Hampson, F.O., Maule, C.J. (editors). *Canada Among Nations 1990-91.* Ottawa: Carleton University Press. 25–40.

—. 1991–92a. Betting on Moral Contracts. *Optimum,* 22(3):45–53.

—. 1991–92b. The Best Is Enemy of the Good. *Optimum,* 22(1):7–15.

—. 1992a. The Strategic State. In Chrétien, J. (editor). *Finding Common Ground.* Hull: Voyageur Publishing. 85–101.

—. 1992b. L'heure juste dans la formation en management. *Organisation,* 1(2):41–51.

—. 1993a. Sciences transversales et savoirs d'expérience : the Art of Trespassing. *Revue générale de droit,* 24(2):269–281.

—. 1993b. État postmoderne : mode d'emploi. *Relations*, 587, 17–19.

—. 1994a. Reinventing Governance. *Opinion Canada*, 2(2):1–5.

—. 1994b. Paradigms of Governance. In Cottrell-Boyd, M. (editor). *Rethinking Government*. Ottawa: Canadian Centre for Management Development. 29–42.

—. 1994c. Grandeurs, limites et scandales : fondements éthiques du financement des systèmes de santé. In Larouche, J.M. (editor). *Ethique, santé et société*. Ottawa: Center for Techno-Ethics. 21–46.

—. 1995. Institutional Evolution in an Information Age. In Courchene, T.J. (editor). *Technology, Information and Public Policy*. Kingston: John Deutsch Institute for the Study of Economic Policy. 197–229.

—. 1996a. The Strategic State (Part 1). *Ciencia Ergo Sum*, 3(3):257–261.

—. 1996b. Le fruit dont l'ignorance est la saveur. In Armit, A., Bourgault, J. (editors). *Hard Choices or No Choices*. Toronto: Institute of Public Administration of Canada. 47–58.

—. 1996c. Gouvernance distribuée et habitus centralisateur. *Mémoires de la Société Royale du Canada*, Series VI, Vol. 6, 425–439.

—. 1997a. The Strategic State (part 2). *Ciencia Ergo Sum*, 4(1):28–34.

—. 1997b. The Strategic State (Part 3). *Ciencia Ergo Sum*, 4(2):148–154.

—. 1997c. The Burden of Office, Ethics and Connoisseurship. *Canadian Public Administration*, 40(1):55–71.

—. 1997d. Slouching Toward a New Governance. *Optimum*, 27(3):44–50.

—. 1997e. States, Communities and Markets: The Distributed Governance Scenario. In Courchene, T.J. (editor). *The Evolving Nation-state in a Global Information Era: Policy Challenges*. Kingston: John Deutsch Institute for the Study of Economic Policy. 25–46.

—. 1997f. Ethics, Leadership and the Military. *Optimum*, 28(1):47–54.

—. 1999. *Oublier la Révolution tranquille — Pour une nouvelle socialité*. Montreal: Liber.

Paquet, G., Pigeon, L. 1995. Toward a Transformation of the Public Service. *Optimum*, 26(1):47–55.

Paquet, G., Roy, J. 1995. Prosperity Through Networks: the Small Business Strategy That Might Have Been. In Phillips, S. (editor). *Mid-life Crises — How Ottawa Spends 1995*. Ottawa: Carleton University Press. 137–158.

Paquet, G., Shepherd, R. 1996. The Program Review Process: A Deconstruction. In Swimmer, G. (editor). *Life Under the Knife*. Ottawa: Carleton University Press. 39–72.

Paquet, G., Taylor, J.H. 1986. The Marksmanship of Research Grants Programs: An Evaluative Framework. *University of Ottawa Quarterly*, 56(4), 117–137.

Paquet, G., von Zur-Muehlen, M. (editors). 1987. *Education Canada? Higher Education on the Brink*. Ottawa: Canadian Higher Education Research Network.

—. (editors). 1989. *Edging Toward the Year 2000*. Ottawa: Canadian Federation of Deans of Management and Administrative Studies.

Paquet, G., Wallot, J.P. 1987. Nouvelle-France, Québec, Canada: A World of Limited Identities. In Canny, N., Pagden, A. (editors). *Colonial Identity in the Atlantic World*. Princeton: Princeton University Press. 95–114.

Parizeau, J. 1988. Transition. *Canadian Public Administration*, 31(1):1–11.

Passaris, C. 1985. Multicultural Connections. *Policy Options*, May, 6(4):27–28.

Pavitt, K., Soete, L. 1981. International Differences in Economic Growth and the International Location of Innovation. In Giersch, H. (editor). *Emerging Technologies: Consequences for Economic Growth, Structural Change and Employment*. Tubingen: J.C.B. Mohr. 105–133.

Pearce, D., Markandya, A., Barbier, E.B. 1989. *Blueprint for a Green Economy*. London: Earthscan Publications Ltd.

Pelletiere, J.C. 1989. Public vs. Private: A Wavering Line. *The Bureaucrat*, Summer, 57–60.

Perlmutter, H.V. 1965. *Toward a Theory and Practice of Social Architecture*. London: Tavistock.

Perrenoud, P. 1987. Sociologie de l'excellence ordinaire. *Autrement*, 86, 62–75.

Perrings, C. 1987. *Economy and Environment*. Cambridge: Cambridge University Press.

Perroux, F. 1960. *Économie et société*. Paris: Presses Universitaires de France.

—. F. 1970. *Industrie et création collective*. Paris: Presses Universitaires de France.

Peter, K. 1978. Multicultural Politics, Money and the Conduct of Canadian Ethnic Studies. *Canadian Ethnic Studies Association Bulletin*, 5.

Peterfreund, S. 1976. Education in Industry — Today and in the Future. *Training and Development Journal*, 30(5):30–40.

Peters, T. 1992. *Liberation Management*, New York: Alfred A Knopf.

Piore, M.J. 1995. *Beyond Individualism*. Cambridge: Harvard University Press.

Pirsig, R.M. 1991. *Lila — An Inquiry into Morals*. New York: Bantam Books.

Polanyi, K. 1957. The Economy as Instituted Process. In Polanyi, K., Arensberg, C.M., Pearson, H.W. (editors). *Trade and Markets in the Early Empires*. New York: the Free Press. 243–270.

—. 1968. *Primitive, Archaic and Modern Economies*. New York: Anchor Books.

Polanyi, M. 1958. *Personal Knowledge*. Chicago: University of Chicago Press.

—. 1996. *The Tacit Dimension*. New York: Doubleday.

Popper, K. 1972. *Objective Knowledge*. Oxford: Oxford University Press.

Porter, L.W., McKibbin, L.E. 1988. *Management Education and Development: Drift or Thrust into the 21st Century?* New York: McGraw Hill.

Proulx, P.P. 1986. Free Trade Is Not Enough. *Policy Options*, January, 11–15.

Putnam, R.D. 1993. *Making Democracy Work*. Princeton: Princeton University Press.

—. 1995. Bowling Alone: America's Declining Social Capital. *Journal of Democracy*, 6(1):65–78.

—. 1996. The Strange Disappearance of Civic America. *American Prospect*, 24, 34–48.

Ramos, A.G. 1981. *The New Science of Organizations*. Toronto: University of Toronto Press.

Ravetz, J.R. 1986. Usable Knowledge, Usable Ignorance: Incomplete Science with Policy Implications. In Clark, W.C., Munn, R.E. (editors). *Sustainable Development of the Biosphere*. Cambridge: Cambridge University Press. 415–432.

Rawls, J. 1971. A Theory of Justice. Cambridge: Harvard University Press.

Reich, R.B. 1991. *The Work of Nations*. New York: Alfred A. Knopf.

Regens, J.L., Rycroft, R.W. 1989. Funding for Environmental Protection: Comparing Congressional and Executive Influences. *The Social Science Journal*, 26(3):289–301.

Reisman, S. 1985. Canada–United States Trade at the Crossroads: Options for Growth. *The Canadian Business Review*, Autumn, 12(3):17–23.

Resnick, M. 1994. Changing the Centralized Mindset. *Technology Review*, 97(5):32–40.

Ricks, T.E. 1996. The Great Society in Camouflage. *Atlantic Monthly*, 278(6):24–38.

Rittel, H.W.J., Webber, M.M. 1973. Dilemmas in a General Theory of Planning. *Policy Sciences*, 4, 155–169.

Roberts, L.W., Clifton, R.A. 1982. Exploring the Ideology of Canadian Multiculturalism. *Canadian Public Policy*, 8(1):88–94.

Robinson, J.B. 1982. Backing into the Future: On the Methodological and Institutional Biases Embedded in Energy Supply and Demand Forecasting. *Technological Forecasting and Social Change*, 21(3):229–240.

—. 1987. *Designing a Sustainable Society for Canada*. Waterloo: University of Waterloo. (Mimeo)

Roots, F. 1988. The Brundtland Challenge: Background and Objectives. In Davidson, A., Dence, M. (editors). *The Brundtland Challenge and the Cost of Inaction*. Halifax: Institute for Research on Public Policy. 75–91

Rosell, S.A. (editor). 1992. *Governing in an Information Society*. Montréal: Institute for Research on Public Policy.

Rosenbaum, W.A. 1985. *Environmental Politics and Policy*. Washington: Congressional Quarterly Press.

Rosenberg, N. 1982. *Inside the Black Box: Technology and Economics*. Cambridge: Cambridge University Press.

Ross, M. (editor). 1954. *Our Sense of Identity*. Toronto: Ryerson Press.

—. 1961. *The New University*. Toronto: University of Toronto Press.

Rotstein, A. 1984. *Rebuilding from Within*. Ottawa: Canadian Institute for Economic Policy.

Rugman, A.M., D'Cruz, J.D. 1991. *Fast Forward*. Toronto: Kodak Canada, Inc.

Sarna, A.J. 1985. The Impact of a Canada–U.S. Free Trade Area. *Journal of Common Market Studies*, 23(4):299–318.

Schaffer, D.L. 1988. Theodore J. Lowi and the Administrative State. *Administration and Society*, 19(4):371–398.

Scheler, M. 1958. *L'homme du ressentiment*. Paris: Presses Universitaires de France.

Schellenberg, J.A., Druckman, D. 1986. Bargaining and Gaming. *Society*, 23(6):65–71.

Schick, F. 1984. *Having Reasons — An Essay on Rationality and Sociality*. Princeton: Princeton University Press.

Schon, D.A. 1971. *Beyond the Stable State*. New York: Norton.

—. 1983. *The Reflective Practitioner — How Professionals Think in Action*. New York: Basic Books.

—. 1987. *Educating the Reflective Practitioner*. San Francisco: Jossey-Bass.

—. 1995. Causality and Causal Inference in the Study of Organizations. In Goodman, R.F., Fisher, W.R. (editors). *Rethinking Knowledge*. Albany: State University of New York Press. 69–101.

Schon, D.A., Rein, M. 1994. *Frame Reflection*. New York: Basic Books.

Schrag, C.O. 1980. *Radical Reflection and the Origin of the Human Sciences*. West Lafayette, IN: Purdue University Press.

Schumacher, E.F. 1973. *Small Is Beautiful — A Study of Economics as if People Mattered*. London: Blond & Briggs.

—. 1977. *A Guide for the Perplexed*. New York: Harper & Row.

Schwartz, J. 1989. The Rights of Nature and the Death of God. *The Public Interest*, 97, Fall, 3–14.

Science Council of Canada 1977. *Canada as a Conserver Society — Resource Uncertainties and the Need for New Technologies*. Ottawa: Science Council of Canada. Report 27.

—. 1986. *Placing Technology Up Front: Advising the Bilateral Trade Negotiators*. Ottawa: Science Council of Canada. Council Statement, May.

Scitovsky, T. 1976. *The Joyless Economy*. Oxford: Oxford University Press.

Scorsone, S.A. 1990. The World Has a Mid-life Crisis. *The Globe and Mail*, 21 June.

Sen, A. 1987. *On Ethics and Economics*. Oxford: Basil Blackwell.

Senge, P.M. 1990. *The Fifth Discipline*. New York: Doubleday.

Sérieyx, H. 1993. *Le Big Bang des organisations*. Paris: Calmann-Lévy.

Servan-Schreiber, J.L. 1986. *Le retour du courage*. Paris: Fayard.

Shapiro, G., Sico, A. (editors). 1984. *Hermeneutics: Questions and Prospects*. Boston: University of Massachusetts Press.

Shearer, R.A. 1986. The New Face of Canadian Mercantilism: The Macdonald Commission and the Case for Free Trade. *Canadian Public Policy*, 12(suppl.):50–58.

Sheridan, W. 1987. *Le multiculturalisme canadien : questions et tendances*. Ottawa: Parliamentary Library. Bulletin d'actualité.

Shklar, J. 1989. Giving Injustice Its Due. *Yale Law Journal*, 98, 1135–1151.

Shubik, M. 1982. *Game Theory in the Social Sciences*. Cambridge, MA: MIT Press.

Simon, H.A. 1960. *The New Science of Management Decision*. New York: Harper & Row.

Slater, D.W. 1967. Economic Policy and Economic Research in Canada Since 1950. *Queen's Quarterly*, 74, 1–20.

Smith, A. 1976. *An Inquiry into the Nature and Causes of the Wealth of Nations*. Oxford: Clarendon Press. p. 688.

Solo, R.A. 1975. The Economist and the Economic Roles of the Political Authority in Advanced Industrial Societies. In Lindberg, L.N. et al. (editors). *Stress and Contradiction in Modern Capitalism*. Toronto: D.C. Heath & Co. 99–113.

Solow, R.M. 1971. The Economist's Approach to Pollution Control. *Science*, 173, 498–503.

Spicer, K. 1988. The Best and Worst of Multiculturalism. *The Ottawa Citizen*, 13 July.

Stasiulis, D.K. 1980. The Political Structuring of Ethnic Community Action: A Reformulation. *Canadian Ethnic Studies*, 12(3):19–44.

—. 1988. The Symbolic Mosaic Reaffirmed: Multiculturalism Policy. In Graham, K.A. (editor). *How Ottawa Spends*. Ottawa: Carleton University Press, 81–111.

Stavins, R.N. 1989. Using Economic Incentives to Protect the Environment. *Policy Review*, 48, 58–61.

Steed, G.P.F. 1988. *The Canada–US Free-trade Agreement: A Canadian Science and Technology Viewpoint*. Ottawa: Science Council of Canada.

Stewart, J.B. 1993. Whales and Sharks. *The New Yorker*, February 15, 37–43.

Stinchcombe, A.L. 1990. *Information and Organizations*. Berkeley: University of California Press.

Stobaugh, R., Yergin, D. (editors). 1983. *Energy Future* (3rd Ed). New York: Vintage.

Stokey, E., Zeckhauser, R. 1978. *A Primer for Policy Analysis*. New York: Norton.

Storper, M. 1996. Institutions of the Knowledge-based Economy. In *Employment and Growth in the Knowledge-based Economy*. Paris: Organisation for Economic Co-operation and Development. 255–283.

Stroup, R.L. and Shaw, J.S. 1989. The Free Market and the Environment. *The Public Interest*, 97, 30–43.

Strange, S. 1996. *The Retreat of the State — the Diffusion of Power in the World Economy*. Cambridge: Cambridge University Press.

Taguieff, P.A. 1987. *La force du préjugé*. Paris: La Découverte.

Tarondeau, J.C., Wright, R.W. 1995. La transversalité dans les organisations ou le contrôle par les processus. *Revue française de gestion*, 104:112–121.

Taylor, C. 1985. Alternative Futures. In Cairns, A., Williams, C. (editors). *Constitutionalism, Citizenship and Society of Canada*. Toronto: University of Toronto Press. 183–229.

Taylor, F.W. 1911. Principles of Scientific Management. New York: Harper & Row.

Thompson, J.B. 1981. *Critical Hermeneutics*. Cambridge: Cambridge University Press.

Tisdell, C.A. 1981. *Science and Technology Policy — Priorities of Governments*. London: Chapman & Hall.

Toner, G. 1986. Stardust: the Tory Energy Program. In Prince, M.J. (editor). *How Ottawa Spends — 1986-7: Tracking the Tories*. Toronto: Methuen. 119–148.

Torgerson, D. 1986. Between Knowledge and Politics: Three Faces of Policy Analysis. *Policy Sciences*, 19, 33–59.

Toulmin, S. 1988. The Recovery of Practical Philosophy. *The American Scholar*, 57(3):227–352.

Trebilcock, M.J. 1985. The Politics of Positive Sum. In Courchene, T.J. et al. (editors). *Ottawa and the Provinces: The Distribution of Money and Power*. Toronto: Ontario Economic Council. Vol. 2, 235–250.

Trebilcock, M.J., Pritchard, R.S., Hartle, D.G., Dewees, D.N. 1982. *The Choice of Governing Instruments*. Ottawa: Economic Council of Canada.

Tremblay, G. 1991. Economie en état d'urgence. *La Presse*, 11-12 September.

Tully, J. 1995. *Strange Multiplicity*. London: Cambridge University Press.

Tully, S. 1993. The Modular Corporation. *Fortune*, February 8.

Tussman, J. 1977. *Government and the Mind*. New York: Oxford University Press.

—. 1989. *The Burden of Office*. Vancouver: Talonbooks.

Tversky, A., Kahneman, D. 1981. The Framing of Decisions and the Psychology of Choice. *Science*, 211, 453–458.

Uhr, J. 1992. Public Accountabilities and Private Responsabilities: the Westminster Word at the Crossroads. Presented at the Annual Meeting of the American Political Association, Chicago, 3–6 September.

Uslaner, E.M. 1987. Energy Politics in the USA and Canada. *Energy Policy*, 15(5):432–440.

Valaskakis, K. 1990. *Canada in the Nineties*. Montréal: Gamma Institute Press.

Varzeliotis, A.N.T. 1985. *Requiem for Canada*. Vancouver: Alcyone Books.

Vertinsky, I. 1987. An Ecological Model of Resilient Decision-making: An Application to the Study of Public and Private Sector Decision-making in Japan. *Ecological Modelling*, 38, 141–158.

Vicere, A.A. 1992. The Strategic Leadership Imperative for Executive Development. *Human Resource Planning*, 15(1):15–31.

Vickers, G. 1965. *The Art of Judgment*. London: Methuen.

von Bertalanffy, L. 1968. *General System Theory*. New York: George Braziller.

von Foerster, H. 1988. La construction de la réalité. In Watzlawick, P. (editor). *L'invention de la réalité*. Paris: Seuil. 45–69.

von Hayek, F. 1952. *Scientism and the Study of Society*. Glencoe, IL: The Free Press.

von Wright, G.H. 1971. *Explanation and Understanding*. Ithaca, NY: Cornell University Press.

Waldo, D. 1980. *The Enterprise of Public Administration: A Summary View*. Novato, CA: Chandler & Sharp.

—. 1985. An Agenda for Future Reflections: A Conversation with Dwight Waldo. *Public Administration Review*, 459–467.

Watkins, G.C. 1987. Living Under a Shadow: U.S. Oil Policies and Canadian Oil Pricing. In Gordon, R.L., Jacoby, H.D., Zimmerman, M.B. (editors). *Energy: Markets and Regulation*. Cambridge: MIT Press.

Watson, C. 1987. *Governments and Higher Education — The Legitimacy of Intervention*. Toronto: Ontario Institute for Studies in Education.

Watzlawick, P. 1978. *La réalité de la réalité*. Paris: Seuil.

Webber, A.M. 1993. What's So New About the New Economy? *Harvard Business Review*, 71(1):24–42.

Weinberg, A.M. 1972. Science and Trans-science. *Minerva*, 10, 209–222.

Westell, A. 1984. Economic Integration with the USA. *International Perspectives*, November-December.

White, S.K. 1991. *Political Theory and Postmodernism*. Cambridge: Cambridge University Press.

Wilensky, H.L. 1967. *Organizational Intelligence*. New York: Basic Books.

Wiley, N. 1977. Review of Habermas' "Legitimation Crisis." *Contemporary Sociology*, 6(4):416–424.

Williams, T.A. 1979. The Search Conference in Active Adaptive Planning. *Journal of Applied Behavioral Science*, 15(4):470–483.

—. 1982. *Learning to Manage Our Futures*. New York: Wiley.

Williamson, O.E 1975. *Markets and Hierarchies*. New York: Free Press.

—. 1985. *The Economic Institutions of Capitalism*. New York: Free Press.

Willson, B.F. 1980. *The Energy Squeeze — Canadian Policies for Survival*. Ottawa: Canadian Institute for Economic Policy.

Wittgenstein, L. 1953. *Philosophical Investigations*. Oxford: Blackwell.

Wolfe, A. 1989. *Whose Keeper?* Berkeley: University of California Press.

Womack, J. 1969. *Zapata and the Mexican Revolution*. New York: Knopf.

Zaleznik, A. 1991. L'absence de leadership et la mystique managériale. *Gestion*, 16(3):15–26.

Zussman, D., Jabes, J. 1987. *Survey of Managerial Attitudes*. Ottawa: Faculty of Administration, University of Ottawa (mimeo).

—. 1990. *The Vertical Solitude*. Halifax: Institute for Research on Public Policy.

Ziman, J. 1991. A Neural Net Model of Innovation. *Science and Public Policy*, 18(1):65–75.

PRINTED AND BOUND
IN BOUCHERVILLE, QUÉBEC, CANADA
BY MARC VEILLEUX IMPRIMEUR INC.
IN APRIL, 1999